L

• We believe that highbrow and LOWBROW have given way to no brow
• The LESS you know the smarter you are, since everything we were brought up to believe is wrong

M

• We believe that MAXIMALISM has more to offer than minimalism
• We believe that we are all a MINORITY OF 1
• We believe that MODERN LIFE is rubbish
• We believe the MISSIONARY POSITION is best left to missionaries

N

• We believe it's easy to say NO. But better to say Yes
• We do not believe in the NEW YORK TIMES
• We believe that we are all born NAKED and the rest is drag (Thank you, Ru.)
• We believe in NEW SENSE from Nonsense, and that old sense is a Nuisance

O

• We believe OPRAH will inherit the Earth
• We believe that no ONE THING is too out there to be in here
• And when it comes to being OUT, we are all Outcasts
• We believe that the most OVEREXPOSED people are also the least revealed

P

• We believe that PORNOGRAPHY is a vital civilizing force
• We believe PLAY is the new Work
• We believe in PRONOIA, that the universe is working for you rather than against you
• We believe that POLITICS is Passe
• We believe that some words sound better than others. Like PAMPLEMOUSSE

Q

• We believe in QUEENS. Hello

R

• We believe REALITY is overrated. We don't need to see that. But we love to watch

S

• We believe the SUPERFICIAL is often the most profound
• We believe SOUP cans can be art
• We believe you can talk to STRANGERS. But not get in their cars. Necessarily
• We believe everyone is the STAR of their own musical. But no one may be watching
• We believe this is the SCREEN AGE. Watch what happens
• We believe a SHORT ATTENTION SPAN is more than made up for by a broad attention range (Thank you, Doug Rushkoff)
• We believe the SIXTEENTH MINUTE can be better than the fifteen minutes before it

T

• We believe in TOTAL TELETRANSFORMATION. Beam us up!
• We believe that we turn on TELEVISION to be turned on
• We believe that there is nothing more natural than TECHNOLOGY

U

• We believe that today's UNDERGROUND is tomorrow's mainstream
• We believe that every one of us is a UNIQUE BRAND
• We believe that UGLY is the new beautiful

V

• We believe VEGAS is the pinnacle of modern architecture
• We believe VIDEO did not kill the radio star, it merely hurt her feelings

W

• We believe the WRAPPING'S the thing.
• We believe it really is a WORLD OF WONDER

XYZ

• We believe that the answer to 'Y brand X?' is ZZZ!

The World According to Wonder

The World According to Wonder

PHOTOGRAPHY *by Idris Rheubottom & Tony Craig*

TEXT *by Fenton Bailey & Randy Barbato*

ADDITIONAL PHOTOGRAPHY

by Mathu Andersen and Alex Grace

ART DIRECTION *by Trey Speegle*

ENNIS BELEY

1980–1996

Welcome to WOW

173
109
117
21
142
149
51

362
203
255
237
290
202
259

Welcome to WOW!

YOU DO WHAT YOU LOVE.

And then the next thing you know, 20 years have passed.

At first we were just going to have a big party. Twenty years! Woo hoo! But then Billy Luther came up with the idea that we should do a book of portraits joining the dots of the different people we have worked with over the years.

Like the best ideas, it seemed so simple and clear. And even a way to give back a little something. But had we known the amount of work that would go into publishing a book, we probably would have just stuck with the party.

Idris Rheubottom and Tony Craig very generously agreed to shoot the pictures. They tirelessly and (almost) without complaint went here, there, and everywhere shooting people big and small, famous and unfamous, all on their own time.

Eventually they had shot over 200 portraits.

Thairin Smothers and Chris Wereski ran logistics and bookings with great patience. Then we turned to our old friend Trey Speegle (joined by Emiliano Neri) to design the book and he pointed out that a collection of portraits would beg some kind of explanation. So we

OPPOSITE PAGE: Randy and Fenton photographed by Paul Morgan for *Esquire* magazine, London, July, 1991

Right in front of our eyes we had seen the world go Pop. Things on the edges of the culture drifted to the center

thought, OK, we can write an introduction. But then Lauren Zalaznick thought that we had a story to tell. Something that required more than an introduction. Chapters.

And come to think of it, right in front of our eyes we had seen the world go Pop. The Berlin Wall came down and pop culture became the planet's Esperanto. Things on the edges of the culture drifted to the center, and the outer limits became the mainstream.

By the turn of the century Pop was no longer a mere teenage indulgence, it was the very engine of our civilization. And it was insatiable in its appetite for new stars, new trends, new scandals.

Not only did we have a front row seat, we also did a turn on the catwalk. Drag became mainstream. Being gay became cool. In 1996 we directed a music video for Ultra Naté's new single "Free." She was a downtown diva, an underground club talent, and her song became a gay anthem for freedom in every respect. Next thing you know – OK, it was 14 years later – the song was the official theme for Home Shopping Network. From popping poppers to popcorn poppers.

And reality TV, that most maligned of all genres in that most maligned of all mediums, did to television what rap did to rock and roll – took it over and re-invented it.

So 50,000 words later (and thanks to the diligent copy-editing skills of Stephen Saban aided and abetted by Tom Wolf), here's our story. And, as the story of people who didn't invent YouTube, the iPad, or Facebook, it's kind of fitting it's all told in a coffee table book. Because no one reads coffee table books.

So just flick through and enjoy the pictures of – to name but a few – Pamela Anderson, Tammy Faye Bakker, Wayne Brady, Chaz Bono, Leigh Bowery, Pete Burns, Andy Cohen, Divine David, Elvira, Linda Evangelista, Macaulay Culkin, Fantasia, Carrie Fisher, Sarah Ferguson Duchess of York, Larry Flynt, Boy George, Seth Green, Bobcat Goldthwait, Hugh Hefner, Perez Hilton, La Toya Jackson, Kaeto Kaelin, Monica Lewinsky, Norman Mailer, Imelda Marcos, Dylan McDermott, Ultra Naté, Rosie O'Donnell, Kelly Osbourne, Camille Paglia, Joey Ramone, RuPaul, Chloë Sevigny, Tori Spelling, Dita Von Teese, John Waters, Oprah Winfrey, Carnie Wilson, and Holly Woodlawn.

We hope everyone who appears in this book will read just far enough for us to thank them for giving their time to sit for us, and for being in our lives. And if by some terrible oversight you aren't in it, your turn will come in Volume 2. But whether you are in the book or not, please know that it is a world of wonder because of everyone in it. Especially you. Thank you.

OPPOSITE PAGE: Fenton and Randy dumpster diving outside the World of Wonder office, photographed by Idris + Tony. Hollywood, California, April 20, 2010

OF
CREAM
FLAVORED CREAM
LIDS
DO NOT PARK
NO HAZARDOUS
WASTES ACCEPTED
CAUTION
KEEP OFF!
CAUTION
LOAD EVENLY!

Total Teletransformation

IT REALLY ALL BEGAN WITH *Videodrome*. Cronenberg's fetish-fantasy about the netherworld of cable television, where strange shows transmitted in the dead of night had the ability to turn you into a freak with a video vagina and a compulsion for snuff games. *Long live the new flesh!* ♦ Notionally a horror film, *Videodrome* was really a piss-take on the culture's ingrained belief that TV has evil powers to turn us into the walking dead. Because TV – in spite of being a miracle of science and technology – has somehow been cast as the bane of culture, the end of civilization. Studies claim it is responsible for everything from mental retardation to the early onset of puberty – not to mention causing unspeakable crimes. *We wanted in!*

At the time, we were broke, living in a sixth-floor walk-up in crack-infested Alphabet City. It had that inverse kind of glamour that people bedazzle as "bohemian": drug dealers, addicts, hookers, and even a psychotic murderer. The fag-end of the American dream. *We loved almost every minute of it!*

There was a lone club, the Pyramid, on Avenue A and 7th Street – the very edge of civilization. There was something about the place. It pulled people in. Fabulous drag artistes. Hapi Phace. Tabboo. Faye Runway. Sister Dimension. Lypsinka. And occasionally, from Atlanta, the not-yet-famous RuPaul and Lady Bunny. Todd Haynes debuted his notorious *Karen Carpenter* film there. Victor Weaver and Trey Speegle hosted "Straight to Hell" strip parties on Sunday nights.

And on hand almost every night was Nelson Sullivan, a gentleman charmer with the most languid southern drawl and a fag in his mouth, videotaping everyone and everything. That camera was like a pirate's parrot, permanently perched on his shoulder. He said that one day he was going to edit his thousands of hours of material into a public access cable show. But on July 4, 1989, he dropped dead of a heart attack.

OPPOSITE PAGE: Randy, Fenton, and Kitty the Cat on the couch at the office, photographed by Rich Renaldi, World of Wonder's office, 80 Varick Street, New York City, 1991

We were broke, living in a sixth-floor walk-up in crack-infested Alphabet City. It had that inverse kind of glamour that people bedazzle as "bohemian"

Nelson's death was our call to action. We didn't really know what public access was, but we soon learned. Cable companies had to make a couple of channels available for local community access. In other words, people could make their own shows and get them on TV. Simple as that. They could be about whatever they wanted them to be. There was no editorial screening process. Slots were assigned on a first-come, first-served basis. Manhattan's public access channels presented a glittering seam of talent. Willa Sands – possibly tipsy – hosting *Happy Hour*. John Wallowitch – no less tipsy – banging out "Sing Along in Lithuanian" on the piano and knocking back Long Island Iced Teas. He was friends with Warhol, reportedly. Mrs Mouth, who painted a face on her upside-down chin then talked about picking her nose. And, for the adults, *Voyeur Vision,* where viewers could call in and talk to comely Lynn lying on a bed, touching herself where they requested. And veteran fixture Robin Byrd, in her trademark crocheted bikini, introducing strippers. It was pure *Videodrome,* but without the inconvenience of sprouting a video vagina.

We figured there was no reason we couldn't make a public access show, so we came up with the idea of *Flaunt It! TV*, a talk show taped once a week at New York's Limelight nightclub, and hosted by us. Quentin Crisp, Kate O'Toole, Sigue Sigue Sputnik, Michelangelo Signorile, Michael Musto, and a monosyllabic Stephen Saban were some of the long-suffering guests on the short-lived show. It wasn't exactly ratings gold. It ran for four episodes before we collapsed in exhaustion, followed by a prolonged period of deep depression. Not that failure ever stopped us. In the long run it was our fuel.

Meanwhile, everyone at the Limelight was buzzing about "Disco 2000," a sick and twisted circus run by a kid called Michael Alig. Not so long ago he had taken us out to dinner (McDonald's. Cheap) to consult with us about promoting club events. Now he was practically running New York City nightlife and, he crowed, had $50K saved to put down on a condo. Meanwhile, we were relying on our jar of loose change to get through the weekend. Life can be so unfair sometimes.

A bit later, we were in London (pursuing another incredibly successful – NOT – career as a musical act called The Fabulous Pop Tarts) flipping through – count 'em – all four of the UK's TV channels. We really didn't feel like watching a documentary about fish, a cooking show, a game of snooker, or an Open University show on colloids. You see, British television at the time was under severe regulation to educate and entertain – and that often translated as a license to bore. We yearned for some good old Manhattan Cable.

And that was it.

The idea.

We would license clips from our favorite shows and bundle them together into a single program. The result was *Manhattan Cable,* a series that would run in various iterations (*Made in the USA, USTV,* and *TV Pizza*) for four seasons on Channel Four UK.

Having decided that we were not cut out to be on camera, we cast about for a host. Actress Lisa Edelstein, stylist Victoria Bartlett, pop star David Yarritu, and fashion designer John Bartlett (in a fabulous poncho) all auditioned for a role that, in the end, went to fiesty redhead Laurie Pike. Laurie was a '90s take on Modern Millie, with a shock of red hair and boyish looks. She was as fearless about fisting in a sex club as she was about hanging with the mole people in their tunnels below Grand Central Station. Nothing bothered her and everything was interesting to her. Her foil was Bill Judkins, the show's official

THIS PAGE: The inimitable Mrs Mouth; Nelson Sullivan and Michael Musto at Nelson's home in the meatpacking district; Kenny Kenny and Quentin Crisp, photographed by Michael Fazakerley

love magnet, and they were joined from time to time by designer Albert Crudo and RuPaul, who thoroughly immersed himself in the lifestyles of the hookers of the meatpacking district. Segment producer Jim Wilson perhaps found some early inspiration doing a piece on East Village killer Daniel Rakowitz, who kept his girlfriend's head in a locker at Port Authority and fed the rest to squatters in Tompkins Square Park. He would later go on to be one of the producers of *The Lovely Bones*. Wilson, not Rakowitz. He also met his wife Liz while doing a piece on Kostabi World. Kostabi was a thoroughly '80s artist who had a post-Warhol factory, planned to build the world's tallest skyscraper, and had just published a vast book about himself that we judged to be the height of vaingloriousness. It was slightly bigger than the book you hold in your hands now. Hello.

Producing *Manhattan Cable* wasn't the smoothest process. This was our first television show and the suits were nervous. So nervous that Michael Attwell, the executive in charge of the show at Channel Four, announced he was flying in immediately to see what we had. The only problem was we didn't really have anything, apart from the title sequence. So we managed to persuade the people running the new JumboTron in Times Square (then as novel as the billboards of Marky Mark in his underwear) to play it, and had Michael Attwell meet us there for a drink at the appointed hour. *Look up!* He was duly impressed. And then – pure luck – Matt Dillon walked up and tapped us on the shoulder. We had met him once or twice casually through mutual friends. "Hey man, is that your show? Cool shit!" Or something like that. Michael, who like the rest of us thought Matt was the second coming, flew back to London completely happy.

When the show launched, the audience immediately connected with the clips; they had never seen anything like it before. It was all so wild and wanton, completely without motive. A non-stop cavalcade of characters and catch phrases. It was often assumed that we were laughing at these people. But it was not mockery. We were, as Lady Miss Kier put it, "gagging on the lovely extravaganza." With nothing but a cardboard box and a few bits of string, these people, these pioneers, put on a show. And what a show! They didn't edit themselves, they didn't care what people said. They were exuberant. And they were making a whole different kind of television, TV not weighed down by rules, worried about ratings, or advertisers. It was TV that was free to be whatever it wanted to be. It felt truly punk. *The revolution was being televised!*

Today these clips are on the internet and called viral videos. But this was before the web. We aren't making grandiose claims here. *If only we had invented YouTube.* Instead, we had simply made a show, with some bits that made you laugh and some that made your toes curl.

Once *Manhattan Cable* was greenlit we made the bold step of moving from our East Village apartment to an office loft in Tribeca, near the Holland Tunnel. Right across from the entrance. It hadn't seemed like a problem when the agent showed us the place late one night over the Christmas holiday. It was delightfully quiet. But the first morning we moved in – and every morning after – we would wake to horns and fumes wafting up from gridlock below. Note to selves: real estate agents are so smart.

We needed a staff. Enter rain-soaked Alison Pollet. She had an encyclopedic knowledge of all things television and a brand new Gucci bag and was so worried about it getting wet that she decided to stay the whole day. She came back the next morning. And so on. Maria Silver who flew over from England on a one-way ticket, had even less mobility. At the time, our loft had a *Being John Malkovich*

FROM LEFT: Sister Dimension at Wigstock; The Lady Bunny, photographed by Michael Fazakerley; Lorraine Bowen, one of the British stars of *Takeover TV*, photographed by Nigel Bowen; Deaundra Peek, one of the legendary Peek Sisters who appeared on *Manhattan Cable*, photographed by Michael Peligrinon

Stills from *Flaunt It! TV*, World of Wonder's first-ever show, hosted by Randy and Fenton. Guests included (left to right, top to bottom) Kate O'Toole; James St James and Michael Musto; Teddy Rapunzel and Randy (we all had hair back then); singer John Sex; Stephen Saban, editor of the original *Details*; Quentin Crisp; Neal X of Sigue Sigue Sputnik; Nelson Sullivan; Tish and Snookie, singers and owners of Manic Panic; singer Dean Johnson; drag king Murray Hill; Michael Alig; and Michelangelo Signorile, author and broadcaster.

Nelson Sullivan (front and center next to RuPaul) was inseparable from his video camera. His 24/7 videotaping of New York's downtown scene inspired us to forego pop stardom and become TV producers instead

FROM TOP LEFT: Michael Musto, Trade, David Goldman aka Betty Jack DeVine, Albert Crudo, Randy, RuPaul, Nelson Sullivan, and Fenton, photographed by Dick Richards outside his Atlanta house, 1988

With nothing but a cardboard box and a few bits of string, these people, these pioneers, were putting on a show. And what a show!

floor, a half-height space in which you could not stand up. Producer Isabel Tang moved in, pursued by a trail of Porsche-driving men. Somehow she would emerge in a full ball gown or complete riding gear to go on an endless series of social functions. While they all could not have been more different, they could not have been more glamorous and fun to work with. For a time, Mary Harron, director of *I Shot Andy Warhol* and *American Psycho,* was a lodger, along with RuPaul.

"It's the new Factory!" exclaimed Bob Colacello one day. The place had its moments. Joey Arias sat – do not attempt this at home – on a champagne glass and then fell asleep on someone's desk. Jose and Luis (Madonna's dancers from "Vogue") dropped by at the peak of their hotness. And Queerdonna, the three-hundred-pound tribute artiste, did irreparable damage to our floors performing her version of "Erotica."

From time to time Michael Alig would also pop in. From being slightly annoying and squeaky clean, he was now slightly annoying and completely drug-addled – though always charming and sharp as a tack. By this point, he and his Club Kids had become a national movement and were on all the talk shows and magazine covers. It would be so good to make a documentary about them, we thought, but everyone turned us down. They just didn't get it. So, in a word, NO.

It was also NO to our history of pornography idea, NO to our drag queen variety show idea called *Stars of the Future*, and NO to our documentary series on Andy Warhol. NO to our show following real estate agents. NO to our idea of a quiz show in which the prize is a million dollars. NO to marooning people on a desert island Robinson Crusoe-style. It was scary. Here we were rattling around in this giant loft with rent to pay and everyone saying how wonderfully creative and edgy we were... and then saying NO NO NO NO NO NO NO.

We got used to hearing that word so many times we became immune to it. Besides, we know now that NO is the beginning of YES.

Thank goodness for *Takeover TV*, where we invited people in the UK to make their own TV – like US public access. It was a simple idea to transplant *Manhattan Cable* to Britain. There were no public access channels in the UK; however, the last few years had seen the introduction of inexpensive, easy-to-use camcorders that (for the first time) could record broadcast-quality footage. Now that the means of production was finally being thrust into the hands of the people, we reached out to the people who were doing it for themselves. Case in point, Adam Buxton.

It was after midnight in an edit suite in London's Soho, and we were editing the show's presentation reel for *Takeover TV*. All we really needed was a great clip to kick things off. There were two piles of tapes that had been pre-screened: YES and NO. Nothing in the YES pile seemed that good. So we turned to the NO pile and picked the tape off the top. "Too clever for its own good," the Post-It note said. And indeed it was. Adam Buxton wore a satellite dish on his head and was shouting at the camera as if the viewer was hard of hearing, "My name is Ken Korda and you're all rubbish." We thought it was genius and so did Peter Grimsdale, the commissioning editor. NO really is the beginning of YES.

Takeover TV ran for four seasons on Channel 4. In addition to one of the first television appearances of Graham Norton and work by Edgar Wright (*Shaun of the Dead*) and Hammer and Tongs (*Hitchhiker's Guide to the Galaxy*), what got the series noticed was a talking bottom called Norman Sphincter. With a pair of eyes scrawled on the top cheek, jiggling both cheeks gave the impression that his plumber's crack

was talking. Hilarious stuff. When it became known that the bottom playing Norman belonged in real life to the son of a prominent conservative MP and cabinet member, he – not the MP – was forced into early retirement.

Sad as Sphincter's demise was, *Takeover TV*'s true breakouts were Adam Buxton and his friend Joe Cornish. They quickly became the stars of *Takeover TV*'s spin-off series, *The Adam and Joe Show,* consisting of the antics of two slacker students laboring for months in a cramped bedsit creating versions of *Titanic*, *Star Wars*, *Showgirls,* and other Oscar heavyweights, starring animated stuffed toys. Among other things. One time, they showed up at a friend of a friend's house promising a fabulous living room makeover. While he and his girlfriend went down to the pub, Adam and Joe set about trashing the place. Hilarity – and profanity – ensued when the occupants returned. In *Vinyl Justice* they would show up dressed as policemen at the homes of pop stars like Gary Numan. They would search their record collections for musical infractions and hand out humiliating punishments on the spot. (We later remade *Vinyl Justice* for VH1, starring then-unknown Wayne Brady and Barry Sobel.) For their television work, Adam and Joe won a Royal Television Society Award. The ceremony was so uniquely British, recipients weren't allowed to make acceptance speeches; they had to go up to the dais, collect their trophy, and then return obediently to their seats. No red carpet. No designer gowns. No Governors Ball. Very Hogwarts – but without the magic.

The Adam and Joe Show ran for four hit seasons, after which they were climbing the walls of their bedsit and begged to be let out. They have since gone on to glamorous careers for which we have no problem taking sole credit.

Shock Video

As Masha says to Max in *Videodrome*, "It has something that you don't have, Max. It has a philosophy and that is what makes it dangerous." We quickly evolved ours. Instead of documentaries (yawn) we were making clipumentaries, perfectly honed for our shortened attention spans. *Takeover TV* was not about technology, it was about clicknology. *Push a button, anyone can do it!* It was all sort of a McLuhanesque joke, or so we thought until someone pushed the "record" button and Los Angeles burned.

The LA Riots happened because a guy with a video camera taped Rodney King getting the crap beaten out of him by some cops. Not since the Zapruder footage of Kennedy's assassination had there been such a clip. And when a jury decided that it had not seen what everyone had seen with their own eyes, LA erupted. *The video revolution had arrived. For real.*

A week later, we were on the ground in South Central handing out video cameras to people caught up in the riots to keep video diaries of their lives for the next 12 months. Among them was Charles Denny, a reformed Cripps gangleader; Ennis Beley, a young kid who lived around the corner in his grandpa's dry-cleaning store; Bob Tur, a helicopter pilot who had hovered above the scene at the flash point of the riots; and Reggie Brumfield, a guy who took his video camera and filmed the looting and mayhem as it kicked off. We wove their video journals into a two-and-a-half-hour feature for BBC2 called *LA Stories.*

And then the Big One happened. The Northridge earthquake in January, 1994, upended our office and made up our minds. We would move from New York to Hollywood permanently. Besides, it was a good time to buy. Our real estate agent was Debbie Berg. She was tiny, but drove a gold

OPPOSITE PAGE: Title stills from *Manhattan Cable, TV Pizza*

THIS PAGE: *United States of Television*, and *Takeover TV*, all clip show series – or, as one might call them today, aggregations of user-generated content – produced for Channel 4 UK

Adam and Joe were two slacker students creating versions of Hollywood hits with stuffed toys

Mercedes the size of a boat. By sitting on a Yellow Pages she could just about see over the dashboard. What was it about real estate agents?

And then came the Really Big One: OJ Simpson taking off down the freeway after the murder of his ex-wife. We knew we were in the right place as we watched helicopter pilot Bob Tur reporting the drama in all its compelling non-eventness. It didn't end with the chase. Watching OJ's white Ford Bronco parked in the driveway of his home as night fell was the very definition of Andy Warhol's dream of a show called *Nothing Special*, in which nothing happened (though Bronco sales spiked 25%). In the days to come, it became a reality soap opera as an array of stars sprang from the woodwork. Kato Kaelin, who lived in the guest house. Carol Lieberman, the media shrink who had a car with license plates to match. Elaine Young, who had sold OJ his Brentwood home.

New twists and turns were revealed daily. There was the mysterious lawyer Robert Kardashian, who was seen carrying one of OJ's bags away from the scene. Caught on tape, it was assumed that the bag contained bloody clothes or some other incriminating piece of evidence. "What's in the bag, Mr Kardashian?" became a refrain. There was much ballyhoo about the forensic experiment conducted by local news reporter Patrick Healey, who purchased ice cream from the same shop as Nicole Simpson then drove it back to the crime scene to see how much it melted. Hard to say what this proved, but it played well that night at 11.

Traditional media decried this trivialization of hard news. They called it soft-core infotainment. But as with the polar ice caps, so with Nicole's fateful ice cream. *We had passed the point of no return.*

Right on time came a book, *Media Virus,* written by a young renegade academic, Douglas Rushkoff. His thesis was that the mediasphere was not some technological construct, but an organic extension of ourselves. In today's world, he argued, an idea that excites people will *"probably duplicate itself and spread through the datasphere without any further effort on the part of the individual who initiated it. It no longer matters if it is 'alive' or not; like the ocean, the weather, or a coral reef, it behaves as it is."*

What strange new beast was this?

Come on down, Reality TV!

You can trace the evolution of the genre from this beginning point. It's in its DNA. Quite literally. Robert Kardashian's ex-wife and three daughters are the stars of the monster hit, *Keeping Up with the Kardashians.*

In the same way that rap has overtaken rock, so "reality" has overtaken fiction. Reality is a broad church that contains everything from observational documentary soaps to competition elimination shows. But the OJ phenomenon was a bi-winning combination of both; there was the day-to-day soap opera followed by the televised trial as elimination game show. We ended up making two films about OJ – one right in the thick of it for the BBC called *OJ Mania: The Media Trial of OJ Simpson,* and a couple of years later *Juror #5* for HBO, in which Deena Mullen recounted her experience as a juror in the civil trial.

We also made a documentary called *Videos Vigilantes and Voyeurision* that tried to make sense of the new videocracy. We were living in 1994; in other words, just 10 years after Orwell's *1984*, but we were in such a completely different world than his nightmare vision. Take Big Brother himself. Instead of some nasty totalitarian lens watching our every move, *Big Brother* was a fun entertainment show just then beginning to garner attention in the Netherlands. People *wanted* to be on camera. They wanted to be watched, they wanted

THIS PAGE: Title still from *The Adam and Joe Show*, with Adam Buxton and Joe Cornish; Barry Sobel and Wayne Brady, faux cops / hosts of the US version of *Vinyl Justice*; transmission card, with Adam Buxton, his dad Nigel Buxton, and Joe Cornish as Teletubbies

TOYTANIC

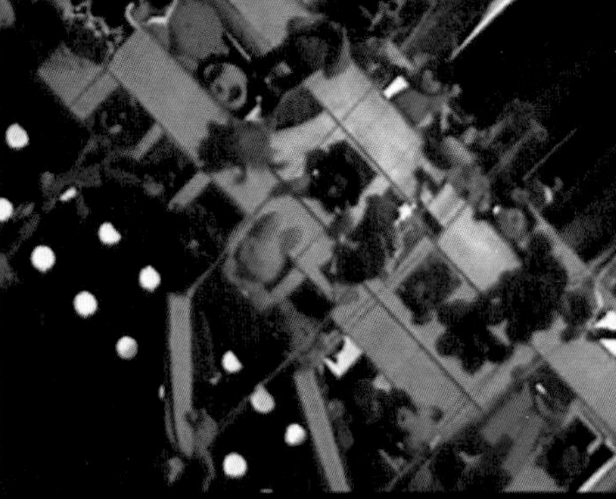

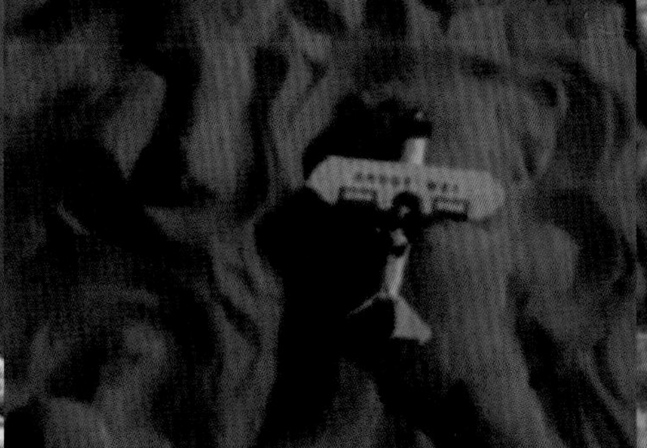

Stills from Adam and Joe's *Toymovies*, taking on *Trainspotting*, *Toytanic*, and *The English Patient*.
Joe would go on to be one of the co-writers of Spielberg's *Tintin*. Clearly this early work played a critical role in that later success

to be seen. Instead of a controlling eye, the camera lens was the way to validation, the way people could transform themselves from nonentities into celebrities.

All just a long way of saying it's not that the revolution will be televised, but that the revolution *is* television.

But if we had a plan, nothing could have been further from the truth.

The afternoon that Sheila Nevins – head of documentaries at HBO – called, we thought someone was playing a joke. We had been trying to reach her for months, but she wasn't one of those people who just picked up the phone when you called. She had seen our documentary *Videos, Vigilantes and Voyeurism* and wanted to buy it for HBO. So she invited us into her office for some frozen yogurt (even though it was midwinter) and talked about the few tweaks here and there that she wanted to make. Over the next few months we would completely remake and reshoot the film. It even got a new title: *Shock Video.*

Shock Video wasn't just about social injustice caught on tape, it was also about other outrageous things, like sex and nudity on television around the world. The show was a hit and devolved into an annual Christmas TV-titty treat. Defying a more considered analysis (boring!) we now needed an endless supply of puns (fun!) to accompany the bouncing boobs and jiggling peni. You might say we went from semiotic to semi-idiotic, from analysis to anal warts, and so on. John Waters signed on to narrate an episode (following in the footsteps of Marcia Brady, RuPaul, and Ann Magnuson), then read the script and made a dignified retreat. Even the creator of *Desperate Living* and *Female Trouble* had a reputation to protect. It all came to a head, so to speak, with *Shock Video 10*, which has never aired. HBO's in-house lawyer called to tell us that he had reviewed the show and vomited into his trash can after watching the clip from a British network show called *Detox Camp,* in which unhealthy eating habits were purged via a series of coffee enemas and contestants were given chopsticks and told to pick through their pooh.

Corn? I don't remember eating corn!

You could say that British TV had changed in a few short years. And that Sheila Nevins changed our lives.

THIS PAGE: Sheila Nevins (left), President of Documentaries at HBO, in a Photoshop mashup of Fenton (center) and Randy (right) as Siegfried and Roy

08:23:02:21
TC

SHOCK
VIDEO II

Shock
VIDEO
turn on
TV

Shock
Video
4
TURN ON
TV 96

SHOCK
VIDEO
5
TURN ON
TV 97

shock
video
TURN ON TV
98

THE BEST OF
THE WORST OF
SHOCK
VIDEO
REFRIED

SHOCK VIDEO
2000:
TURN ON TV

Laurie Pike

JOURNALIST

Host of *Manhattan Cable.* We loved her from the moment we met her at *Paper* magazine. The Cincinnati native popularized words like "gagging" and endeared herself to the British viewing public with her trademark elongated "hellooooo"

THIS PAGE:
PHOTOGRAPHED BY PAUL MORGAN
LONDON STUDIOS, SEPTEMBER 10, 1991

OPPOSITE PAGE:
PHOTOGRAPHED BY IDRIS + TONY
AT HOME, KOREATOWN, LOS ANGELES,
JULY 17, 2009

Laurie was a ’90s take on Thoroughly Modern Millie… nothing bothered her and everything was of interest to her

Michael Musto

COLUMNIST, AUTHOR, PROVOCATEUR

Longest-reigning King of Downtown. Michael writes the weekly La Dolce Musto column in New York's *Village Voice*, as well as his La Daily Musto blog, and is the author of three books

PHOTOGRAPHED BY IDRIS + TONY
THE VILLAGE VOICE OFFICES,
NEW YORK CITY, JUNE 12, 2009

Robin Byrd

TV PRESENTER, QUEEN OF PUBLIC ACCESS

Host of *The Robin Byrd Show*, her adult series on public access that has been running for 30 years and has taped over 1,500 episodes

PHOTOGRAPHED BY IDRIS + TONY
CENTRAL PARK, NEW YORK CITY,
APRIL 21, 2010

Kato Kaelin

RADIO AND TV PERSONALITY

One of the celebrities created by the OJ scandal (he lived in Simpson's guest house), Kato is much smarter than he ever got credit for

PHOTOGRAPHED BY IDRIS + TONY
WORLD OF WONDER PRODUCTIONS,
HOLLYWOOD, CALIFORNIA,
JANUARY 26, 2010

"Everyday to me is like opening a wrapped gift. I'm so full of happiness to find a gift and even happier that the gift is life"

–KATO KAELIN

Edward Temple Morris

RADIO PERSONALITY

His bare bottom was the popular recurring character Norman Sphincter on *Takeover TV*. Norman was forced into early retirement by the revelation that Eddie is the son of a baron and British government minister

PHOTOGRAPHED BY ALEX GRACE
CLAPHAM COMMON, LONDON,
NOVEMBER 29, 2010

Luis "Xtravaganza" Camacho

DANCER

Madonna's adorable dancer forever associated with "Vogue" was interviewed in our Wigstock documentary for the BBC

PHOTOGRAPHED BY IDRIS + TONY
WORLD OF WONDER PRODUCTIONS,
HOLLYWOOD, CALIFORNIA, JULY 16, 2010

Leigh Bowery

ARTIST

It's hard to think of a title that does justice to his particular kind of genius. Remembered as the muse of painter Lucian Freud, he was also the visual inspiration for Michael Alig and the Club Kids

PHOTOGRAPHED BY MICHAEL FAZAKERLEY
LIMELIGHT NIGHTCLUB,
NEW YORK CITY, 1992

Bill Judkins

WRITER, SALOON PROPRIETOR

Co-host and official "love magnet" of *Manhattan Cable*. We were classmates with Bill in the NYU graduate film program

PHOTOGRAPHED BY IDRIS + TONY AT HOME, BROOKLYN, NEW YORK, JUNE 29, 2010

Albert Crudo

ARTIST

Downtown fixture and artist who appeared on *Manhattan Cable* before making a splash in the art world selling his limited edition Barbie Poop

PHOTOGRAPHED BY IDRIS + TONY
23RD AND BROADWAY, NEW YORK CITY,
MARCH 9, 2010

Leo Braudy

ACADEMIC

Professor of English at the University of Southern California and author of the definitive – and perhaps only – history of fame, *The Frenzy of Renown*. We interviewed Leo for the original *Shock Video* and numerous other productions

PHOTOGRAPHED BY IDRIS + TONY AT HOME, LOS FELIZ, CALIFORNIA, JANUARY 22, 2010

Douglas Rushkoff

WRITER

Doug is a Marshall McLuhan for the digital era and author of *Media Virus*, a book that completely inspired us

PHOTOGRAPHED BY IDRIS + TONY
GREENWICH VILLAGE, NEW YORK CITY, MARCH 5, 2010

Nathan Anderson

ACTOR

Nathan was the pizza delivery boy in the series *TV Pizza*, hosted by Laura Kightlinger. Everyone had a crush on him. He looks exactly the same today as he did then. He went on to appear in Roland Emmerich's American remake of *Godzilla*

PHOTOGRAPHED BY IDRIS + TONY
TAMARIND AND FRANKLIN AVENUES, HOLLYWOOD, CALIFORNIA, APRIL 27, 2010

Wayne Brady

TV HOST

While still an unknown, Wayne was half of the wacky cop duo (Barry Sobel was the other half) in the US version of *Vinyl Justice*, a segment originally in *The Adam and Joe Show*. Wayne went on to become star of *The Wayne Brady Show* and host of *Let's Make a Deal*

PHOTOGRAPHED BY IDRIS + TONY
WORLD OF WONDER PRODUCTIONS,
HOLLYWOOD, CALIFORNIA, JULY 13, 2010

Isabel Tang
PRODUCER, DIRECTOR

Isabel worked on *Manhattan Cable* and developed *Pornography: The Secret History of Civilization.* She also wrote the book that accompanied the series

PHOTOGRAPHED BY ALEX GRACE
PEACOCK YARD STUDIO, KENNINGTON, LONDON, JUNE 9, 2011

Alison Pollet

AUTHOR

Alison, perched on the hood of an old Routemaster bus (because she now lives, alas, in the UK) was our very first US employee

PHOTOGRAPHED BY ALEX GRACE
SHOREDITCH BUS DEPOT, LONDON,
MARCH 4, 2010

Ennis Beley

STUDENT PHOTOGRAPHER

Ennis was the youngest person in our BBC feature documentary *LA Stories*. He evolved into a talented young photographer and became an important part of the WOW family. Sadly, he was murdered in a drive-by on the streets of South Central shortly before his sixteenth birthday.

PHOTOGRAPHED BY LAUREN GREENFIELD
LOS ANGELES COURTHOUSE,
MARCH 5, 1993

Reggie Brumfield

CINEMATOGRAPHER

Reggie grabbed his camera and headed into the eye of the storm as the LA riots began in April, 1992, shooting incredible eyewitness footage smack in the thick of it. His video diary in *LA Stories* documented his attempts to get into the TV production business

PHOTOGRAPHED BY IDRIS + TONY
FLORENCE AND NORMANDIE AVENUES (FLASHPOINT OF THE LA RIOTS), SOUTH CENTRAL LOS ANGELES, JULY 15, 2010

Adam Buxton

TV PERSONALITY, WRITER

One half of *The Adam and Joe Show*. Funny, charming and, above all, brilliant

PHOTOGRAPHED BY ALEX GRACE
WHITECHAPEL STUDIO,
LONDON, FEBRUARY 9, 2010

Joe Cornish

FILM DIRECTOR,
SCREENWRITER

The other half of *The Adam and Joe Show*. Joe Cornish recently wrote and directed *Attack the Block* and was a co-writer on Steven Spielberg's *Tintin*

PHOTOGRAPHED BY ALEX GRACE
PEACOCK YARD STUDIO, KENNINGTON, LONDON, JUNE 9, 2011

Carol Lieberman

MEDIA THERAPIST

Carol grabbed headlines for her analysis of the psychodynamics of the OJ case. She was interviewed in our BBC documentary *OJ Mania: The Media Trial of OJ Simpson.*

PHOTOGRAPHED BY IDRIS + TONY
BEVERLY HILLS, CALIFORNIA,
JULY 14, 2010

Bob Tur

TV REPORTER, HELICOPTER PILOT

Bob reported live from the flashpoint of the LA riots, found OJ fleeing on the freeway in his white Bronco, and covered Madonna's Malibu wedding to Sean Penn. He was one of the characters in *LA Stories* who made a video diary about his life in LA in the wake of the LA riots

PHOTOGRAPHED BY IDRIS + TONY
AT HOME, SANTA MONICA, CALIFORNIA, APRIL 24, 2010

Kate O'Toole

ACTRESS

Kate was one of the first guests on our first-ever television show *Flaunt It! TV*. Despite that indignity, she has remained a loyal friend ever since and popped by to get her photo taken just after her father, Peter O'Toole, got his star on Hollywood Boulevard's walk of fame

PHOTOGRAPHED BY THAIRIN SMOTHERS
WORLD OF WONDER PRODUCTIONS,
HOLLYWOOD, CALIFORNIA, APRIL 30, 2011

Trey Speegle
ARTIST

A canvas print of his paint-by-numbers YES painting, originally created for Stella McCartney, hangs in our office to bring positive vibes to our meetings and – hopefully – turn NO (we won't be in your show) into YES (we live for the opportunity!). He is also the designer of this book

PHOTOGRAPHED BY IDRIS + TONY
AT HOME, MEATPACKING DISTRICT,
NEW YORK CITY, MAY 25, 2010

It's not that the revolution will be televised, the revolution *is* television

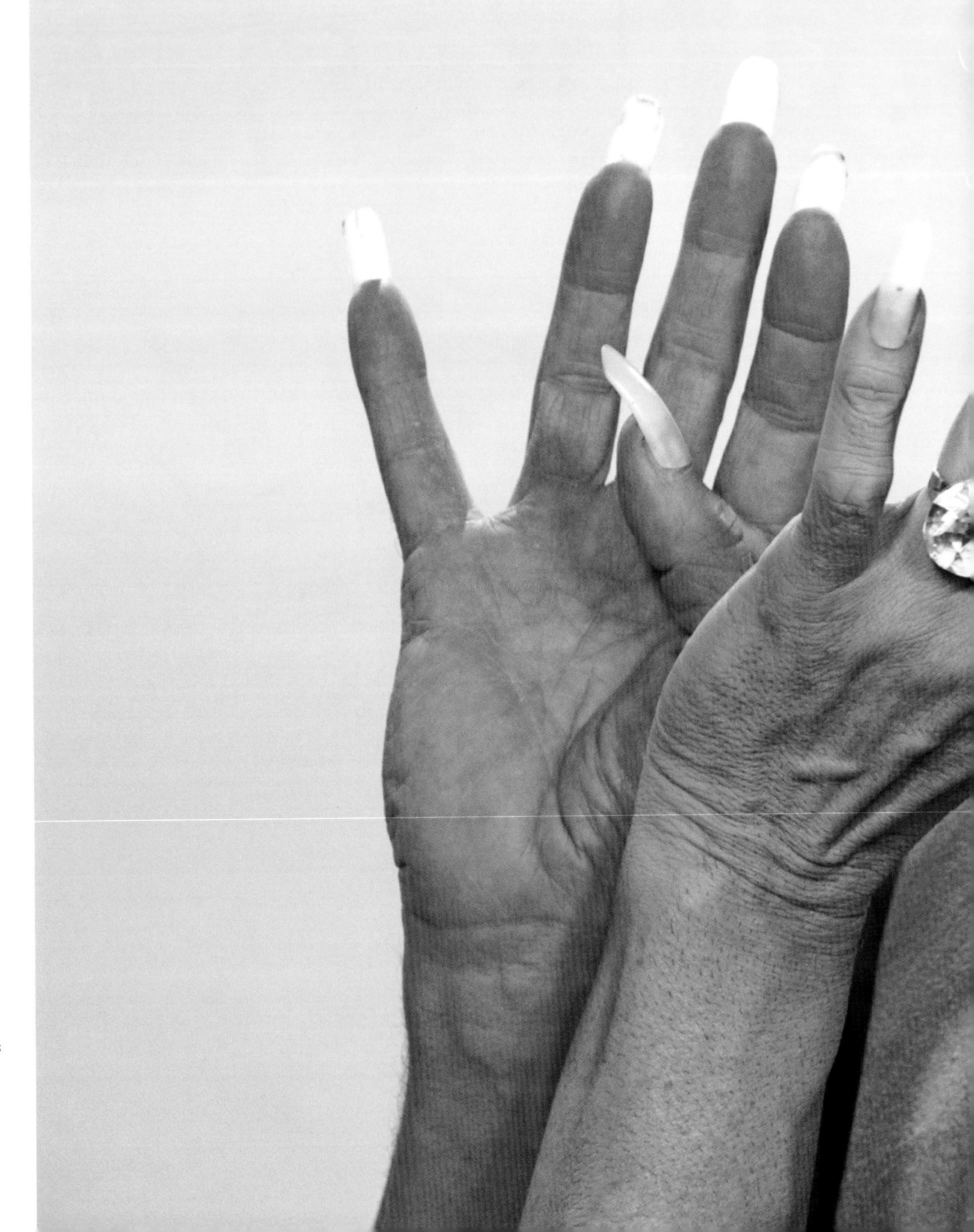

Halstead

PERFORMER

His star turn as Barbra Streisand on the phone trying to acquire a dog with a very specific bark was our all-time favorite clip on *TV Pizza*

PHOTOGRAPHED BY THAIRIN SMOTHERS
WORLD OF WONDER PRODUCTIONS,
HOLLYWOOD, CALIFORNIA,
DECEMBER 15, 2010

Drag & Things of That Nature

ONE AFTERNOON IN 1991 while we were sitting at our desks making busy, RuPaul walked into our office. *Sashay, shanté.* ♦ We had first set eyes on Ru about six years earlier, in Atlanta. He wore football shoulder pads with streamers, a jock strap, waders, and a frightwig. The kind of outfit you might wear to get noticed in a club – albeit a very twisted one. But Ru wasn't in a club waiting around for anyone to snap his picture.

In 1989 Fenton and Randy dressed in drag to go to Lady Bunny's Wigstock in Tompkins Square Park, around the corner from their East Village apartment. Randy has made sure that all visual evidence has been destroyed. Fenton was not so careful

He had a bucket and brush and was wheatpasting posters of himself all over the city. The xeroxed posters said, simply, "RuPaul is EVERYTHING."

We have always loved drag and seen it as the most fabulous of all the plastic arts. To us, Ru was its Andy Warhol. It wasn't just the towering inferno of his frame; behind the mascara was a soul as gentle and wise as ET.

"You're born naked and the rest is drag!" Ru has said more than once. So true. Drag is a fabulous act of self-invention. Taking the canvas of oneself and conjuring up – often with nothing more than a wig and a pair of heels – a completely new persona.

Ru came to see us that day because he wanted us to manage him. He had a demo and a catchy song called "Supermodel" that he'd written with Jimmy Harry and Larry Tee. We had never managed anyone but, based on our (ahem) glittering career in the music biz, he thought we might be helpful.

It didn't go that well at first. Every record label turned us down. No. No. No. But that didn't stop us. We sent the demo to Tommy Boy, a hardcore indie hip-hop label the least likely to sign a big old drag queen. We'd just met the label's co-owner Monica Lynch because we had interviewed her about some controversy over rap lyrics for the pilot of *Manhattan Cable*. We could not have been more surprised when she called us up and offered Ru a deal.

From then on it didn't take that long. Erwin Gorostiza designed the cover art. Mathu and Zaldy did Ru's hair,

RuPaul's
DRAG RACE
Mondays 9/8c
Season Premiere Feb 1

Logo
LogoTV.com

Here was a big black man in a blonde wig and high heels right in the heart of pop culture. And the best part is America didn't blink

wardrobe, and make-up. We pitched in and directed the video for basically 99 cents. And "Supermodel" walked the runway up the charts. *You better work, bitch*. And he did. And we did too. But it didn't feel like work because it was so exhilarating and exciting.

We also produced and directed Ru's other music videos ("Back to My Roots," "Shade Shadey," "Don't Go Breaking My Heart") and a Christmas special for Channel 4 that starred Elton John, Boy George, La Toya Jackson, En Vogue, Little Richard, and, natch, a bevy of downtown drag queens like Linda Simpson, Billy Beyond, Sherry Vine, Taboo, Ffloyd, etc etc.

If it looked like an overnight success, it certainly wasn't. Ru had worked tirelessly for years, hustling, performing, and wheatpasting. He always knew he was a star. He just had to be patient while the rest of the world caught up. Eventually, inevitably, the time was right.

Right time, because drag was at a kind of cultural tipping point. Uptown, you had the legendary vogueing balls of Harlem that Jennie Livingston immortalized in her landmark documentary, *Paris Is Burning*. Then that magpie Madonna swooped in and turned "Vogue" into one of her hugest hits, most memorable videos, and an international phenom.

Meanwhile, downtown, the Pyramid Club's Lady Bunny had created a monster hit with Wigstock, an all-day drag festival held in Tompkins Square Park. We called this kind of drag Superdrag, because it drew its inspiration from DC comics, TV commercials, and Saturday-morning cartoons. It didn't seem to have much to do with gender or anything trans at all.

We wanted to make a feature documentary about it, but settled for making a 10-minute piece for the BBC's highbrow arts magazine, *The Late Show,* created by Michael Jackson. The likes of Salman Rushdie and Rem Koolhaaus were the show's usual subjects. Not drag queens. Roly Keating, then the show's editor, pulled us aside and whispered in our ears that we would have to make "a cultural adjustment up." A daunting prospect. So we packed the show with famous intellectuals, from Fran Lebowitz to John Waters, plus white-hot stars like Madonna's stunning voguers Jose and Luis, who just giggled a lot and looked hot.

But our favorite interview had to be with Camille Paglia whose book *Sexual Personae* had made her infamous – and feared. Yet that day in Philadelphia she could not have been friendlier as she scampered down the steps of the University of the Arts talking a mile a minute. A few people can speak in entire sentences and fewer still in complete paragraphs. Professor Paglia was the only person we've ever met who spoke in entire chapters…

"For me, the drag queen is a Holy Man, someone who enacts all the mysteries of woman's power in the universe. At the same time, the drag queen, in their mastery of the arts of elegance, grace, style, and so on, is a work of living theater. I've always taken drag queens very seriously. And for me, the drag queen has a more authentic sense of sex roles – much more historically based – than feminism. I feel that in order to reform feminism and bring it back to a sense of reality about woman, we must study the drag queen and the tradition of drag. Sometimes drag has been used for humor, but for me, the purest and most essential drag is that haughty and aristocratic style of voguing. Voguing, thanks to Madonna, has been brought out into the public arena and forces feminism to confront its failures in aesthetics. Aesthetics is the huge vacuum at the heart of feminism. It's the absence of an aesthetic. For me, the drag queen is the only person today who in the Western world, is keeping alive the idea of beauty, which is regarded as divine by Plato. The revival of the Renaissance, The Birth of Venus *and so on. We see at that moment for the great Florentine artists that beauty is of enormous spiritual value. Today, the drag queen is a marginalized person without any kind of social status and without money. All available resources*

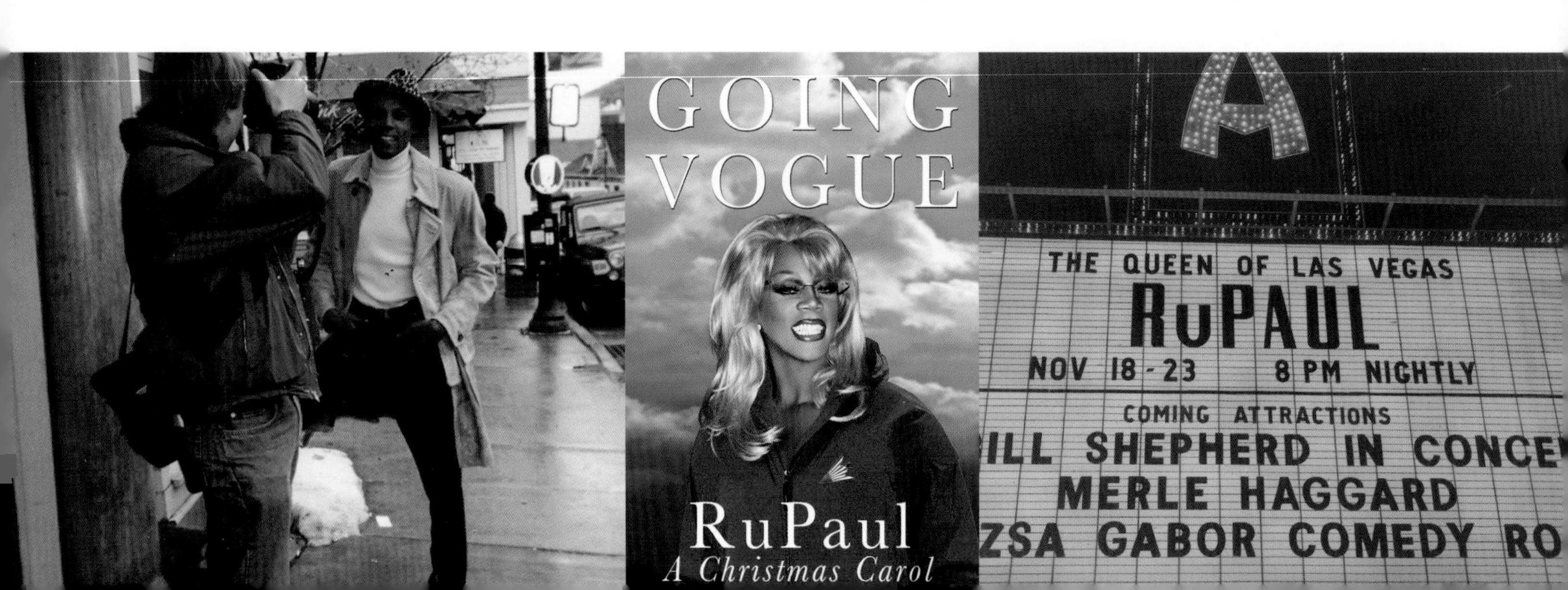

are devoted to living and embodying this ancient ideal of beauty that was made into an art form in Egypt. Five thousand years of Western tradition go into the drag queens enactment of sexual personae.

The drag queen for me is a hero of imagination. The drag queen is like the great avant-garde artist, the great bohemian artists of the 19th century. Starving in a garret and giving everything for Art. It's the tradition of Keats. If a painter in Paris had money, it would not go to food. It would go to buying paint. In Paris Is Burning *there was a moment when one person said, "The people will come to these shows hungry; they will spend their money for a piece of fabric." I think, how wonderful! I honor such a man! I honor a person who would scant the body, torture the body for one beautiful moment, one beautiful gesture. That is part of the nobility of the drag queen. The drag queen is a pagan saint.*

Western culture is a combination of two traditions. That is, the Judeo-Christian and the Greco-Roman, the pagan. And all the complexities of our culture come from the tensions between these two traditions. For me, drag is an enormous Art form that belongs to the pagan line. They are part of this ancient tradition of the Great Mother. I think that the cult of the Great Mother returns at various points in history. Right now, we have a very kind of sentimental, sludgy goddess cult that's everywhere in feminism. It's all about Nature and how we find the goddess within, and so on and so forth, when in fact the drag queen had it more authentically. This idea of the cosmic mother who is in some way a dominatrix, a bitch goddess. And that is very close to the way in Hindu cult they still honor Kali, a divided being who is both positive and negative, who is both benevolent and destructive. It seems to me the drag queen in her perfect hauteur, arrogance, and bitchiness enacts that. Enacts the full range of woman's emotion. Today there's a sentimentality about woman in American feminism. Woman is benevolent and nurturing and hand-holding. Oh, it just makes me nauseous! Okay? To me, the drag queen is a great, great model. I have been influenced by drag queens. Like Madonna, I identify strongly with them. The drag queen is a great feminist model. A drag queen is all woman and all man. A drag queen looks fabulous, has mastered all the arts of elegance and style. At the same time, don't mess with a drag queen! They'll punch you out! They'll just kick off their shoes and hike up their skirt and POW! [punches the air] *I like that! I'm very combative! I'm confrontational! And it seems to me the drag queen has the street-smarts, this canniness of how to survive on the street. There's an enormous range here from street sensibility to High Art.*

So it seems to me the drag queen should be taken much more seriously. The drag queen is not just some sort of trashy thing that's on the edge of society. Of course, I must point out: I also honor the prostitute. The prostitute is not a victim! Ugh! I cannot stand the way feminism is centered around victims today. The victimology is so oppressive. The prostitute is not a victim! The drag queen is not a victim! The prostitute to me commands the sexual realm. And she is an outlaw. And the same thing with the drag queen. The drag queen commands. I had the good fortune to have just very briefly known a drag queen in New York. A Hispanic drag queen who died of AIDS about five years ago. And this drag queen was so haughty he would barely speak to me. OK? And I just felt honored to be in her presence. She was like six-four, OK? Very haughty and thin. Would live in abandoned houses. Would eat like three grains of rice a day. All right? Everything was devoted to thinking about the great Hollywood stars. And to remembering their lives.

So to me the drag queens live in that world, recreate that world that's been lost. Because for me, Meryl Streep? Ugh! [spits] *Meryl Streep! I mean, this is a star? Oh, give me a break! To me, a star is like Dietrich. A star is like Bette Davis. A star is like Hedy Lamarr. That's a face I want to look at on the screen. My sense of beauty, and my honoring of beauty has totally separated me from contemporary feminism.*

I feel that there are two realms of existence. Almost like a fifth dimension. All right? There is a world of concrete reality around us, and there is this world – this

OPPOSITE PAGE: RuPaul being photographed on Main Street at the 2000 Sundance Film Festival in Park City, Utah; RuPaul Christmas card, posing as Sarah Palin, 2009; the marquee of the Sahara Hotel in Las Vegas, a favorite haunt of both Elvis and the Rat Pack, 1994

THIS PAGE: A billboard on Sunset Boulevard for RuPaul's debut album, Supermodel of the World, 1993; the title still from *The RuPaul Show*, which ran for 99 episodes

Sketch by Mathu and Zaldy for RuPaul's iconic outfit for the "Supermodel" video shoot. August 24, 1992

The program cover for RuPaul's headlining appearance in Las Vegas, photographed by Albert Sanchez Jay Ahrend Studios, Hollywood, California, October 4, 1994

Drag Race was the chance to make TV about TV. It deconstructs then reconstructs, bedazzles, and teases the genre of competitive reality. It's a show in drag

enormous world – that has its own laws and that has been going on for thousands of years. The world of Art. Abasing the body like a Hindu ascetic, or like a monk of the Middle Ages, the drag queen, has stepped over into that other realm. The realm of Art. That drag queen is not in the least pathetic, OK, for neglecting his physical care. On the contrary, he's made himself into a saint. He's made himself into a heroic, a mystic who has an expanded consciousness and has expanded our insight into what humanity is, what civilization is".

To us, Camille Paglia's words were Bolivian marching powder, inspiring us to build RuPaul into as big a brand as possible and deliver on that campaign promise of his: "RuPaul Is Everything." Like RuPaul himself often said, so long as we are in the nursery why not play with all the colors in the crayon box? And he had a list. He actually had a list of all the things he wanted to accomplish. No, really. Record deal. Cosmetics deal. Book deal. Talk show. Headline in Vegas.

Of course, any supermodel worth her salt simply had to have a cosmetics modeling contract, so when the opportunity presented itself for Ru to become not only the face of M•A•C Cosmetics, but also to be its first-ever spokesperson, we knew we better not f*ck it up. On the plane ride up to Canada to meet Frank and Frank who were the founders and owners of the company (one was the business, the other the creative), we agreed to ask for a generous six-figure sum.

Frank and Frank could not have been more delightful. We spent the day meeting people, exploring ideas, getting to know each other, and then – as the time to catch our return flight neared – it was finally time to talk business. How much would it take? business-Frank wanted to know. We looked at each other. Neither of us wanted to speak. Then when the number was said out loud, Randy blanched. We had doubled the figure we'd come up with. There was a stunned silence in the room that seemed to last so long we were sure we would miss our plane."OK," said business-Frank. "Done."

Next on the list, a book. Our old friend Victor Weaver, former editor of the mythic gay rag *Straight to Hell,* brought us into Hyperion Books, Disney's then-new imprint, where he was the director of design. Done!

And don't forget the talk show. That is where we first met the amazing Jeff Gaspin and his cohort, the legendary Lauren Zalaznick. Co-hosting with Ru was Michelle Visage, who brought along Billy B to do her makeup. Mathu and Zaldy continued to work their magic with hair, makeup, and couture for Ru.

At the time, VH1 had a ratty old studio on the West Side that smelled like a men's locker room. If we could stand the smell, we could make the show. Michael Rourke came in and produced what would be a booker's dream show:

Cher, Diana Ross, Debbie Harry, Mary J Blige, Chaka Khan, Mary Tyler Moore, Olivia Newton John, Cyndi Lauper, Little Richard, Whoopi Goldberg

THE MOST POPTASTIC NAMES:
Backstreet Boys, 'N Sync, Usher, Belinda Carlisle, Duran Duran, Erasure, Fergie (before Black Eyed Peas)

CAMP'S STALWART CLASSICS:
La Toya Jackson, Jerry Springer, Martha Wash, Lynda Carter, Joan Rivers, John Waters, Isaac Mizrahi, Adam West

GUILTY PLEASURES:
Jackie Collins, Jeff Stryker, Vanna White, Charo, Susan Lucci

A WHOLE LOAD OF WTF:
Maria Shriver, Neil Patrick Harris, Mark Hamill, Ivana

Trump, Molly Ringwald, Linda Blair, Dennis Rodman

AND SOME SO STARRY THEY HAVE LEFT THE PLANET:
Robert Palmer, Bea Arthur, Anna Nicole Smith, Rick James, Gary Coleman, Marilyn Chambers, Tammy Faye Messner, Eartha Kitt

RuPaul's Talkshowtini with its unique combination of greats, poptastic names, camp classics, guilty pleasures, and lashings of WTF, ran for 99 episodes.

It also – along with *Pop Up Video* and *Behind The Music* – gave VH1, a channel hitherto laboring under the shadow of MTV, its own identity for the first time.

The Ru experience had many highs along the way. Elton John called to re-record his Kiki Dee duet, "Don't Go Breaking My Heart," with RuPaul. There was the RuPaul doll by Jason Wu. The box read "99% plastic, 1% woman." There was the march on Washington, at which Ru walked on stage and, pointing to the White House, told the quarter million strong throng that it was time to "paint the mutha pink." What was so exciting was that here was a big black man in a blond wig and high heels right in the heart of pop culture. As Ru once said, "Every time I bat my eyelashes, it's a political act." And the best part is America didn't blink. It felt like change had come to America.

Gentlemen, Start Your Engines...

But it was a moment, not an eternity. Shortly after the march, the much-anticipated repeal of the ban on gays in the military got thwarted by Don't Ask, Don't Tell. The enormous wave of goodwill that brought Ru into the hearts and minds of America ebbed as it had flowed, and eight years of Bush followed.

The other day we were in a pitch for a series about endangered species.

"But have you done any rare-animal shows before?"
"As a matter of fact we have," Randy replied. "Drag queens were an endangered species. Until *RuPaul's Drag Race*."

It's certainly true that drag queens had a hard time getting on TV. Drag queens were too extreme, would frighten viewers away, did not represent middle America, etc etc. So the road to *RuPaul's Drag Race* was a long and winding one. Ten years long. Even before *Project Runway* took off we had batted around the idea of a nationwide search for America's next top drag queen. And then when word began to spread that a new gay channel called Logo would be launched, we were first in line knocking on the door. The welcome was a little muted.

"You guys are so great," an executive said with an uncomfortable glance at their watch. Translation: you guys are just too gay. Actually, another executive even *said* that. Joking, of course. But the early Logo did not want to frighten the neighbors. It wanted to present the idea of gays as the guys next door. Regular suburban folk. Exuberants need not apply. It's a common concern. Every Gay Pride you hear the same complaints that the drag queens and fisters just ruin it for everyone. So in the end we just gave up pitching them.

When Tom Campbell, whom we had known even before moving to LA, joined World of Wonder as executive in charge of development, he immediately brought up RuPaul. At every development meeting, after a warm-up of Diana Ross YouTube clips on the conference-room screen, the RuPaul drag competition conversation would inevitably come up. Having met such resistance to our drag pitches in the past, we weren't convinced we would be able to find a home. Eventually, we relented and took *Drag Race* out. Brian Graden and Dave Mace were at the new and improved Logo, and they recognized that the world had moved on. We were now all a part of the "Will and Grace generation." And the drag queen blend-

OPPOSITE PAGE: Stills from our short Wigstock documentary for the BBC's *The Late Show* featuring Professor Camille Paglia (author of *Sexual Personae*), Jennie Livingston (director of *Paris Is Burning*), and John Waters

THIS PAGE: RuPaul, Lady Bunny, and David Dalrymple at Laurie Weltz's champagne and truffle party in New York a year or so before "Supermodel" became a hit. The judges' panel on *RuPaul's Drag Race*: Michelle Visage, Ru, and Santino Rice; Randy and Fenton strangling Linda Simpson dressed as an elf for *RuPaul's Christmas Ball*, 1993

ed Charisma, Uniqueness, Nerve, and Talent to create an aspirational and spiritually uplifting cocktail for us all.

Of course *Drag Race* is a balls-out gay show, but it was also the chance to make TV about TV. It deconstructs then reconstructs, bedazzles, and teases the genre of competitive reality. It's a show in drag.

It was also made for next to nothing – which explains the soft-focus glow that covered everything in the first season. Besides, it's not just true for drag queens and porn stars; none of us really looks our best in hi-def.

Drag Race became a family reunion of sorts, bringing together people we have known for decades: RuPaul, Tom Campbell, Mathu Andersen, Michelle Visage, Santino Rice, Billy B, Zaldy, Chris McKim, Steven Corfe, James McGowan, Thairin Smothers.... One way or another their connection to RuPaul and the WOW family existed long before this show and coming together to work on *Drag Race* became a full-circle moment.

From the outset, the show connected and became the channel's most-watched show of all time. Just goes to show that in these jaded times we could all do with a little more C.U.N.T. in our lives. But when it comes to drag, less is less, and we needed more. One day, we were in the control room (basically a broom closet with aspirations) watching the monitor while the girls were waiting in the Interior Illusions Lounge for the deliberations to happen. We were totally mesmerized. "Uhmm guys, there is another TV show right here." Voila, *Untucked!*

...May The Best Woman Win

But wait, there's more! Drag is not just for queens, it's a church for all. Given that we are all born naked and the rest is drag, you don't have to be a man pretending to be a woman to be a drag queen. And at *RuPaul's Drag U*, assisted by a faculty of professorial queens from previous seasons of *Drag Race*, real women are helped to find their inner queen and draguate with honors.

At the end of the show they get to walk the runway in front of their friends and loved ones. Why a runway? Because life is a runway, and a runway for us all to walk. You don't have to have long legs, be wrapped in Prada, or have the face of a supermodel. Fat or thin, young or old, beautiful or ugly, it's really all about showing up, and then walking the walk.

It's really all about finding the you of you. Are you good enough? Yes you are, bitch!

THIS PAGE: Rubama! This composite of RuPaul portraying both the president and the first lady, a promotion for the first season of *RuPaul's Drag Race*, was dreamed up by Monica Lewinsky and executed by Mathu Andersen. It went viral on the world wide interweb

OPPOSITE PAGE: The poster for *RuPaul's Drag U*, the show that takes real women and turns them into drag queens for a day

America's first school of fierce is now in session.

Ru had a bucket and brush and was wheatpasting posters of himself all over the city

RuPaul

SUPERSTAR, SUPERMODEL OF THE WORLD

We had known RuPaul since he was a mandrogynous act in Atlanta. A few years after moving to New York and becoming the toast of the town he asked us to manage him because he said he saw reflected in Randy's eyes the list of everything he wanted to achieve: record deal, book deal, talk show, cosmetics contract, and so much more

PHOTOGRAPHED BY MATHU ANDERSEN
CULVER CITY, CALIFORNIA,
SEPTEMBER 9, 2010

RuPaul doll

COLLECTIBLE PLASTIC PLAYTHING

Jason Wu, who designed the doll, became world-famous overnight when he designed a dress Michelle Obama wore to an inaugural ball in 2009

PHOTOGRAPHED BY IDRIS + TONY
WORLD OF WONDER PRODUCTIONS,
HOLLYWOOD, CALIFORNIA, APRIL 25, 2010

Mathu Andersen
ARTIST

Mathu, creative producer of *RuPaul's Drag Race* and *Drag U*, also does RuPaul's hair, makeup, and is a celebrated photographer

PHOTOGRAPHED BY IDRIS + TONY AT HOME, SILVER LAKE, LOS ANGELES, APRIL 22, 2010

Lady Bunny

PERFORMER, DJ, BLOGGER

Bunny is a permanent member of the faculty on *RuPaul's Drag U.* She and Ru have been friends since their early days together in Atlanta

PHOTOGRAPHED BY MATHU ANDERSEN
CULVER CITY, CALIFORNIA, APRIL 1, 2010

Bebe Zahara Benet

PERFORMER

Winner, *RuPaul's Drag Race* season one. As Ru always reminded us, Bebe came from Camerooooooooooon

PHOTOGRAPHED BY IDRIS + TONY
AT HOME, BROOKLYN, NEW YORK,
MARCH 3, 2010

The road to RuPaul's Drag Race was a long one. Ten years long

Raja Gemini

PERFORMER

Winner, *RuPaul's Drag Race* season three. The secret of her success? "Nothing tastes as good as skinny feels"

PHOTOGRAPHED BY MATHU ANDERSEN
CULVER CITY, CALIFORNIA,
SEPTEMBER 9, 2010

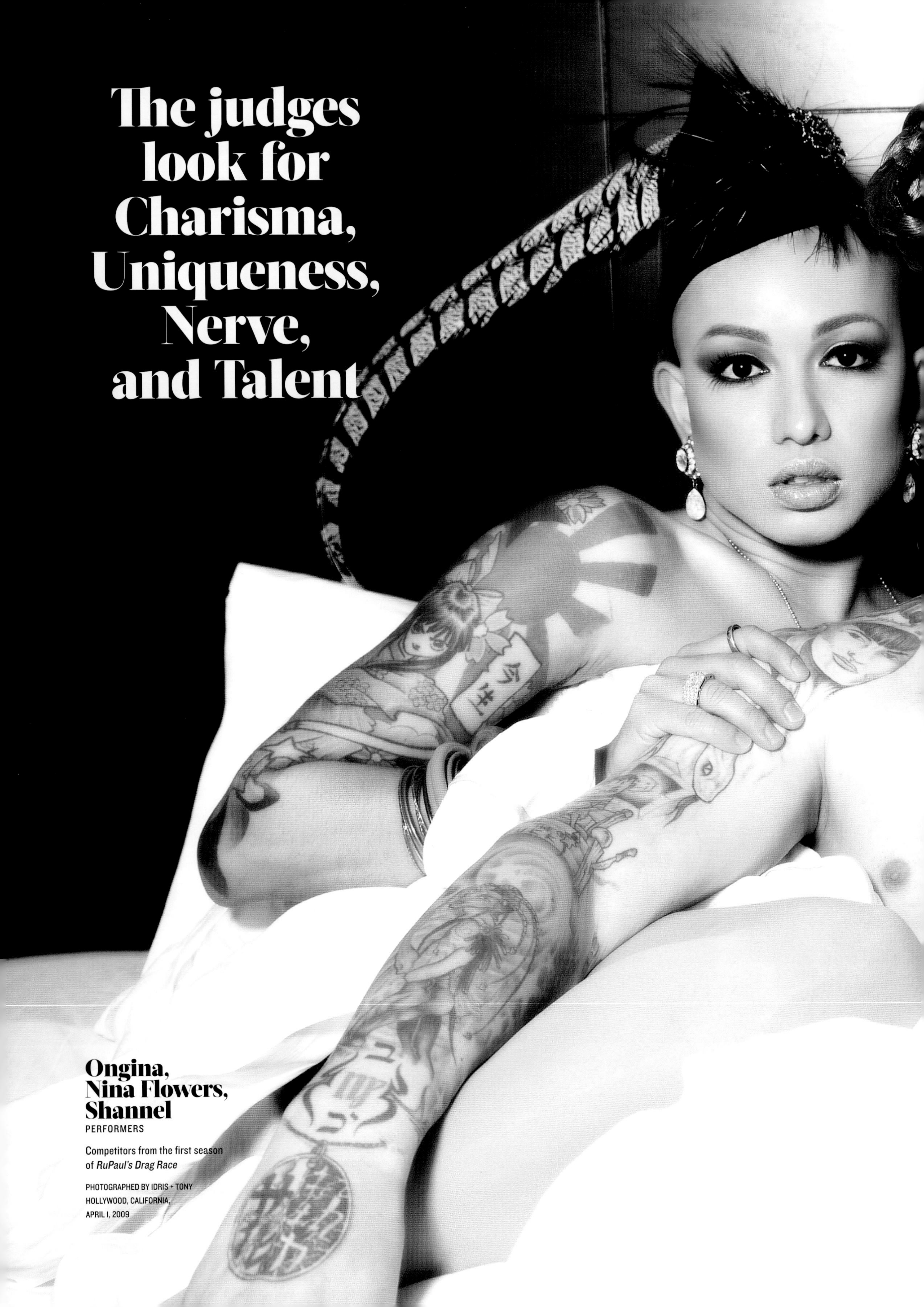

The judges look for Charisma, Uniqueness, Nerve, and Talent

Ongina, Nina Flowers, Shannel
PERFORMERS

Competitors from the first season of *RuPaul's Drag Race*

PHOTOGRAPHED BY IDRIS + TONY
HOLLYWOOD, CALIFORNIA,
APRIL 1, 2009

Tammie Brown

PERFORMER

Competitor, *RuPaul's Drag Race* season one. During the first season's reunion taping, Tammy unforgettably said, "I don't see you out there walking children in nature"

PHOTOGRAPHED BY IDRIS + TONY
WORLD OF WONDER PRODUCTIONS,
HOLLYWOOD, CALIFORNIA,
APRIL 9, 2009

Raven

PERFORMER

First runner-up, *RuPaul's Drag Race* season two. Although she didn't win, she was never at a loss for a winning retort, "Y'know, I wouldn't wear it...but for you, it's cute"

PHOTOGRAPHED BY IDRIS + TONY
WEST HOLLYWOOD, CALIFORNIA,
JANUARY 25, 2010

Latrice Royale
PERFORMER

Competitor, *RuPaul's Drag Race* season four. The audience was outraged when Latrice was sent home on season 4, but were delighted when she picked up Miss Congeniality! She joined the professorial staff of *Drag U* season three

PHOTOGRAPHED BY MATHU ANDERSEN
CULVER CITY, CALIFORNIA,
APRIL 9, 2009

Jujubee
PERFORMER

Competitor, *RuPaul's Drag Race* season two. After making the final three, Jujubee sashayed her way across the US building her fan base. She's been a regular on all three seasons of *Drag U* and returned to compete in *RuPaul's All Stars Drag Race*

PHOTOGRAPHED BY MATHU ANDERSEN
CULVER CITY, CALIFORNIA,
JANUARY 25, 2010

Chris McKim

PRODUCER

Chris was the showrunner and an executive producer of the first four seasons of *RuPaul's Drag Race* and *RuPaul's All Stars Drag Race*

PHOTOGRAPHED BY IDRIS + TONY
CULVER CITY, CALIFORNIA,
SEPTEMBER 3, 2009

Morgan McMichaels
PERFORMER

Competitor, *RuPaul's Drag Race* season two and professor on *RuPaul's Drag U*

PHOTOGRAPHED BY IDRIS + TONY
LOS ANGELES, CALIFORNIA,
JANUARY 25, 2010

> “The drag queen is a Holy Man, someone who enacts all the mysteries of woman’s power in the Universe”
>
> –CAMILLE PAGLIA

Alexis Mateo

PERFORMER

Competitor, *RuPaul’s Drag Race* season three. Alexis liked to keep it to the point, “What you see is what you get, bitches.” BAM!

PHOTOGRAPHED BY MATHU ANDERSEN
CULVER CITY, CALIFORNIA,
SEPTEMBER 9, 2010

Piyah Martell

PERFORMER

Guest star on *RuPaul's Drag Race* season four. At first, the network resisted featuring a transgendered person with Caudal Regression Syndrome, but the result is one of the most amazing and moving episodes ever

PHOTOGRAPHED BY MATHU ANDERSEN
CULVER CITY, CALIFORNIA,
AUGUST 3, 2011

Chad Michaels

PERFORMER

Top three, *RuPaul's Drag Race* season four

PHOTOGRAPHED BY IDRIS + TONY, WORLD OF WONDER PRODUCTIONS, HOLLYWOOD, CALIFORNIA APRIL 20, 2010

Elvira

TV PERSONALITY,
MISTRESS OF THE DARK

Goth legend and guest judge on *RuPaul's Drag Race*

PHOTOGRAPHED BY MATHU ANDERSEN
CULVER CITY, CALIFORNIA, JULY 28, 2011

Drag is not just for Queens. It's a church for all

Dita Von Teese

BURLESQUE PERFORMER

Special guest on *Untucked: RuPaul's Drag Race* season three and *RuPaul's Drag Race* season two. Dita famously told one contestant, "I wouldn't leave my man in a room alone with you"

PHOTOGRAPHED BY MATHU ANDERSEN
CULVER CITY, CALIFORNIA, AUGUST 29, 2011

Kelly Osbourne
TV PERSONALITY

Guest judge on *RuPaul's Drag Race, Drag U, and All Stars*. Kelly notoriously told one contestant, "F*ck you for having the most amazing body, ever"

PHOTOGRAPHED BY
MATHU ANDERSEN
CULVER CITY, CALIFORNIA,
AUGUST 12, 2011

Manila Luzon

PERFORMER

First runner-up, *RuPaul's Drag Race* season three. As she explained afterwards, "So if Raja dies of old age then maybe I'll get the crown"

PHOTOGRAPHED BY MATHU ANDERSEN
CULVER CITY, CALIFORNIA,
AUGUST 29, 2011

Sharon Needles

PERFORMER

Winner, *RuPaul's Drag Race* season four. "I'm beautiful, spooky, and stupid" or, as Princess said to her, "You are exactly the type of guy that I go for. Like, that whole meth look"

PHOTOGRAPHED BY
MATHU ANDERSEN
CULVER CITY, CALIFORNIA,
AUGUST 29, 2011

Phi Phi O'hara

PERFORMER

Competitor, *RuPaul's Drag Race* season four

PHOTOGRAPHED BY
MATHU ANDERSEN
CULVER CITY, CALIFORNIA,
AUGUST 29, 2011

Linda Simpson
PERFORMER, JOURNALIST, PLAYWRIGHT

The very busy actress and party promoter is not only the founder and editor of the pop culture zine *My Comrade*, but also the author of such dark and hilarious plays as *The Emperor's New Codpiece*

PHOTOGRAPHED BY IDRIS + TONY
TIMES SQUARE, NEW YORK CITY, APRIL 10, 2010

In Drag U real women are helped to find their inner queen, and draguate with honors

Downtown Julie Brown
TV PRESENTER

Winner, *RuPaul's Drag U* season two (celebrity episode)

PHOTOGRAPHED BY IDRIS + TONY
AT HOME, MARINA DEL REY, CALIFORNIA,
JULY 22, 2011

Nolan Luther Bailey

LITTLE KID

Nolan Luther Bailey age 4 1/2 on the set of *RuPaul's Drag Race*. "I believe the drag queens are the future"

PHOTOGRAPHED BY JONATHAN CLAY HARRIS
CULVER CITY, CALIFORNIA AUGUST 13, 2011

Santino Rice

FASHION DESIGNER

Santino became famous as the villain on *Project Runway* season two, but found love as a permanent judge on *RuPaul's Drag Race*.

PHOTOGRAPHED BY IDRIS + TONY
CULVER CITY, CALIFORNIA,
JULY 31, 2009

Merle Ginsberg
JOURNALIST

Judge on the first two seasons of *RuPaul's Drag Race* and contributor to *Hollywood Fashion Machine*

PHOTOGRAPHED BY IDRIS + TONY
CULVER CITY, CALIFORNIA,
JULY 31, 2009

Michelle Visage

RADIO DJ, TV PERSONALITY

Co-host on *The RuPaul Show* and judge on *RuPaul's Drag Race*

PHOTOGRAPHED BY
MATHU ANDERSEN
CULVER CITY, CALIFORNIA,
SEPTEMBER 7, 2010

La Toya Jackson

MUSICIAN

Guest judge on *RuPaul's Drag Race* season three. We first worked with La Toya on *RuPaul's Christmas Ball*, spoofing the famous *Mommie Dearest* scene where Joan and Christina have it out. La Toya was priceless playing Ru's daughter. And now she has her own show on OWN

PHOTOGRAPHED BY
MATHU ANDERSEN
CULVER CITY, CALIFORNIA,
SEPTEMBER 7, 2010

Mike Ruiz
PHOTOGRAPHER, MODEL

In addition to being a frequent judge on *Drag Race*, the hot Q scene photographer is also the co-founder of Miahaus Studios

PHOTOGRAPHED BY IDRIS + TONY
LOS ANGELES, CALIFORNIA,
JANUARY 25, 2010

Phoebe Price

MILLINER

Guest, *RuPaul's Drag Race* season two

PHOTOGRAPHED BY IDRIS + TONY AT HOME, HOLLYWOOD, CALIFORNIA, APRIL 15, 2010

Am I good enough? Yes you are, bitch!

Larry Tee
MUSIC PRODUCER

Larry Tee, a crucial member of the sadly missed band The Now Explosion ("Put your arms in the air, show your underarm hair") has known RuPaul since the old days in Atlanta and co-wrote Ru's iconic debut hit "Supermodel"

PHOTOGRAPHED BY ALEX GRACE
AT HOME, HOXTON, LONDON,
JULY 17, 2010

Tom Campbell

SENIOR VICE PRESIDENT OF DEVELOPMENT AT WORLD OF WONDER

The life force of *RuPaul's Drag Race* and the world's biggest Diana Ross fan (second only to RuPaul) poses as all three of the Supremes

PHOTOGRAPHED BY IDRIS + TONY
WORLD OF WONDER PRODUCTIONS,
HOLLYWOOD, CALIFORNIA,
JULY 9, 2009

Jimmy Harry

MUSIC PRODUCER

The co-author of RuPaul's break-out hit "Supermodel" also composed the *Party Monster* and *The Eyes of Tammy Faye* soundtracks. And capped all that winning a Golden Globe with Madonna for 'Masterpiece'

PHOTOGRAPHED BY IDRIS + TONY
AT HOME, HOLLYWOOD, CALIFORNIA,
APRIL 15, 2010

Lucian Piane

MUSIC PRODUCER, SONGWRITER

Lucian aka RevoLucian has produced two of RuPaul's albums and also created the viral hit "Bale Out," a techno mash-up of Christian Bale's infamous on-set outburst

PHOTOGRAPHED BY IDRIS + TONY
AT HOME, HOLLYWOOD, CALIFORNIA,
NOVEMBER 20, 2009

RuPaul
SUPERSTAR, SONGWRITER

Ru surveys the proofs of his book *Workin' It!*

PHOTOGRAPHED BY IDRIS + TONY
WORLD OF WONDER PRODUCTIONS,
HOLLYWOOD, CALIFORNIA,
JANUARY 22, 2010

Women with Balls

WHO RUNS THIS MUTHA? GIRLS! ♦ We love women with balls. Behind the screen, we have worked with some of the ballsiest women in the business: Sheila Nevins, Lauren Zalaznick, Laura Michalchyshyn. All fiercely intelligent, fun executives with an untamable oomph factor. And then, in front of the camera, we have been drawn to women who live out-loud-and-proud. Not just RuPaul, but Tammy Faye, Heidi Fleiss, Pamela Anderson, Carrie Fisher. If it is a man's world – and frankly we're really not so sure – you gotta have balls. Hollywood has always been an object lesson in this...

Hollywood Broads

After we first relocated to LA, there was something so luxurious about being in Hollywood. People say LA has no center, but it does, it's called Hollywood and we lived there, up the road from Mann's Chinese Theatre, next door to the Magic Castle, and a stone's throw from Yamashiro. The Roosevelt Hotel – where the first-ever Academy Awards were held – was at the bottom of our hill and had a coffee shop where we got our morning lattes. It was exciting to go there every morning, stand in line with the tourists on vacation, and know that we actually lived here. We didn't have to go home somewhere on a long-haul flight. We lived in the Magic Kingdom. Our home was within walking distance of our office – not that we ever walked – Crossroads of the World, LA's first outdoor shopping mall that was a collection of Hansel and Gretel cottages and other architectural whims. Randy's office had a lighthouse above it. For real. To live and work here for a negligible rent seemed incredible.

One day, Marc Juris and Jessica Falcon found their way to our lighthouse. They were from AMC and wanted us to make a series for them that would be called *Hollywood Fashion Machine* and would talk

The eyeshadow crucifix designed by David Littleton as a promotional button for the premiere of *The Eyes of Tammy Faye* at the Sundance Film Festival in 2000

A FILM BY

FENTON BAILEY AND RANDY BARBATO

WORLD OF WONDER PRODUCTIONS, INC. IN ASSOCIATION WITH CHANNEL FOUR & CINEMAX PRESENTS "THE EYES OF TAMMY FAYE"
PRODUCED AND DIRECTED BY FENTON BAILEY, RANDY BARBATO NARRATED BY RuPAUL CHARLES EDITED BY PAUL WIESEPAPE
ASSOCIATE PRODUCERS THAIRIN SMOTHERS GABRIEL ROTELLO DIRECTOR OF PHOTOGRAPHY SANDRA CHANDLER
MUSIC BY JIMMY HARRY POST-PRODUCTION SUPERVISOR EDUARDO MAGAÑA EXECUTIVE IN CHARGE OF PRODUCTION HARRY KNAPP
FOR CINEMAX: PRODUCER JOHN HOFFMAN EXECUTIVE PRODUCER SHEILA NEVINS

The first thing Tammy Faye did when we met was put on her dead mother's glasses. She said she kept them to remind her how Mama saw things. We all see things differently

about costumes and fashion in the movies. The pilot was to be about Edith Head, the legendary costumer and a ballsy woman if ever there was one.

Charming as they were in that first meeting, working for them was really tough. They taught us the importance of storytelling when it came to non-scripted shows. It wasn't enough just to lay out the facts, it was all about ramping it up, ramping it up. "Don't just tell it, *sell it,*" Marc would say, shoving back the umpteenth draft of a script. The whole experience made such an indelible impression on us that when a little stray dog showed up at the office one morning, we named her Edith.

Then there was *Out of the Closet, Off the Screen* a title that told the story of actor William Haines, the Hugh Grant of his day: funny, good-looking, big box office. OK, so he wasn't a woman. But he had balls. His brave decision to live an open and authentic gay life back in the '30s spelled a swift end to his acting career. Not that there weren't gays back then, it's just everyone lived in a closet as big as the Ritz. Except William Haines. After the demise of his on-screen career, he turned trauma into triumph by becoming Hollywood's interior designer to the stars, starting with Joan Crawford – surely one of the world's ballsiest women. With her as his muse, he virtually invented the style that came to be known as Hollywood Regency, a delicious contradiction in terms that took a hint of modernism, a dollop of kitsch, and beat it into a mayonnaise splashy enough for Hollywood, yet classy enough to be considered tasteful. Maximal minimalism. The point, then, is not that behind every great man there's a woman, but that behind every ballsy woman there's a gay man.

Not everyone we covered was dead. We were able to do an episode of Hitchcock's strategic use of costumes, most memorably with Tippi Hedren in *The Birds*. What she wore in the actual film was pretty minimal; just one outfit. She had gone on a daytrip flirtation to Bodega Bay when the birds attacked, leaving her stranded without a change of clothes. But for the press tour to promote the film, Edith Head created an entire wardrobe. Amazingly, she still has several pieces of the wardrobe from *The Birds* tour, and even more amazingly, can fit into every single outfit. She modeled each one for us while the lions and tigers roared their approval on The Shambala Preserve where Tippi Hedren resides.

Slightly less felicitous was our experience with Jane Wyman. At some point after her divorce from Ronald Reagan she moved to Palm Springs, where she presumably terrorized the sleepy desert community. She was a no-nonsense kind of woman, every bit as intimidating as the matriarch role she played on *Falcon Crest*. Halfway through a convoluted question, she barked, "Young man, are you mumbling or asking a question?"

But we had the mother of all experiences with Faye Dunaway. The subject was the fashion in the crime caper *Bonnie and Clyde*. We arranged to have a limo pick her up and bring her to the hotel for the interview. But no company would pick her up. A warning sign, perhaps? In the end, she drove herself. On her arrival at the suite, she stuck out her hand. Not to shake, but for the money we had agreed to pay her for the interview. Our understanding had been that she would invoice. But she didn't want to invoice and she didn't want a check. She wanted the full amount before the cameras started rolling. Randy frantically ran from one ATM to another. Unable to secure all the cash, Dunaway wrote up a contract on the spot guaranteeing that the balance would be delivered to her the following morning.

With legal taken care of, Faye turned to the crew: "Each of you tell me who you are, and what you do." One by one the crew stepped forward and accounted for themselves. She listened, and then with grim satisfaction dismissed most of them.

You! You can stay and reposition these lights.

In the end, all that remained of an elaborate lighting set up was a light as bright as the sun not two inches from her face.

Very good. What's your first question?

She had agreed to an hour, which she not unreasonably figured would be when the 60-minute tape ran out. So as we were changing tapes, she said, "I believe I said I would give you an hour and now that the tape has run out, the hour is up."

The amazingly unflappable producer David Schiff had the temerity to tell her that it was actually only a forty-minute tape. So Faye had to sit there for another twenty minutes.

And the point of all this really is just to say that these stars, perhaps as a result of having had to invent themselves out of nothing, had balls of steel. If that sounds like a dis, just consider the countless stars fucked over countless times by movie-biz chauvinists. She was just making sure she got hers.

The Eyes of Tammy Faye

Sometimes the title comes first. And then you just have to make the film. This was the case with *The Eyes of Tammy Faye*.

The first thing Tammy did when we met was put on her dead mother's glasses. She said she kept them to remind her how mama saw things. It could have been ghoulish. Actually, it was. A little. But in that moment she made the point that we all see things differently because we are all looking through different lenses. She also reminded us that no matter how different our points of view or how harshly we judge others, it's all just temporary anyway.

The lens that Tammy Faye loved the most was the camera lens. And it loved her right back. Amazing really, because Tammy didn't have a lot to work with. She was tiny. OK, so Hollywood could always forgive the vertically challenged as long as they had the eyes. But Tammy hardly had any eyes either, just two tiny raisins bordered with stumpy eyelashes. It's what she did with those eyes – those unmistakeable eyes – that was the secret of her success.

Almost half a century before James St James pronounced "If you've got a hunchback, throw a little glitter on it, honey," she did just that. With false eyelashes glued on and her mascara tattooed, Tammy made her eyes pop. She painted her face like Warhol's Marilyn years before Warhol even thought of it. It was a look that was perfect for television, which in those days was an upstart trashy medium no one really respected.

From the moment we met her we liked her. Yes, the eyes were what first grabbed our attention, but with them came warmth, love, and laughter. At a time when most Christian preachers, especially in the South, wouldn't even consider saying the word "gay," Tammy was hugging and loving us – even the PWA's.

The televangelism thing gets a lot of people worked up – poor widows sending in money they can't afford to spend in return for what, etc. The fact is that television has always been a completely commercial medium and anyone who thinks there is a safe divide – or any divide at all – between commercials and content needs a reality check.

Besides, Jim and Tammy were happy to give something in return. While most televangelists like to tell you that you will burn in Hell unless you send money NOW, Jim and Tammy built a theme park and holiday camp. Instead of burning in the fires of Hell, you could take a ride down the water flume. And everyone was welcome. This "come one, come all" approach was more than revolutionary among Christian circles. It was heresy. Jerry Falwell made it his mission to stop them. He

OPPOSITE PAGE: Tammy Faye, Randy, Marlena McCarty (who designed the film titles for *The Eyes of Tammy Faye*), and Fenton upstairs at Trattoria Dell'Arte in New York, December, 1999; Mike Rysavy, Chris McKim, Randy, Naomi Trejo, Dan Snyder, Thairin Smothers, Tammy Faye, Fenton, and Alicia Gargaro-Magaña outside LA's Off Vine restaurant, 2005

THIS PAGE: Tammy Faye eating ice cream in the sub-zero weather at Sundance 2000 during the ice cream-and-coffee klatsch to promote *The Eyes of Tammy Faye*, a brilliant idea conceived by publicists Tom Chen and David Magdael; a sendup of the Tammy Faye T-shirt; Randy and Fenton manhandling Tammy Faye in Park City

LIFE. BEYOND AN EYESHADOW OF DOUBT.

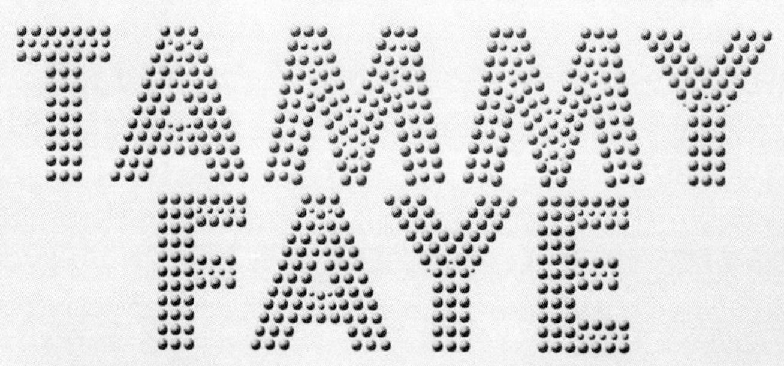
A WE: WOMEN'S ENTERTAINMENT ORIGINAL DOCUMENTARY
TAMMY FAYE
Death Defying
WE : WOMEN'S ENTERTAINMENT PRESENTS A WORLD OF WONDER PRODUCTION 'TAMMY FAYE : DEATH DEFYING'
EXECUTIVE PRODUCERS FENTON BAILEY & RANDY BARBATO PRODUCER/DIRECTOR CHRIS McKIM PRODUCER ALICIA GARGARO EDITOR MIKE RYSAVY MUSIC MICHAEL COHEN
PRODUCTION MANAGER DEVON SCHNEIDER POST PRODUCTION SUPERVISOR TOM WOLF POST PRODUCTION MANAGER JASON BRYAN HEAD OF PRODUCTION DAVID SCHIFF CONSULTING PRODUCER DANIEL SNYDER
ASSISTANT EDITOR NAOMI TREJO SOUND MIXER JIM CORBETT ONLINE EDITOR EDUARDO MAGANA AUDIO POST FACILITY MIX MAGIC, HOLLYWOOD FOR WE DIRECTOR FOR PRODUCTION KATHLEEN FARRELL
MANAGER OF PRODUCTION THERESA PATIRI PRODUCTION COORDINATORS DANA APREA LYNN HELLENBRECHT EXECUTIVE PRODUCER FOR WE ROSEANNE LOPOPOLO
WORLD OF WONDER

We
women's entertainment
www.we.tv

cunningly managed to steal Jim and Tammy's ministry right out from under their noses, deftly destroying their reputations in the process.

But Tammy was not in the least bit bitter and took insult, mockery, and prejudice in her stride. While filming with her in DC, a group of schoolkids mocked her to her face, calling her "butt cheeks." Tammy didn't blink. She gathered them round and said, "C'mon, let's take a picture." In an instant the hecklers became fans. Like she sang, "Jesus takes a frown, turns it upside down and, whoops, there comes a smile."

At the beginning of filming she was divorced, her second husband was in jail, and she was living in Palm Springs. We drove out there to discuss the idea of making a documentary, but she came to the door camera-ready.

"Let's do it, guys!"

We had a camera – of course – but we didn't have lights and it was too dark to film inside. So we decided to shoot outside. It must have been 120 in the shade. She wore a wig, full makeup, and her Sunday best. In our shorts and T-shirts we were melting in the heat, but Tammy didn't even break a sweat. As she described how both her husbands had been railroaded and how she had become a national joke, the tears flowed. Jim J Bullock would later point out, "After the nuclear holocaust there will be three survivors: roaches, Cher, and Tammy Faye."

With the interview done, we asked her to sign the release. "Now, you're not going to make fun of me, are you?" she asked.

Cut to a couple of years later when the film was premiering at the Sundance Film Festival. We were all on tenterhooks. No one had really heard much about Tammy Faye since the scandal that made her a laughing stock back in the mid-'80s. Her daytime talk show had failed and she had survived a bout of colon cancer. When the film ended, a moment of silence hung in the air. Shit, they didn't like it. And then the applause *exploded*. As we stepped out with Tammy, the crowd rose to its feet. This was more than applause. It was wave after wave of heartfelt love for an amazing woman. It had an intensity you could feel. Just remembering that moment still gives us goosebumps.

Today people still say, "Oh, I love that film," and give us such nice compliments. But really all we did was push "record" and remember to take the lens cap off. OK, we did more than that. We added puppets – but, again, that was her idea. "Everybody loves puppets," Tammy told us one day.

Jim and Tammy were more than compassionate. They were broadcast pioneers. They built an entire ministry and television empire out of shows with puppets made of empty paper towel rolls and a couple of old yogurt pots. Their DIY style of television – essentially a public access show in its origins – pioneered the kind of come-into-our-living-room cosy-casting that is the staple of breakfast TV. Together they spoke the language of television so fluently, so effortlessly, and so incessantly that suddenly they had a hugely successful ministry on their hands.

Jim and Tammy built an entire ministry and television empire out of shows with puppets made out of a couple of old yogurt pots

While Tammy was ill with cancer she was still keen to film. She participated in *Death Defying*, our film directed by Chris McKim, and *One Punk Under God*, our series about her son, directed by Jeremy Simmons. A few days before she died, she called Larry King and asked him to interview her. She looked dreadful, ravaged with cancer. But she still had the eyes, not only because the lashes were superglued in place and the mascara tattooed on, but because she always knew it was all about the eyes. And she knew – as we all should by now – that the most important eye of all is the eye of the camera lens. It was the way that she reached out and touched so many.

We will never forget the eyes of Tammy Faye.

THIS PAGE: Publicity shot of Tammy Faye with husband Jim in the early days of their ministry. Cute homemade puppets were the key to their success. Director and producer Chris McKim shoots Tammy Faye for our 2005 WEtv documentary *Tammy Faye: Death Defying*, so-called because Tammy just refused to succumb to the cancer that doctors said gave her only months to live. She would live for several more years

Monica In Black and White

January 16, 2002, the Television Critics Association.

"Monica!"
"Monica!"
"Over here, Monica!"
"Monica! After September 11, can't you just let the country move on?"
"How do you feel about the stain you brought on the presidency? "
"On your right! Monica! Why are you putting yourself in the spotlight again?"
"Monica, why don't you just curl up and die?"

That one even drew a gasp from the audience.

"You said they'd be nice," joked Monica in what subsequently would be reported as "a pathetic wail."

She didn't have a chance. She said that she just wanted to set the record straight. But they didn't care about our film, *Monica in Black and White,* and they didn't care about the record. They just wanted to rip her to shreds.

We so should have seen it coming.

♦

Everyone's got an opinion about Monica. People smirk. Roll their eyes. Crack jokes. When Sheila Nevins first got us in the room with Monica, we were struck by how pretty she was. She quickly put us at our ease, explaining she was no stranger to people being surprised that someone about whom so many ugly things have been written could be attractive in person.

The film's format would be simple, Monica would field questions from an audience of law students. Law students because Monica wanted to talk about the legal issues and shed light on the way she had been manipulated and coerced by prosecutors. Monica would not be protected by a host. She would be up on stage, alone. And the students would be free to ask her anything they wanted. But it soon became apparent as she walked out to lukewarm applause for the first of several question-and-answer sessions we were filming at Cooper Union, that the law students hadn't come prepared with legal questions. Instead, they wanted to know what she called the president when she was alone with him. Which is what we all wanted to know. Because this was not about law. This was about love.

And as Monica chatted openly about it, it looked a lot like love. They chatted on the phone about nothing. They exchanged silly gifts. But, in a series of stunning betrayals, Monica's fairytale became a nightmare, and her romantic reverie became a sexual grotesque.

Cue the wicked witch, Linda Tripp, with a tape recorder for a broomstick. And the handsome prince (that's what she called her Bill, "Handsome"). On January 26, 1998, the day before the State of the Union address, Bill denied the state of his union with Monica when he said, "I did not have sex with that woman." More Pinocchio than Prince Charming.

But, initially, Monica was glad of this disavowal, since it was their plan. "It's people's natural inclination to lie about sex," said Monica. Besides, telling the truth about sex is a dangerous business. When D H Lawrence put the sex in romance in *Lady Chatterly's Lover,* he ended up on trial for obscenity. Madonna's book *Sex* almost derailed her career. The Starr Report would prove to be no less controversial. Casting himself as the long suffering clean-up guy (subtly underscored by his habit of taking out the trash as he left his home chit-chatting with reporters), Starr autopsied Monica and Bill's affair, detailing every sexual gesture and moment. Extramarital affairs aren't that unusual, but what is unusual is to

THIS PAGE: Monica Lewinsky with Fenton and Randy backstage between tapings of *Monica in Black and White* at Cooper Union in New York City, April 3, 2001

OPPOSITE PAGE: The poster for *Monica in Black and White.* Between shooting the documentary in April of 2001 and its airing in March of 2002, 9/11 drastically changed the landscape

America Undercover
SUNDAYS

monica
in black and white

Media, Mayhem, Monica

PRODUCED AND DIRECTED BY FENTON BAILEY RANDY BARBATO EDITED BY JEREMY SIMMONS DIRECTOR OF PHOTOGRAPHY TEODORO MANIACI MUSIC JIMMY HARRY
CO-PRODUCER GABRIEL ROTELLO LINE PRODUCER JERRY KUPFER ASSOCIATE PRODUCER MONA CARD SOUND EDITING DAVID STEINBERG
FOR HBO: PRODUCTION EXECUTIVE SUSAN BENAROYA PRODUCTION ASSOCIATE SARA BERNSTEIN SENIOR PRODUCER LISA HELLER EXECUTIVE PRODUCER SHEILA NEVINS

HBO

PREMIERES SUNDAY, MARCH 3, 10PM/9C

Monica was there to recover her dignity. Like Peter Pan she wanted her shadow back. The audience wouldn't let her have it

see moments of illicit passion clinically listed in a criminal report. The subjects' passion was cleverly crafted to become the reader's revulsion. And so the Starr Report was the crowning betrayal of Monica. Thanks to it, we know more about her than we have a right to know about any individual. And because she retains not a shred of privacy with which to cover herself, she has also been stripped of the dignity and respect any fellow citizen enjoys. To say she has been a victim of an invasion of privacy is a considerable understatement. Informational gang rape is more like it.

Not that she got much sympathy from the audience. Why did she talk? they asked her. Because she was threatened with jail, because she was under oath. Why does she continue to talk about it? they asked her.

But that was why they were there. This was the show they had come to see.

Patiently, Monica said she would give anything to have her anonymity back but she also had to set the record straight: She never meant this to become public, she signed a false affidavit to cover it up. Yes, she told a few friends. But there's a difference between telling someone something in private and having it revealed in public. There's a difference between confiding in someone over the phone and hearing it played back in the offices of the FBI. There's a difference between something you write and then delete from your computer, and seeing it published in a government report and distributed over the internet.

But why, the audience kept on, didn't she put herself out to pasture in Nebraska or Nova Scotia?

As the back-and-forth went on, it became clear that the audience and Monica were engaged in some kind of struggle. Linda Williams in her book *Hardcore* characterizes the evolution of pornography as "a frenzy of the visible," describing the way the medium is forever striving to show sex more explicitly, more realistically, and more close-up. It's ultimately an exercise in futility, because the thing we seek to see cannot be shown. It was no different in Monica's case; the audience came frenziedly seeking the visible, the striptease of her soul. The more Monica gave, the more they wanted. And yet the more she revealed, the *less* they actually *saw*. Meanwhile, Monica was there to recover her dignity. Like Peter Pan, she wanted her shadow back. But the audience wouldn't let her have it.

Sitting on the dais with Monica as the critics tore her apart at TCA, we felt we had finally lived a tiny bit of what Monica has had to endure.

Shortly after we left the stage, out came Rudolph Giuliani, so-called hero of 9/11. The television critics gave him a standing ovation. They kissed his ass with the same kind of fervor with which they had savaged Monica. It was sick-making.

Listening to one of Linda Tripp's taped calls with Monica one day, we noticed that David Bowie's "Heroes" was playing in the background. It was an epiphany. The song's ache for transcendent heroism paired with the melancholy recognition that this was simply wishful thinking, perfectly captured the plight of all those who, in this episode, aspired to be heroes only to fall short. Bill Clinton, Kenneth Starr, Linda Tripp – they all emerged lesser people. But not Monica.

She did her best. She refused to wear a wire to trap the president. And where everyone else got to walk away and go on to other things, she paid for all this with the loss of her good name.

THIS PAGE: The crew pass for the Monica tapings; Monica mugging with Fenton and Randy at World of Wonder's Christmas party, 2008; title still of *Monica in Black and White*

TOP: Imelda Marcos watches a parade in the northern province of the Philippines on SEPTEMBER 11, 2006, honoring the birthday of her late husband, Ferdinand Marcos. BOTTOM: Imelda Marcos gives an impromptu after-dinner performance at the Fort Ilocandia Hotel in Ilocos Norte, September 10, 2006. Note the faux bois carpet tiles

Dictators of Design: Imelda Marcos

Part of the psychosis of dictators is that they often leave behind vast building projects. This gave us the idea for a series on the Discovery Channel about what the dictators who (ab)use their countries as their own personal canvas leave behind.

When Jim J Bullock said that only Tammy Faye, Cher, and cockroaches would survive the nuclear holocaust, he left out another survivor: Imelda Marcos, former First Lady of the Philippines.

At first blush, Imelda Marcos, now in her eighties and elected to the Philippine House of Representatives, was as extraordinaryolicious as any of the characters from *Manhattan Cable*. She always wore butterfly wings – the Asian version of *Dynasty* shoulder pads – and the shoes always matched the dress. But she was also driven by a vision easier to dismiss than it was to understand.

If you believe the things you read about Imelda, you would expect someone feared and despised by her own people. But everywhere she went – and it was impossible for her to have orchestrated this – people flocked to her. Perhaps she just had that royal charisma, someone who doesn't so much need your attention as simply commands it. But then she would do these nutty things. Like getting up after dinner and serenading her guests with an impromptu cabaret set that channeled Liza Minnelli, disco, and traditional Pinoy songs. It was as strange, compelling, and unfathomable as the faux bois carpet tiles beneath her feet. It was, by the way, approaching midnight and she had been up since dawn. At breakfast that morning, she appeared in the coffee shop of our hotel with a plastic bag. She sat herself down and rummaged through the bag, pulling out stock certificates, gold bullion records, and statements from the Bank of England. She was worried that we thought – like the rest of the world – that she had looted her country. Her point was that they were multimillionaires before they even came to power, and she had the documents to prove it.

After the impromptu concert, she wanted to show us her rooms. As the tour progressed, a tired-looking assistant set up a slide projector. She wanted to show us a few photos. We begged off. In her hand she held a tiny gun. Was it wise to deny her? Turned out the miniature pistol wasn't an actual weapon, but a slide pointer. For the next couple of hours, Imelda showed us pictures of, well, everything.

HER CHILDHOOD IN LEYTE:
During the war, we were placed by my father in a beach house in Leyte that I thought was paradise, so I always say I was nurtured in paradise. Nature is a great teacher. You look at the landscape, you see a mountain here, you see water here, you see a tree here, the rocks here, the plants here, the flowers here. You put them all together – lump them in one picture, they don't clash. Nature never clash. You put all kinds of flowers in one vase – red, yellow, all kinds of flowers, big, small – they won't clash. Nature never clash.

But human beings clash.

During the war there was so much ugliness in Leyte. I remember going to the beautiful beaches, there were hundreds and thousands dead by the seashore, and crabs were eating the dead, and the stench and the mosquitoes and the flies. Japanese and American dead on either side of the road, ten feet high sometimes. The stench. There were dead in the backyards of our homes. Trucks full of heads put on display by the enemy for all of us to see. There I saw the ugliness of war. This was not done by the beasts of the jungle. This was done by human beings to each other. From then on I saw that nobody wins in a war.

IMELDA AND HER HUSBAND'S TIME IN POWER:
Our Philippine cultural genesis is via a divine bamboo that was split to create man, who was called 'the strong'

THIS PAGE: Title still from *Dictators of Design*; Imelda shows us around the Fort Ilocandia Hotel, September 10, 2006

OPPOSITE PAGE: Green is Imelda's favorite color and everything always matches; Imelda checks her makeup before we interview her, September 12, 2006; the license plate on Imelda's Mercedes-Benz. IRM are her daughter's initials

and woman who was called 'the beautiful.' It's the complete opposite of the Western concept where Adam was the first creation of God, and from the rib of Adam came Eve. There were doubts about whether women had souls because we were just extension of men and, worse, it is suspected that we women were named Eve because it's the root word for evil. Adam, the weakling, succumbed to the evilness from Eve and so paradise was lost, and the legacy is Original Sin.

Well, President Marcos and myself were very sensitive to our cultural genesis. And he said, "Power is for peace not for war," and I said, "Beauty is not for conquest, beauty is not for seduction, prostitution. Beauty is for nurturing, caring, loving, mothering," and mothering in Latin means selfless endless love, endless giving, and so I said, "The role of beauty is an endless giving." In the end the only things we keep are those we give away, and mothering is selfless and endless love. Even death does not diminish a mother's love. Almost everybody remembers their mothers and still feel their mothers' love long after they've gone. And this is the role of everybody. The role of everybody is really endless and selfless giving. That is how we should use power and beauty.

When Ferdinand became president he said to me, "As president I am father of the country. As first lady, you are mother to the country. I will build a strong house for the Filipino people, and you make it a home." So I reflected, what makes a home? Love. What is love made real? Beauty. Beautiful tradition, beautiful values, beautiful art, beautiful things, beautiful culture.

I said to people, "Why don't you improve your houses and fix them up and make them nicer?" They said, "Oh, we're so poor ma'am. All we have here is coconut and bamboo." So I said, "I am going to make not only a house made out of bamboo, but a mansion. Not only a house made of coconut, but a palace." So I made a coconut palace and I built a bamboo mansion. And they could not tell me that there were not enough coconuts because the Philippines was producing 87% of the world's coconut oil.

And people were asking me, "Mrs Marcos, what is your role as first lady?" Well, I had to be a star that people would look up to. Mass follows class, never class follows mass. I said, "I have to be a star and then also at the same time a slave." So my role was star and slave. I had to enslave myself, work so hard from day to night, so that everybody becomes a star.

HER LEGACY:
Who is Imelda? Was she a genius? No! Who was Imelda? Did she have a great mind? No! Is she a great artist? No! What did Imelda have? What Imelda had was common to everybody – common sense. And common sense is bringing out what is natural in you. Everybody has what Imelda had. All we have to do is use our common sense.

Life is not only to be extravagantly generously giving, but to give it all, because in the end the only things we keep in life are those we give way. Money and power you take with you only up to the grave, but beauty and love will live beyond your grave until infinity.

In the end I was born because I was loved. The Lord had me created because of love. I just follow him. What is love? It is giving, caring, nurturing.

And this is the great creativity of the creator that each and every one was made unique. Even identical twins are not the same. Every drop of rain, every grain of sand is unique. What a bore if everybody was first lady. Once I was asked, "Mrs Marcos, would you want to be cloned like Dolly the sheep?" I said, "Don't you think one Imelda is enough?"

It was now almost three in the morning. We had seen hundreds of slides of buildings. We had seen plans for tunnels, power plants, we had seen

Once Imelda was asked if she wanted to be cloned like Dolly the Sheep. "Don't you think one Imelda is enough?" She replied

numerological and symbolic charts showing the order of the universe, but now she was watching a grainy black-and-white news clip: Imelda is at a function when suddenly, from the front of the crowd, a man leaps on her, like a lion, and unleashes a frenzy of stabbing. Imelda watches, rapt.

The first few seconds I was even joking at myself and asking the Lord, "This is a program for beautification and cleanliness campaign and here comes an assassin with a knife, so ugly and so dirty." I said, "Lord, I'm so committed to beauty, why did you have this man with this ugly knife to kill me? He should have placed at least a yellow ribbon – a beautiful ribbon to balance it off."

The Filipino culture is committed to what is beautiful. Even as we greet each other, we don't say good morning, good afternoon, we say beautiful morning, beautiful afternoon, beautiful evening. We are brainwashed to beauty.

This is the reason I couldn't understand why when I did beautiful things and built beautiful buildings or did anything beautiful, it was luxury, it was excessive, it was vulgarity. I did a little research on it and found out that the word "vulgar" derives from a Greek word meaning overly beautiful. Then I stopped worrying because I have no problem. And I can't do anything about it anyway.

They tell me, Imelda you're cross-eyed. I look at the mirror, I'm not cross-eyed. It's a waste of time to be angry. Instead of being angry I have compassion for the person that tells me that I am cross-eyed when it is not true because the poor girl or man sees ugliness instead of what is normal, natural, and true. Why would you be angry, when they see ugliness where there is only beauty? In my case I see beauty everywhere. I see beauty in everything including garbage. And I create beauty. When the government stole my jewelry, I began making jewelry out of garbage.

Anna Nicole's Dark Roots

No one had much time or patience for Anna Nicole. Probably because she was stunningly, ravishingly beautiful. We had hoped she would come aboard for our re-examination of who she really was, but we never quite got to her. Instead, we ran up against a strange but intriguing guy, Howard K Stern. A flat-footed lawyer cum bodyguard in a suit, wearing shoes that made his feet look enormous.

All our entreaties to Anna had failed, so we decided to tell Anna's story by taking a look at her roots. Who were her parents, her siblings? It was time for an intervention. We had flown her cousin Shelly from Meja Texas to meet with Anna. They had grown up together, yet had become estranged over the years.

Ding dong, we rang the doorbell and out came Howard the self-appointed officiant at a funeral yet to happen.

We explained. He rebutted. We countered. He threatened. We left – though not before Shelly slipped a heartfelt note under Anna's front door telling her not only how much she wanted to see her, but also where she was staying, etc.

Less than 30 minutes later, a limo pulled up outside cousin Shelly's hotel and scooped her off for an evening – we assume – of Hollywood glamour. Unfortunately, it was without us or our cameras. But it was OK. Truly, it was more important that they were reunited. Besides, the next morning we interviewed Shelly with the Hollywood sign as our backdrop. Every few minutes she paused to throw up.

It was the lack of access to Anna that inspired Gabriel Rotello to pen *The Ballad of Anna Nicole*, which would become the narration for the film.

THIS PAGE: RuPaul and Anna Nicole Smith on the set of *The RuPaul Show*, 1998, in happier days; title still from *Dark Roots*, our unauthorized look at Anna Nicole Smith

OPPOSITE PAGE: The segments in *Dark Roots* were linked by a brilliant bluegrass ditty written in about twenty minutes by the doc's producer and director, Gabriel Rotello

The Ballad of Anna Nicole
by Gabe Rotello

Ya'll gather round
To hear ~~our~~ my story
Of a ~~strippers~~ young girl's dreams
of fame & glory.

From ~~the~~ a stripper's stage
She became a star —
And a ~~rich mans~~ millionaire's wife
~~She went too far~~! Oh, she went far!

She wore diamond rings
She had rhinestone boots
But ~~her~~ the secret was
She had dark, dark roots.

and add in some additional verses here and there, like:

A new career
She now persued
By posing naked
In the nude.

Her fame shot up
Then it crashed back down
when the papers dragged her
Through tabloid town.

Now ~~hostle~~ hauled before
Their inquisition
They tried her for
Her blond ambition

As the ~~[illegible]~~ scandals raged
Like a yeast infection
Her career went zooming
In the wrong direction.
(is this too mean?)

Ballad of Anna Nicole

Y'all gather round
To hear our story
Of a young girl's dreams
Of fame and glory

From the stripper's stage
She became a star
And a millionaire's wife
Oh, she went far

She wore diamond rings
She had rhinestone boots
But the secret was
She had dark, dark roots

In chicken grease
She feared she'd drown
So Vicky flew
To Houston town

Every night she prayed
'Til she was blessed
With Dr. Johnson's
Double D-cup breasts

As aches and pains
And the hurts embrace her
She turned to Xanax
And a tequila chaser

A new career
She now pursued
By posing naked
In the nude

Her beauty and grace
And her buxom breasts
Were noticed by
A prince from Guess?

Her fame shot up
Then it crashed back down
When the papers dragged her
Through tabloid town

Her kin folk wondered
As her jewels got bigger
Was she a true lover
Or a plain gold digger

She thought getting hitched
Was half the battle won
She sure didn't count on
Old Howard's son

As the scandals rage
Like a yeast infection
Her career goes zooming
In the wrong direction

Now hauled before
Their inquisition
They try her for
Her blonde ambition

When she was alive
No one would have her
But they fought like cats
Over her cadaver.

Well she's laughing last
From the great beyond
Cause she died in shape
And she's still a blond...

So there it is
Our peculiar story
Of a young girl's dreams
Of fame and glory

...Is she good or bad
People still dispute
But they all agree
She had dark, dark roots.

Heidi Ho Heidi Hi

Sometimes you set out to tell one story, but end up telling another.

On the first day of filming *Heidi Fleiss: The Would-Be Madam of Crystal*, things got off to a rocky start. Our DP, Goro, was preparing to film Heidi and the young woman we thought was her assistant in their car when an argument broke out. Heidi punched her in the face and snatched her bag. As the assistant screamed, Heidi got out and hopped into the camera car. "Let's go," she said. Thus began our bumpy ride with Heidi.

Over the previous five years, we had talked with her off and on about doing a number of projects together, but none ever took off. We were fans of her entrepreneurial spirit and no-nonsense personality. On the one hand, she was never afraid to speak the truth, yet on the other hand, she never spilled the beans. She knew the secrets of Hollywood's most powerful, but she never betrayed them, even though it meant going to jail.

Even before we began to film, we met with her at her novelty sex shop on Cahuenga Boulevard. During the entire meeting, Heidi never stopped sweeping. She had a broom and kept sweeping bits of dirt and dust into mounds. Sweep, sweep, sweep. That should have been our first clue. Crystal. The meth to her madness.

Sometime in 2006, Heidi announced she was going to open a brothel for women. It was the perfect hook for a film and Heidi had us convinced it would be her big second act. She had a vision: architects, land, a business plan, and passion. What a film this would be. But we had a nagging, uneasy feeling. The brothel was going to be located in Crystal, Nevada. Just outside of Parumph, a Vegas-adjacent haven for characters and eccentrics. The name of the place alone should have been our second clue.

We tried to track the story of the brothel, but very early on it became clear that no ground would be broken, no brothel would be built. Instead, there were midnight excursions into the desert to gather rocks. By this point, the penny finally dropped that Heidi had a habit. She was erratic, mysterious, unpredictable. It was impossible to stick to any kind of schedule. There were abrupt mood swings, and more than once she tried to get us thrown off the project.

Stuck out in Crystal with Heidi and her broomstick and endless sweeping, things looked very bleak.

Then a funny thing happened. Heidi introduced us to her next-door neighbor, a bedridden former madam who lived in a double-wide trailer. Inside, she kept dozens of exotic birds. Rare macaws. Parrots. Birds of all shapes and sizes. Some in cages, some roaming free. The din was unbelievable. The smell, not so great. But every time Heidi stepped into this crazy world, she transformed into a loving, caring soul. One bird in particular, a scarlet macaw named Dalton, she was particularly fond of, and the two formed an instant bond. He would sit on her shoulder for hours, soothed by her endless sweeping.

And then, sadly, the old madam died. It wasn't entirely a surprise. She was very sick. And Heidi – who seemed barely capable of looking after herself properly, let alone other living things – took in all of the old lady's birds, and added a huge aviary onto her house.

In so many ways it was better than if she had built that brothel. Because in her bird sanctuary, we got to really see Heidi, the Heidi beneath the Hollywood Madam, the Heidi hidden in the addict. When Dalton died Heidi raged, cried, and sobbed. We saw

THIS PAGE: Stills from *Heidi Fleiss: The Would-Be Madam of Crystal*, a very surprising and unexpected love story

She's in the middle of nowhere
trying to learn some new tricks.

HEIDI FLEISS
THE WOULD-BE MADAM OF CRYSTAL

HBO DOCUMENTARY FILMS IN ASSOCIATION WITH WORLD OF WONDER PRESENTS A FILM BY FENTON BAILEY & RANDY BARBATO
"HEIDI FLEISS: THE WOULD-BE MADAM OF CRYSTAL" ASSOCIATE PRODUCER SHAM IBRAHIM MUSIC COMPOSED BY DAVID BENJAMIN STEINBERG DIRECTORS OF PHOTOGRAPHY DAVID KEMPNER & GORO TOSHIMA
EDITED BY LANGDON PAGE CO-PRODUCED BY MONA CARD DIRECTED AND PRODUCED BY FENTON BAILEY & RANDY BARBATO FOR HBO: SUPERVISING PRODUCER NANCY ABRAHAM FOR HBO: EXECUTIVE PRODUCER SHEILA NEVINS

MONDAY, JULY 21, 9PM HBO

DANCE
DONT
BULLFIGHT!
Manolo
looking for
CHARO
CHARO
Manolo
looking for
CHARO
Charos
CLUB
Manolo
looking for
CHARO

what no one had ever seen before, or actually even thought possible: Heidi in love.

It doesn't always end happily ever after. Heidi stopped speaking to us long before the film was done. She has never spoken a single word about the film and we haven't heard from her since.

Women With Bulls

When it comes to women with balls, sometimes the balls were steel (Imelda), sometimes the balls were men's (Heidi), sometimes they were eight balls (Anna Nicole), and sometimes they were metaphysical (Tammy Faye). In one case they belonged to a bull.

We first met Charo when she guested on *The RuPaul Show*, but it was her guest appearance on our VH1 show, *Viva Hollywood*, when we really bonded. She invited us into her trailer as she was doing her makeup. She explained how she felt we had a lot in common, because she knew that we had worked with RuPaul and she too was someone who had created her character. The Charo everyone knew and loved was a construct. Behind the curves, the hair, and mangled English was a business woman, a classically trained musician, and a loving mom and wife. Then she put down her makeup brush and took our hand and said with complete solemnity that she would be there whenever we needed her.

From that point on, we called Charo for a number of appearances and favors, and did our best to continue to work with her. And she always showed up and turned it out. One day she called needing a favor. She explained she had a new club track coming out, "España Cañí," and had an idea for a music video – did we have any ideas on how she could get it made?

Anything for Charo. So we provided the studio, crew, and editing; she provided the costumes, dancers, and...a bull. Yes, she showed up at WOW for the shoot with a baby bull ready for its close-up. Charo lured it into the elevator with a huge baby bottle and proceeded to dance with that bull, changing costumes three times. The song went on to be a huge club hit for Charo and the bull moved into her Beverly Hills home. So you could say she's a woman with bull's balls.

FROM LEFT: Stills from the video we made for Charo's "España Cañí" (means Spanish Gypsy) starring her baby bull, shot in the World of Wonder studio, on September 18, 2008

BELOW: Candis Cayne, Randy, Charo, and Lady Bunny photographed by Jeff Hobbs, March 16, 2011, on the set of *Drag U*

Tammy Faye Bakker

TV EVANGELIST

Greg Gorman kindly let us use this image for our 1999 Christmas card

PHOTOGRAPHED BY GREG GORMAN
LOS ANGELES, CALIFORNIA,
OCTOBER 26, 1998

"I don't judge people. We're all made out of the same dirt. And God doesn't make any junk"

–TAMMY FAYE BAKKER

Jay Bakker

CHRISTIAN PASTOR

Our series on the Sundance Channel about the fabulous Bakker boy, *One Punk Under God*, continued our saga with the Bakker family. Thanks to showrunner Jeremy Simmons, it brilliantly managed to explore the son's relationship with his mother and, especially, his father

PHOTOGRAPHED BY IDRIS + TONY
BROOKLYN, NEW YORK, MAY 11, 2010

Jim J Bullock

TV PRESENTER, ACTOR, COMEDIAN

Jim poses with a portrait of Tammy, a prop from *The Jim J and Tammy Faye Show*. He perhaps put it better than anyone else when he borrowed Jimmy James' words: "After a nuclear holocaust, all that will be left are cockroaches, Tammy Faye, and Cher"

PHOTOGRAPHED BY IDRIS + TONY
WORLD OF WONDER PRODUCTIONS,
HOLLYWOOD, CALIFORNIA,
JANUARY 22, 2010

Charo
MUSICIAN, PERFORMER

Charo lives with her miniature bull in Beverly Hills

PHOTOGRAPHED BY IDRIS + TONY
THE RIVIERA HOTEL, LAS VEGAS, NEVADA, JULY 28, 2009

Heidi Fleiss

MADAME AND ENTREPRENEUR

Heidi stopped talking to us while we were making the documentary, which made finishing it something of a challenge. But, believe it or not, we only wish her well

PHOTOGRAPHED BY GREG GORMAN
HOLLYWOOD, CALIFORNIA,
FEBRUARY 15, 2006

And then a funny thing happened. Heidi fell in love. With a bird

Bobby Trendy

INTERIOR DESIGNER

Although Bobby is not technically a woman, he does have balls. He was our favorite character on *The Anna Nicole Show* and he appears in *Dark Roots*

PHOTOGRAPHED BY IDRIS + TONY AT PHILIP MORRIS, NOVEMBER 12, 2009

Tippi Hedren

ACTRESS

Almost fifty years after starring in Hitchcock's *The Birds*, Tippi could still fit into every one of the outfits Edith Head had designed for her! She is the Founder and President of The Roar Foundation, which funds the big cat animal sanctuary www.shambala.org, northeast of Los Angeles

PHOTOGRAPHED BY IDRIS + TONY
SHAMBALA PRESERVE, ACTON, CALIFORNIA, JULY 9, 2010

Where everyone else got to walk away, she paid with the loss of her good name

Monica Lewinsky

AUTHOR

Monica was uncomfortable with these pictures perhaps because they reveal just how beautiful she is. She has had to live a life unforgiven, which seems especially unfair in a country known for giving people second chances

MAKE-UP BY BILLY B
PHOTOGRAPHED BY IDRIS + TONY
HOLLYWOOD DELL, CALIFORNIA,
NOVEMBER 13, 2009

Bo Derek
ACTRESS

Bo Derek was the host of *The Hollywood Fashion Machine* series on AMC

PHOTOGRAPHED BY IDRIS + TONY
SANTA YNEZ, CALIFORNIA,
JULY 8, 2010

Laura Michalchyshyn

TV EXECUTIVE

The former president of Planet Green and EVP, Programming & Marketing of Sundance Channel greenlit *The Fabulous Beekman Boys*, *Dresscue Me @ Shareen Vintage*, and *Man Shops Globe*. She is surrounded by cute cut-out critters used to promote the first season of *Beekman Boys*

PHOTOGRAPHED BY IDRIS + TONY
NEW YORK CITY, JULY 26, 2010

Lauren Zalaznick

TV EXECUTIVE

The president of NBC Universal Women and Lifestyle Entertainment Networks is known affectionately as LZ. In this photo she reminds us that she knows how to put on a show!

PHOTOGRAPHED BY IDRIS + TONY
CHELSEA, NEW YORK CITY,
OCTOBER 29, 2009

Sheila Nevins

TV EXECUTIVE

If she were so inclined, the president of HBO Documentaries could boast that she has more Emmys than any other living person

PHOTOGRAPHED BY TIMOTHY GREENFIELD SANDERS, NEW YORK CITY, MAY 15, 2010

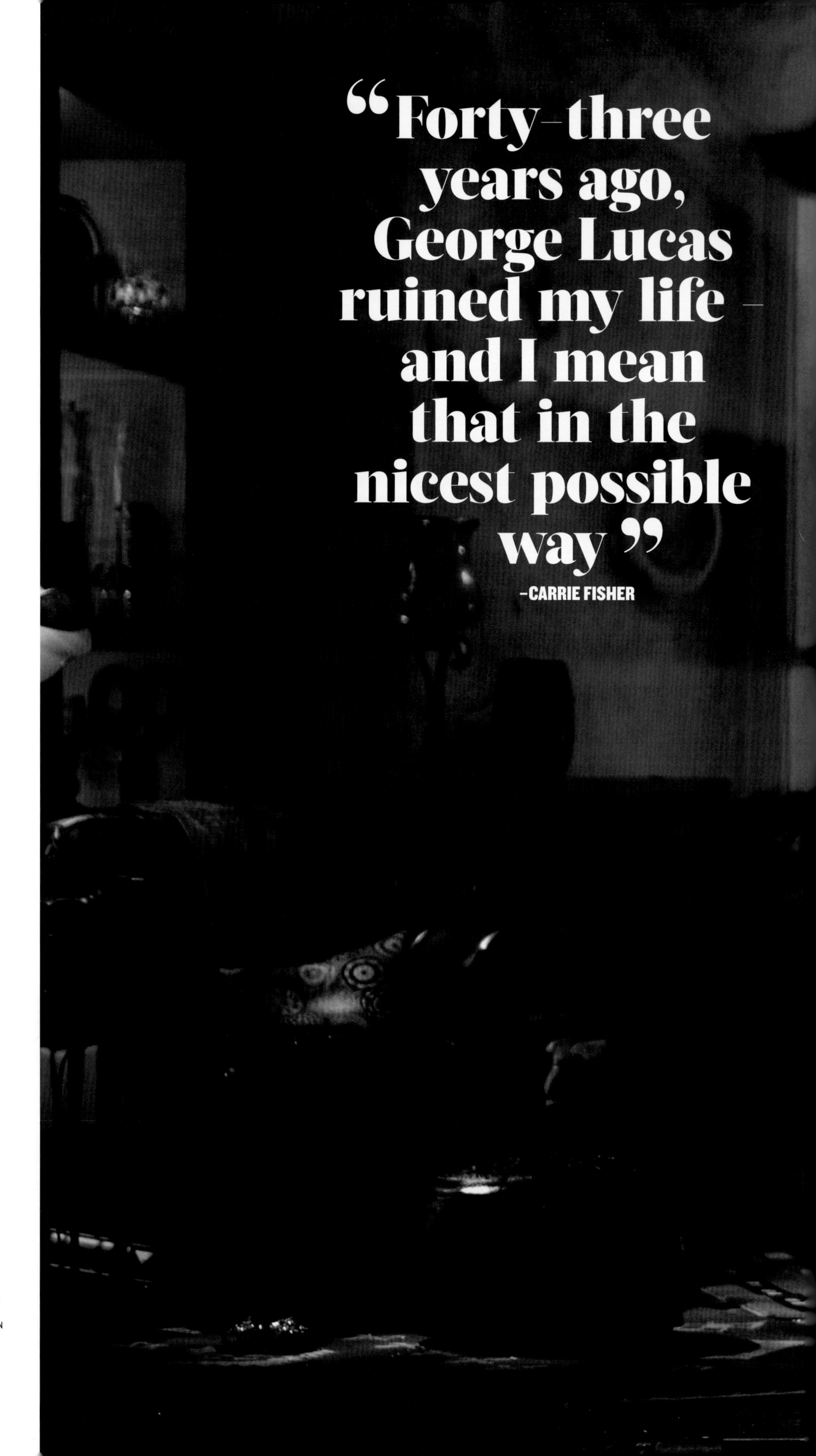

Carrie Fisher

ACTRESS AND AUTHOR

When Carrie Fisher laughs at herself, she makes the whole world laugh with her. We turned her one-woman show, *Wishful Drinking*, into an Emmy-nominated HBO special

PHOTOGRAPHED BY PATRICK HARBRON
SOUTH ORANGE, NEW JERSEY,
JUNE 26, 2010

Party Monster

ONE NIGHT BEFORE CHRISTMAS, in 1996, we sat in the Hollywood Canteen waiting for James St James to arrive for dinner. From the moment he swept into the restaurant, it was clear that he had something on his mind. Throughout dinner he regaled us with the mother of all stories: How Michael Alig had turned from being king of the club kids to club-kid killer; how Michael's roommate Freeze had hammered someone called Angel (so-called because of his habit of wearing feathered wings with a six-foot span) over the head; how Michael had injected the unconscious Angel with Drano; how they had dumped the body in their bathtub and left it for a week or more before hacking the legs off, stuffing the torso in a box, and dumping it into the East River. James apparently knew all the gory details and spared us none.

Fenton and Randy eat ice cream at the Castro premiere in San Francisco of the shockumentary June, 1998

The gist of this amazing story was not unfamiliar. All year long we had heard the rumors of a murder in Manhattan. First there was a blind item in the *Village Voice* by gossip columnist Michael Musto. Then there was a cover story in the *Village Voice* by reporter Frank Owen that named names and went into even more detail. There were also reports in the *New York Post* and *Daily News*, and a bizarre feature in *Details* magazine, complete with pictures by David LaChapelle, anointing Michael as a postmodern murderer – naughty but nice.

But in spite of the press we didn't believe it. In fact, *because* of the press we didn't believe it. We thought Michael had conceived the whole thing as one of his situationist pranks: Angel disappears and Michael goes around telling everyone that he killed him, going so far as to write "Guilty" on his forehead, and just as the police were about to arrest him he would throw a huge party and Angel would come down from the ceiling wearing his wings. It seemed another of Michael's brilliant attention-getting devices, the drumbeat of press merely confirming the success of Michael's clever media virus.

For sure, Michael needed something to give his career a boost. For several years he had been throwing an annual gore-themed party called "Blood Feast," inspired by Herschell Gordon Lewis' similarly titled splatter classic of the '60s. Michael even pictured himself on the invitation with his brains bashed out, a bloody hammer lying nearby. But the novelty of these parties was wearing thin. To have

Party monster
good.
evil.
fun.

The club kids made spectacles of themselves by tottering around on absurdly high platform sneakers, wearing unitards with the butts cut out, and waving kiddie lunch boxes. Initially greeted with derision, the look soon caught on

Angel reappear as if back from the dead would be just the kind of coup that Michael, wunderkind turned drug mess, desperately needed.

And so we waited for the invitation.

♦

We had known Michael almost as long as we had known James. We first met him within a few weeks of his arrival in New York. Still in his teens, he was a shy kid, cute as a button, who had somehow persuaded management he was old enough to work as a busboy at Danceteria.

Instead of joining the existing scene, he quietly created his own. No one paid him any attention as he gathered a bunch of kids around him with wacky monikers like Christopher Comp, Jonathan Junkie, Julius Teaser, and Jenny Talia – "like the mother goose creating all the little fairy-tale characters," as Michael Musto put it. The club kids, as they became known, lived up to their cartoony names with outfits spawned out of a channel-surfing psychosis, sampling consumer and celebrity culture like kids in a candy store. At Disco 2000, Michael's weekly club circus freak show, he created a surreal playground where they could cavort with other post-cartoon creations such as Clara the Carefree Chicken and Dan Dan the Naked Man.

We loved the club kids and their nutty aesthetic, and tried to raise money to make a documentary about them. But we hit a wall. What to us was "modern art on legs" (to borrow Boy George's description of Leigh Bowery, a major inspiration for Michael) was to television executives just a bunch of kids making an exhibition of themselves: "Who wants to know about a bunch of clubbers running round thinking they are famous?"

The fact that these kids did nothing other than wanting to be famous was not just the point, but the whole entire point. In the post-Warhol era, Michael Alig realized that fame was not the reward of a meritocracy. Stardom was a chimera, nothing more than a reflexive act of self-invention. "Don't dream it, be it," as Frank-N-Furter advised. You didn't have to be rich, you didn't have to be beautiful, you didn't even have to do anything. Once upon a time you might have had to be Calvin Klein, Liza Minnelli, or Halston to get into Studio 54. But to get into Disco 2000 all you had to be was fabulous.

And it didn't matter if you had no money; out of nothing other than some ratty wigs and torn tights you could doll yourself up as some Dada bag lady from space and this absurd ensemble – worn with sufficient confidence – would sweep you past the velvet ropes of nightclubs into the VIP rooms. And it didn't matter if you were ugly, either. Perhaps out of revenge for his own wretched school years, these were the very people that Michael wanted to empower – the poor huddled masses fresh out of junior high who didn't fit in.

Moreover, Michael understood that instead of trying to assimilate into the current scene, the trick was to head in the other direction. Instead of trying to look cool, Michael and his gang played the fool and tried to look as ridiculous as possible. The club kids made spectacles of themselves by tottering around on absurdly high platform sneakers, wearing unitards with the butt cut out, and waving kiddie lunchboxes. Initially greeted with derision, the look soon caught on; the lunchbox and platforms became de rigueur.

Michael had big plans for his movement, envisioning the club kids as a brand/lifestyle that would at once copy and satirize the marketeers like Ralph Lauren and Martha Stewart. To maximize press coverage, he started his own magazine, *Project X*. He released a single for Clara the Carefree Chicken on his own record label. Then he persuaded Limelight's owner Peter Gatien to pump millions into Club USA, which, packed with

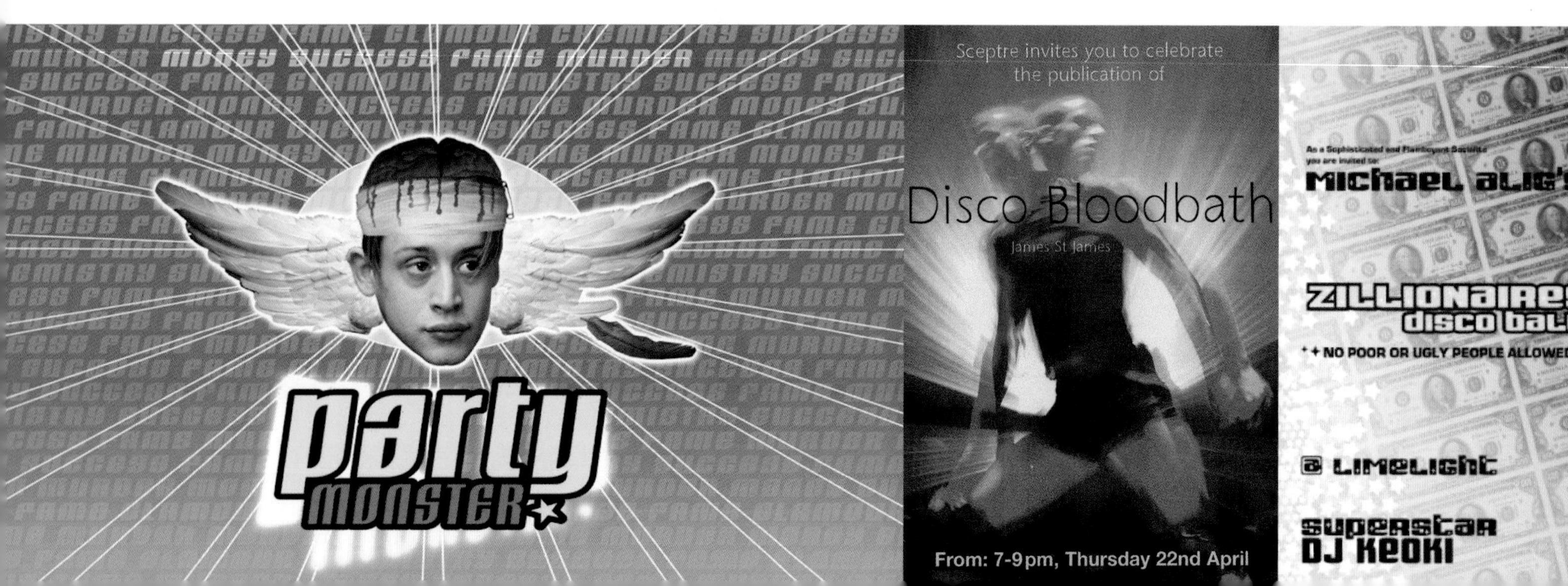

corporate logos and neon, was conceived as a parodic celebration of consumer culture, a simulacrum of Times Square actually in Times Square. In preparation for the opening, Michael went across the country on a club kid talent search. He was a veritable Pied Piper, bringing more misfit toys into his orbit.

But there was another side to Michael's command performance as entrepreneur. From the Filthy Mouth contest to Ida Slapter's champagne enema, Michael was trading in subversion. The person who created the cutesy club kid trading cards also wanted to launch a line of candy in the shape of drugs. There was always this anarchic edge to Michael's plans that made them so tempting. As Ernie Glam said of those buttless pedophile romper suits he made for Michael, "It was some kind of perverted sex clown aesthetic where it was very childish and silly but at the same time kind of nasty and obscene."

Michael's brand of spectacle also depended on escalation. He had a thing about pee. "Urinvited," read one of his invitations. Not a particularly original pun but when the invitation came written on a slip of paper in a vial of pee-colored liquid, the ick factor hit home. Then came Ernie the Pee Drinker, a man who would get on stage and drink a glass of his own pee. And Michael himself got into the habit of peeing into bottles of beer and handing them out as free drinks, and peeing off the balcony of Disco 2000 onto the people below.

Michael never peed on us, but it became clear how far he was prepared to take his commitment to extreme chic when we produced a commercial for the opening of Club USA. When it came time to get paid, we had to wait hours in the lobby of the club for Michael, who finally appeared with the money in loose bills in a brown paper bag. "Oh. Hi. There you are. Count it," he said breathlessly. But we were too gobsmacked by his appearance to count it. It was winter, but Michael was wearing only lederhosen and a flimsy T-shirt. He had a cyst on the back of his neck the size of a grapefruit. But that was nothing compared to the hundreds of puncture wounds all over his body. Lips of flesh curled out like small mouths from the suppurating wounds. We were aghast. But Michael was his usual self: "Oh, some bum threw me through a storefront window," he said with a wave of his hand.

When Michael reached his nadir as a drug mess, he thought he was the coolest. From the catwalk where the supermodels pranced to the sidewalk where River Phoenix expired, heroin chic was all the rage. Michael made sure he was its ultimate exponent: emaciated, a mass of bruises, cuts and sores, limping, covered in shit and piss and vomit. In this revolting extreme, perhaps he thought he was as iconogasmic as Clive Barker's Pinhead. But Michael had crossed a line. The kid who had always laughed at junkies had become one. The life of the party who threw himself down stairs just to stir up more drama was now so fucked up that falling down stairs was all he could do.

Even at this point, we thought that the only person Michael would end up killing would be himself. But as he racked up overdose after overdose with casual flair, repeatedly bouncing back from the brink, it was clear he wasn't going anywhere.

Ghoulishly, it was the tantalizing possibility that Michael might just have murdered someone that secured us some development money, six years after we first conceived the club kid documentary. Since we weren't sure if Michael was going to be arrested or die from an overdose, we wanted to shoot as much footage as possible as soon as possible. One of the first things we filmed was an interview with Michael in James St James' East Village loft. It was August, sweltering, and James' apartment was in a state of junkie disarray,

OPPOSITE PAGE: The poster for the UK release of the movie by Tartan Films; the invite to the launch party for the UK release of James St James' memoir published by Sceptre

THIS PAGE: Mock invitations for real Michael Alig parties used in the movie; graphic for Disco Donuts, a 24-hour coffee shop on 14th Street in New York City and popular late-night stop after a night out at the Palladium

FROM LEFT, TOP TO BOTTOM: Michael Fazakerley's portraits of original club kids at their height: Michael Alig, Astro Earle, Christopher Comp, and James St James. At his New York City studio, one block from Limelight, 1991

OPPOSITE PAGE: Michael Alig actually produced trading cards for the kids, so we did the same for the cast of the movie to promote the UK release

EXCESS ALL AREAS-OCTOBER 17

EXCESS ALL AREAS-OCTOBER 17

EXCESS ALL AREAS-OCTOBER 17

EXCESS ALL AREAS-OCTOBER 17

It was winter, but Michael was wearing only lederhosen and a flimsy T-shirt. He had a cyst on his neck the size of a grapefruit and hundreds of puncture wounds on his body

reeking of cat shit. James himself didn't smell too good. His widow's peak of green hair offset the pallid cast of his skin. But although he looked like death, he was his usual charming self. As we set up, James and Michael showed us how to bake Special K. Once this was snorted, they touched up their makeup and we filmed them. And that was when Michael jokingly said on camera that he had killed Angel. "I killed Angel. And – I'm sorry. That's the kind of thing that gets me in trouble." When pressed, Michael seemed to drift off and the words came slowly, one at a time: "I'm an easy target, because I was with him the day before… he… was… gone." There was a long pause, some more stammering, and then, "I have my own ideas."

Later that night as we were packing up, James said he needed to get out of New York, and that he was thinking of moving to LA. He said he wanted to become a writer. We encouraged him to call us when he arrived in town.

♦

So when James came to the end of this unbelievable story of how Michael had killed Angel there wasn't much more to be said. There certainly was no longer any doubt in our minds. A few days later, Michael was arrested for Angel's murder.

Things happened quickly after that; make of it what you will, but suddenly it wasn't hard to raise the rest of the money to shoot the doc.

Along the way, we met this club kid with red hair called Thairin Smothers. We originally began talking because he had some footage of Angel he had shot. Plus he seemed to know everyone and all the club kids trusted him. He began helping us out on shoots and soon came on board as associate producer. Thairin was different from the others. He was present on – but not immersed in – the scene, and was not lost in a daze of K. He seemed to be watching everything and taking it in. As we got to know him, we learned he had worked on Jerry Springer's show in Chicago before coming to New York with his video camera. When the film was over, he moved to LA and became our receptionist. Now, of course, he is a fantastic producer in his own right and very much at the heart of the whole company, whether it's booking celebrity talent for *Drag Race* or whipping up a batch of guacamole for the potluck office lunches he organizes.

Party Monster: The Shockumentary, as it came to be known, was our first film to go to the Sundance Film Festival. But there was a sense that this was not quite what documentaries were supposed to be about. Before the film, Sundance ran a short PSA-type film about drunk driving. There was, perhaps, *un certain regarde* about the lack of moral positioning. And quite apart from that, something about the story felt untold to us. That we might have missed the real story: the love/hate, twisted-sister bond between Michael and James. So we decided to make a movie about the story.

When we first asked James to write his story as a kind of post-modern *In Cold Blood*, he refused. Somehow, we persuaded him (hint, ca-ching!). Then we took the simply amazing manuscript he wrote and got him a book deal. We wrote a screenplay based on his book, and couldn't resist weaving in a few elements from the documentary. That was all relatively easy compared to the task of persuading financiers to come on board.

Christine Vachon, the legendary producer, suggested we write a mission statement to help get nervous nellies on board:

Disco Bloodbath is a buddy movie with a twist, or a twisted buddy movie. Its focus is the relationship between Michael Alig and James St James, two kids from the Midwest who come to New York where they re-invent themselves as fabulous people. Although it is not immediately clear to

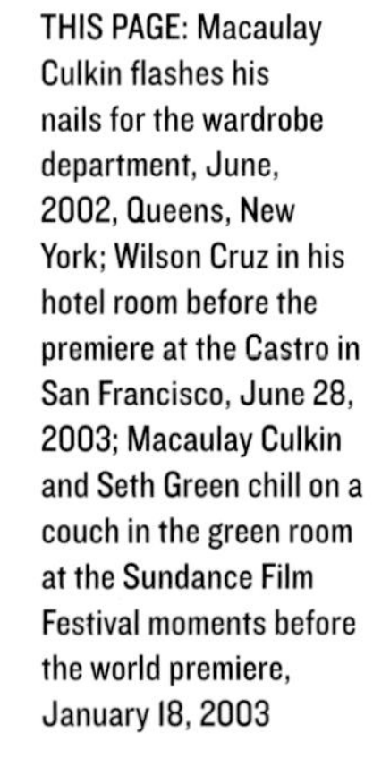

THIS PAGE: Macaulay Culkin flashes his nails for the wardrobe department, June, 2002, Queens, New York; Wilson Cruz in his hotel room before the premiere at the Castro in San Francisco, June 28, 2003; Macaulay Culkin and Seth Green chill on a couch in the green room at the Sundance Film Festival moments before the world premiere, January 18, 2003

James, Michael instantly recognizes that they are soulmates and latches onto him. Shy outsiders as kids, they both learned to hide their feelings behind witty façades, and their bickering and barbed exchanges speak to a deep bond and co-dependency. Of the two, Michael is the quicker study, even though James is smarter and more learned. So although it is James who initiates Michael into New York nightlife, it is Michael who quickly rises to the top.

To get there, Michael was equipped with no special skills or qualifications other than his considerable charisma. He had a twinkle in his eye. A postmodern Peter Pan, he made no secret of the fact that he never wanted to grow up. The way he gulped his words, the way he gestured, projected a child-like vulnerability. Unfazed by being a misfit from the Midwest, Michael gathered around him similarly like-minded souls – the kids who had been teased and bullied in school – and gave them fabulous new club kid identities. They were the Lost Boys to his Peter Pan.

James could see that Michael's chaotic and unruly behavior was a kind of genius performance art. Michael's minting of superstars out of those least likely to be stars parodied society's absurd obsession with celebrity. His attention-getting antics parodied the dysfunctional circuses of our talk show times. His surreal infantility parodied our culture's overriding obsession with youth. The starburst that was Michael inevitably put James somewhat in the shade. But like him or loathe him – and James did both – he found it impossible to resist him. James was not alone in this. Everyone seemed unable to resist the Michael Alig Show.

But just as David Bowie became trapped by his Ziggy Stardust creation, so Michael became hostage to his bratlike persona. He continually had to outdo himself with increasingly outrageous pranks. One day Michael went too far. He murdered Angel. When James first learned about this, he could almost let Michael get away with it. Angel had attacked Michael, hadn't he? But even with Angel reduced to a mere sacrificial symbol, James was forced to recognize that no excuse could justify such a brutal thing. Even the surreal anarchic alternative universe they had created for themselves had to conform.

The goal of the film is to give viewers the ride of their lives, to be seduced by the scene, so that when tragedy strikes they feel implicated and discomfited. James may be the hero but he is a reluctant hero, and we want the audience to feel his sense of loss rather than lofty righteousness as he brings down the curtain on the Michael Alig Show. Instead of demonizing Michael as a freakish killer, we want to make viewers feel the very real connection between him and ourselves. When we look into his heart, we are looking into our own: Who has not at some point in their lives wished that they could stay young forever or stay out all night and never have to go to work? Who has not at some point even imagined killing someone?

Coming out of the theater, the audience should breathe a sigh of relief: There, but for the grace of God, go I.

Now that we had our mission statement, we needed a cast. Everyone agreed the perfect person to play Michael would be Macaulay Culkin, not least because it had been written with him in mind. But he didn't seem particularly inclined to get back in front of the camera after his star turns in the *Home Alone* films made him the most famous kid on the planet.

So God bless Seth Green, because he was the first aboard and applied himself to help secure Mac. And once Mac signed on, we were spoiled with a truly amazing cast whose talents and generosity far exceeded our measly budget. Natasha Lyonne, Chloë Sevigny, Marilyn Manson, Diana Scarwid, Wilson Cruz, Mia Kirshner, Dylan McDermott, and the impossibly delicious Wilmer Valderrama bought a huge amount of goodwill to such a little project. For example, there were no dressing rooms. The only trailer on the entire production was for the wardrobe department and their bazillion costumes.

THIS PAGE: Our dog Edith, with Macaulay Culkin on the phone in the background at the production office in Midtown Manhattan. This photo was taken by Teodoro Maniaci, the movie's DP; Natasha Lyonne, Wilmer Valderrama, Macaulay Culkin (obscured), Chloë Sevigny, Seth Green and Dylan McDermott pose for a group shot by Fenton at the Sundance Film Festival, January 16, 2003

"I killed Angel. And – I'm sorry. That's the kind of thing that gets me in trouble"

We shot digitally on location in New York for twenty-five days and then headed back to LA and buried ourselves in the edit room to have it ready for Sundance. Which we did, in the nick of time.

The goal, of course, in taking the film to the festival was to bag a big fat distribution deal. Which, after the most amazing Bryan Rabin-produced party at Sundance that people still talk about to this day, seemed entirely possible.

So the next morning we expected to open the trades and read all about our multimillion-dollar distribution deal. These articles are in the press all the time during the festival, breathless accounts of all-night negotiations with Harvey Weinstein and Hollywood heavies battling it out in mountainside condos. But all we found was a decidedly ho-hum review in *Variety*. Funny thing about bad reviews is that when you get them no one tells you. People call you to get on the guest list, but they don't call to tell you that you have a crap review. Understandably. But this means you could well be the last to know. As we were.

For months it seemed entirely possible that the movie would skip theatrical distribution and go straight to video. I don't think we had anticipated that at all. And after all the years of work, that was a bitter pill to swallow.

But it was also a critical point. We had finally made a movie. And deep down there was the expectation that life would now be completely different. As if the clouds would part and we'd be whooshed off to Planet Glamour, where life was lived on the red carpet/pool side/gifting suite, and all our friends would be famous and everyone would want to take our picture all the time.

"Glamor is where you're not," Ru once pointed out. So true.

It didn't turn out as planned, but it did turn out as panned. And that's a good thing. Because life is much more fun when you are just living it rather than hurrying through it to get somewhere else. We thought we had to get to Glamourville. But there's no place like home.

So although Steven Spielberg did not call, Marcus Hu and Jon Gerrans from Strand Releasing did. They gave the film a spirited release, and we got to go to Tokyo, Berlin, London, and New York. It was all wildly overstimulating, especially since everyone seemed to assume that making a film called *Party Monster* meant you were one yourself. By the time we reached the Edinburgh Film Festival, we were propping our eyes open with cocktail sticks.

And the party monster himself?

We have stayed in touch over the years. We have never sugar-coated or excused what he did.

One day soon he will emerge, blinking, into a world of apps and iPads, Mob Wives and Kardashians. Very much the ultracrass teletransformed society he anticipated at Club USA in the '90s. He should feel right at home. In fact, the other day on the phone he said he wanted to produce reality shows.

But we want to give James St James the last word. After *Disco Bloodbath* he has written two more books, *Freak Show* (that can only have inspired Britney Spears' classic hit) and the yet-unpublished *Killer Grandpa,* blowing the lid off his family's secret about one of the last lynchings in the US. He also works as co-editor of the WOW Report blog and hosts *Daily Freak Show.* Recently, on the red carpet at Sundance, he interviewed Rosie O'Donnell. They were talking about *Party Monster* and James said, "That's me, I am the original." Rosie blinked and blanched. "You're the killer?" She said, aghast. You can see how James got himself out of that one on YouTube.

FROM LEFT: Randy, Macaulay Culkin, Marilyn Manson, Fenton,photographed by Thairin Smothers; producer Jon Marcus with Fenton on set of Party Monster, Queens, New York, shot by Anthony Pettine, June 5, 2002; the premiere party gets underway in the school library at the Sundance Film Festival, January 22, 2003

CINEMAX REEL LIFE PRESENTS

party monster

He brought life to the New York club scene. He also brought DEATH.

From king of the club kids to club kid killer.

THE MICHAEL ALIG STORY

PRODUCED AND DIRECTED
FENTON BAILEY AND RANDY BARBATO
WORLD OF WONDER PRODUCTIONS

PREMIERES THURSDAY, JUNE 18 AT MIDNIGHT ET/PT

CO-PRODUCER MARIA SILVER CINEMATOGRAPHY JAMIE McEWEN EDITOR SCOTT GAMZON CO-EDITOR TIM ATZINGER
ASSOCIATE PRODUCER GABRIEL ROTELLO PRODUCER JOHN HOFFMAN EXECUTIVE PRODUCER SHEILA NEVINS

Michael Alig went from being king of the club kids to club kid killer

Michael Alig went from being king of the club kids to club kid killer

party monster

From king of the club kids to club kid killer.

THE MICHAEL ALIG STORY

PRODUCED AND DIRECTED
FENTON BAILEY AND RANDY BARBATO
WORLD OF WONDER PRODUCTIONS

PREMIERES THURSDAY, JUNE 18 AT MIDNIGHT ET/PT

CO-PRODUCER MARIA SILVER CINEMATOGRAPHY JAMIE McEWEN EDITOR SCOTT GAMZON CO-EDITOR TIM ATZINGER
ASSOCIATE PRODUCER GABRIEL ROTELLO PRODUCER JOHN HOFFMAN EXECUTIVE PRODUCER SHEILA NEVINS

Michael Alig
KING OF THE CLUB KIDS

Macaulay Culkin
ACTOR

The actor and his subject met before filming began when Macaulay visited Michael in prison on April 27, 2002. Michael, a lifelong fan, was uncharacteristically subdued during their meeting

PHOTOGRAPHED BY THAIRIN SMOTHERS
WORLD OF WONDER PRODUCTIONS,
HOLLYWOOD, CALIFORNIA,
AUGUST 24, 2011

“If you’ve got a hunchback throw a little glitter on it, honey”
–JAMES ST JAMES

Thairin Smothers
PRODUCER

Amazing drag transformation by Billy B

PHOTOGRAPHED BY IDRIS + TONY
WORLD OF WONDER PRODUCTIONS,
HOLLYWOOD, CALIFORNIA,
JANUARY 21, 2010

James St James

AUTHOR, CO-EDITOR OF THE WOW REPORT

When not hosting fabulous Freak Show events around the country, the *Party Monster* author and New York nightlife star likes to relax in his library at home with his longtime companion Harvey

PHOTOGRAPHED BY IDRIS + TONY
AT HOME, HANCOCK PARK, LOS ANGELES,
NOVEMBER 17, 2009

Seth Green

ACTOR AND PRODUCER

Who else could play James St James in the movie version of James' book *Party Monster*? Who else could get so immersed in the role that he would have to call James in the middle of the night to ask how he knocks on a door

PHOTOGRAPHED BY IDRIS + TONY
HOLLYWOOD HILLS, CALIFORNIA,
JANUARY 27, 2010

Daniel Franzese

ACTOR

Daniel played the Rat in *Party Monster* and curated a couple of great shows at the World of Wonder Storefront Gallery

PHOTOGRAPHED BY IDRIS + TONY
GRAND HOTEL, LOS ANGELES, CALIFORNIA, APRIL 13, 2009

Wilmer Valderrama

ACTOR, PRODUCER

Fez from *That '70s Show* was that '90s DJ Keoki in *Party Monster*. It will never cease to amaze us how someone so hot can be so competely lovely. Meetings with Wilmer always last as long as we can possibly make them

PHOTOGRAPHED BY IDRIS + TONY
AT HOME, WOODLAND HILLS,
CALIFORNIA, NOVEMBER 14, 2009

Jon Gerrans
FILM DISTRIBUTOR

Marcus Hu
FILM DISTRIBUTOR

Under their direction, Strand Releasing did an amazing job distributing *Party Monster* and *101 Rent Boys*

PHOTOGRAPHED BY IDRIS + TONY
CULVER CITY, CALIFORNIA, APRIL 9, 2009

Christine Vachon

FILM PRODUCER, KILLER FILMS

The LGBT champion and legendary indie film producer co-produced *Party Monster* with us

PHOTOGRAPHED BY IDRIS + TONY AT HOME, EAST VILLAGE, NEW YORK CITY, FEBRUARY 23, 2010

Natasha Lyonne

ACTRESS

"Go fuck yourself was the theme of the shoot," said photographer Tony. "This image really sums up the message that she wanted to send. It's so her. She was a total pleasure to work with"

PHOTOGRAPHED BY IDRIS + TONY
LOWER EAST SIDE, NEW YORK CITY,
OCTOBER 20, 2011

Who has not wished they could stay young forever, stay out all night and never have to go to work

Wilson Cruz

ACTOR, ACTIVIST

The actor went from playing the HIV+ drag queen Angel in Broadway's *Rent* to the murdered club-kid drug dealer Angel in *Party Monster*

PHOTOGRAPHED BY IDRIS + TONY AT HOME, HOLLYWOOD, CALIFORNIA, NOVEMBER 18, 2009

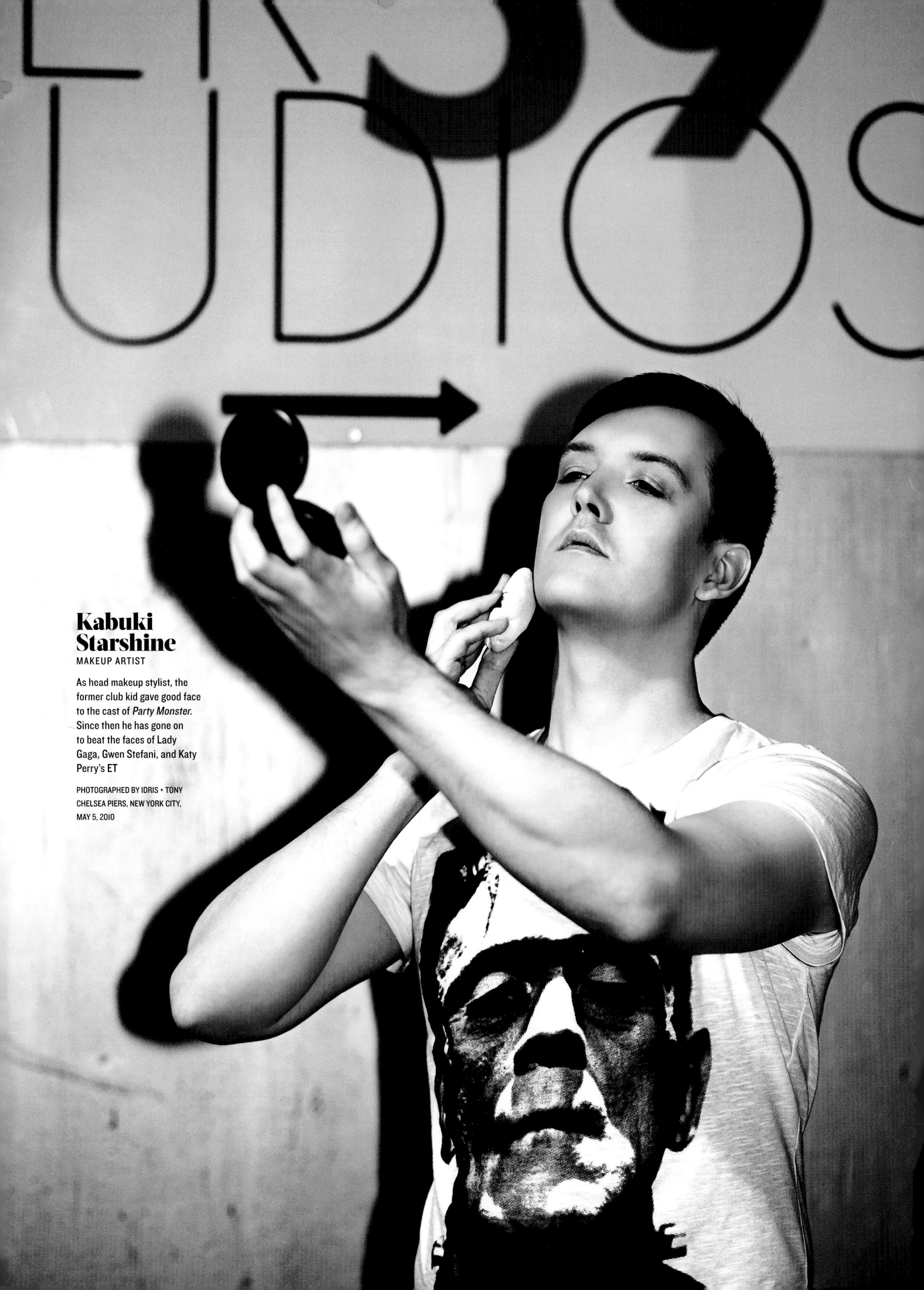

Kabuki Starshine

MAKEUP ARTIST

As head makeup stylist, the former club kid gave good face to the cast of *Party Monster.* Since then he has gone on to beat the faces of Lady Gaga, Gwen Stefani, and Katy Perry's ET

PHOTOGRAPHED BY IDRIS + TONY
CHELSEA PIERS, NEW YORK CITY,
MAY 5, 2010

Bill Coleman

MUSIC MANAGER, PRODUCER

Bill masterminded the release of the *Party Monster* soundtrack and persuaded Felix Da Housecat to produce the old Pop Tarts track "Money Success Fame Glamour" with Macaulay Culkin on vocals

PHOTOGRAPHED BY IDRIS + TONY
BROOKLYN, NEW YORK, JUNE 11, 2009

CSS

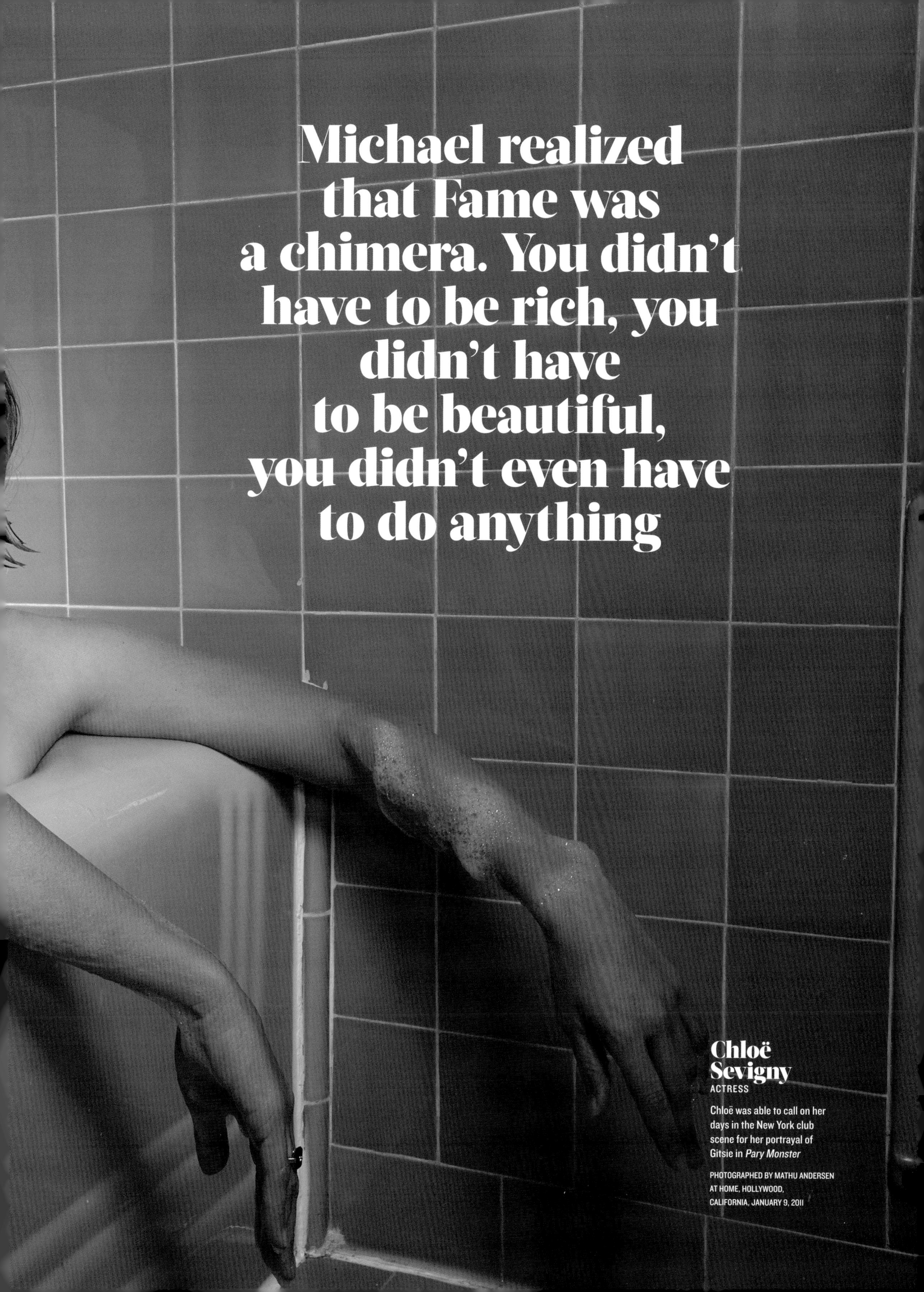

Michael realized that Fame was a chimera. You didn't have to be rich, you didn't have to be beautiful, you didn't even have to do anything

Chloë Sevigny

ACTRESS

Chloë was able to call on her days in the New York club scene for her portrayal of Gitsie in *Pary Monster*

PHOTOGRAPHED BY MATHU ANDERSEN AT HOME, HOLLYWOOD, CALIFORNIA, JANUARY 9, 2011

That's so Gay!

WE ALWAYS LOVED THE PHRASE "that's so gay." Despite its intent as a put-down, it's actually an admission of defeat for the straights, and victory for the gays. "That's so gay" acknowledges that out there, somewhere, is a domain of all gay things, a realm where unicorns frolic and dolphins splash. And it's getting bigger all the time. ♦ Also, "That's so gay" trips so playfully off the tongue that it cannot but put a little gloss on the speaker's lips, no matter how straight they are – or think they are.

The phrase, then, is our version of the Virginia Slims line, "You've come a long way, baby." And we have, because when that slogan was first coined, gay was the love that dare not speak its name. Of course, there was always the gay underground, but such things were not openly spoken about. They were shrouded in shame. It was only in the mid-'80s that the *New York Times* actually used the word "gay" after a vociferous *Outweek* campaign led by Gabriel Rotello and Michelangelo Signorile, among others.

Fenton at airport security with giant lipstick 'liberated' from the VHI Fashion Awards

It's not that gay is such a brilliant word. And it's impossible not to remember Quentin Crisp's quip when asked for his feelings about the gay community: "I'm afraid to say no such happy confederacy exists." But the naffness and even the wrongness of the word has allowed it to stand the test of time in a way that "fabulous" might grate. Anything is better than "homosexual," with its proctological lilt and whiff of medical menace.

And so "that's so gay" shows beyond an eyeshadow of a doubt that we have a place at the cultural table. For example, remember when bad-boy rapper Marky Mark dropped his pants? Shortly afterwards he became a Calvin Klein underwear model. So hot. So street. But it was also – we all can agree – so very very howlingly gay. And the fact that Marky Mark was straight only made it all the more subversive. The mainstream had given itself permission to swing both ways. It was a breathtaking moment in the culture.

A lesser moment, though no less vivid to us, came a few years earlier during the "men in dresses" mini-trend; OK, a trend so minuscule it barely made a blip. It was around the time of Boy George, and the thinking was that if it worked for the Scots in their kilts, why not bankers on Wall Street?

At the time, we had a band called the Fabulous Pop Tarts and, boy, we were so gay. White afro wigs, gold lame togas, crushed velvet suits, etc. But Paul Monroe and Julia Morton, who ran a clothing store and designed some of our outfits, asked if we would feel comfortable

City Boys
on the
verge
of
Country
– THE FABULOUS –
BEEKMAN BOYS
WEDNESDAYS 9PM

planet
green

"Enough already? If it was enough already, we wouldn't have the hate crimes, the suicides. It's not enough already. It's not nearly enough," said Ellen

modeling macho-man skirts for a daytime talk show in Boston called *People Are Talking* or something. Sure, it would be good exposure, right?

The audience politely applauded when a model carrying a briefcase and umbrella strode out wearing a sensible pinstripe number. He looked like a man hurrying to a very important appointment, not a nelly in a dress. They were buying it.

Fenton was up next. But his man dress was a full-length pencil skirt so tapered it was impossible to put one foot in front of the other. As he shuffled out of the wings the audience began to titter. When he had to hop to get up onto the raised dais they collapsed in hysterics.

"He seems to be having a problem with mobility," the host said. The only solution was to yank it up and start striding about.

"It's a cocktail dress, not a hiking outfit," Paul hissed at him as he left the stage.

The man dress never really caught on. But you see our point. Gradually things were becoming gayer.

Except on television (with the exception of local daytime shows in desperate need of content). Just how hard it was to lead an open, honest, and authentic life on TV became clear when Ellen DeGeneres wagered her entire career on coming out, a process that we followed in *The Real Ellen*, our documentary for Channel 4 and Bravo.

It was the longest sustained episode of anticipation ever. Will she, won't she?

After Ellen herself came out on *Oprah,* she went along with ABC's party line that her character on the show would take only "baby steps" towards gayness. But then, she told us, she realized that if she was embarrassed about holding her girlfriend's hand in public, what was even the point of her character coming out? "How am I supposed to say it's OK that I'm gay, but yet I still don't feel I deserve to show affection in public the way other people can show affection?" So she and Anne Heche – her girlfriend at the time – went to the White House and met the president, arm in arm.

The longer it went on – the baby steps, the back and forth – the more trenchant she became. "If you look at just about every sitcom on television, they're about dating and relationships," she said. "And I'm fine with that. But it is interesting that before my character came out, they wanted to focus more on dating and relationships. Then my character comes out and they say, 'Why do you have to focus so much on dating and relationships?' It's just that now it's dealing with a subject matter that everybody's saying, 'Enough already.' It's not enough already, clearly. If it was enough already, we wouldn't have the hate crimes. We wouldn't have the suicides. It's not enough already. It's not nearly enough." Ellen got her way. *Yep, I'm gay*

The night that episode aired on television, you could have heard a pin drop in Hollywood, and all across the country. Forty two million people tuned in. If it had been a movie it would have had an opening weekend of over half a billion dollars.

And the craziest thing of all? This wasn't about Ellen being gay. This was about the character she plays in a sitcom. The problem isn't people actually being gay, it's about being visible, being allowed to be seen and part of the culture.

After the euphoric high of that historic moment, it looked as if Ellen had not only bet the house, but also bet wrong. The show was tanking and people were whispering that her career was over.

Chastity Bono, then media spokesperson for GLAAD, got caught up in the furor when some remarks she

had made got reported as if she was saying that Ellen should concentrate on being funny instead of being gay.

Of course, we all know now that it worked out fine in the end. Ellen wasn't destined to carry on as a sitcom star, just as it was not Chastity's true destiny to be a GLAAD spokesperson. Both would reinvent themselves and enjoy even greater success, rising like Phoenixes from the ashes.

Speaking of unlikely outcomes, later that year we won a GLAAD Fairness Award. It was a new award created for people who, presumably, were fair and – more to the point - able to sell X number of tickets to fill Y number of seats at the Four Seasons in Beverly Hills. Let's just say it was a twist of fête.

It did give us the opportunity to say something as we accepted our award:

Let's not kid ourselves. It's so not a gay old world after all. The world is not a fair place. Working with Ru, Ellen, the club kids from Party Monster, and not to mention 101 male hustlers, we were less struck by the prejudice from the mainstream than that from within our own so-called community. Shame on us!

Time and again people, gay people, have said to us that what we do is all well and good, but that the people are too extreme, too marginal, too freaky, too trashy, too subcultural. Whatever the adjective, what they really mean is too gay.

It's OK to be gay and come out to your parents, wave a flag, march in a parade. What's not OK is to be upper-case GAY. Wave it in people's faces, shove it down people's throats, sashay shanté, or just simply be who you are in all your femmed-out sissy-faggot glory. Well hello – breaking news – there is no such thing as too gay.

We only think there is because we're so obsessed with fitting into the mainstream. With being normal.

But being gay is not about being normal. Gay is gay. Gay is not the same as everyone else. Gay is different. And if we can't be who we are, truthfully who we are – unedited, unconstrained, exuberant – what's the point of even being?

When we chase the mainstream we are chasing an illusion, because the mainstream doesn't exist. No one person is mainstream or normal. Because the mainstream is made up of individuals, each one different, each one unique.

So the way we see it, gay is a metaphor for the human condition; there is no such thing as normal, and we are all a minority of one. Every snowflake is unique.

We are all queer in our own special way.

The responsibility of being gay, then, is not about sameness. It's about difference.

And until we embrace the zaniest, freakiest, and gayest among us, there can be no fairness.

But we realized that practicing what we preached was easier said than done when Sheila Nevins at HBO introduced us to Steve Moore, the HIV positive stand-up guy. It wasn't that Steve wasn't funny – he was – but what could be funny about AIDS, especially from a guy who was HIV positive? The first time we saw his show, the audience laughed nervously at the first couple of jokes, but that wasn't nearly enough for Steve. He threatened to open a vein and take out the first few rows. We didn't know whether to laugh or flee.

Turning Steve's one-man show into the docu-stage show, *Drop Dead Gorgeous*, involved blending his stage performance with archive, interviews, and re-enactments. Re-enactments? In documentaries? We subscribe to the Werner Herzog philosophy that a re-enactment is actually an enactment, because it's not a rehash of anything. It's an exercise in accessing a greater truth, what Herzog has famously called "ec-

OPPOSITE PAGE: Title still and frame grabs from *The Real Ellen Story*, our documentary about Ellen DeGeneres' coming out and her love affair with Anne Heche

THIS PAGE: Ellen sit down interview; Ellen's mom, Anne Heche, and Ellen after a screening of The Real Ellen Story at Outfest, 1998

What could be funny about AIDS especially from a guy who was HIV positive?

static truth." Anyway, the resulting hybrid won us our first Cable Ace award, which was also the last Cable Ace award ever handed out. More importantly, we felt we had stumbled onto an exciting new hybrid of doc and show that we would return to in *Juror #5*, *Monica in Black and White,* and *Wishful Drinking*.

101 Rent Boys

Our second office in LA was up the street from the donut store on Highland and Santa Monica, a popular hangout for hustlers. They were out there all hours of the day and night, and we would often see them on the way to or from pitch meetings. We're just like them, we thought, forever selling ourselves.

At the time, billboards were all over town for the remake of *101 Dalmatians*. That gave us an idea: We would interview 101 hustlers and pay them each $50 not to have sex but to tell us their stories. Then we would edit the interviews into an oral account of sex work. We decided to pay them because it tweaked the documentary tradition that no one gets paid. Besides, they were at work and were taking time out of their busy days, er, nights to tell us their stories. Plus, we gave them the money on camera to keep the transactional nature of their business front and center. We are all brought up to believe that time is money.

Everyone loved our pitch – but no one would buy it. So we would have to film it while we were filming something else. That something else was *The Eyes of Tammy Faye* which we would film by day and *101 Rent Boys* by night. There was some organic overlap, because the business of both revolved around love and money. And both Tammy and our hustlers were ministers of sorts who provided a kind of pastoral care to their flock.

For example, rent boy Steve saw himself as a descendent of a pre-Christian, pagan tradition where priests and priestesses, in return for a contribution, gave of themselves to supplicants. And hustler William compared orgasmic transcendence with the great cathedrals, how the light streaming through the stained glass was deliberately designed to give the worshipper a rush to transport them out of this world.

Yes, many came from broken homes, experienced some kind of abuse when they were young, and had addiction issues. But also, many of them had college degrees. Many of them enjoyed the sex, found it good to be wanted by someone so much that they were willing to pay for it. None of them felt they needed saving, and almost all of them felt good about being professionally engaged in the business of loving people.

Of course, it goes without saying that the hustler's pastoral care brings none of the respect that being a minister enjoys. Often, the chain of abuse started by parents continues uninterrupted. Gangbangers beat them up, police arrest them, johns give them the cold shoulder, and society scorns them. Lex Kyler (#12) told us how the first john he picked up was murdered. The way the police treated the case – as if the man deserved to die because he picked up tricks – inspired him to become a full-time hustler and to fight the callous prejudices against sex workers:

I picked the name Lex Kyler because it was short. I needed something short to fit in an ad. And it has one syllable and two syllables, and that's a pretty basic porn name. I don't use my birth name because it doesn't have the same kind of appeal. And I like to keep some things separate. This is not all I do.

I'm an activist. I just believe that people ought to exercise their right in America to be able to stand up for what they believe in and try to make changes.

The biggest misconception about sex work is that everyone doing it is kind of the same, that we're all cut from the same cloth. There's a broad range of people who work in the business.

The first time I got paid for sex was very very important because it set the tone for a lot of my attitude towards work, especially towards customers. I started out in the street in San Francisco in 1989, just before the big earthquake, I picked up my first client on the street, and it was real exciting.

I wasn't doing it out of desperation; I had just quit a job that I hated, and I thought, you know, what would I want to do? What do I really believe in? I thought, oh, I believe in myself and I'll just push myself and sell my services. And I had no trouble having sex with people I wasn't attracted to. So I thought, if they want to pay for it, then I'll let them.

I picked up my first client – it was such a rush. We went back to his apartment and then he was seeing me like, every week, sometimes twice a week. Then I hadn't heard from him for a while. And a friend of mine told me that the police were looking for me. I later found out that this client had been murdered in his house, and they wanted me for questioning. So I went down there with a friend of mine. The cops asked all sorts of stupid questions. I got really upset when they wanted to find out how we met. I was real cagey about it, because I didn't want to implicate myself, I had brought my friend along as a witness. They were going about it all wrong: It's not about the guy deserved to get killed because he did this, it's about some other person that's a murderer out there, and that's the one you should be going after, instead of trying to say this guy deserved it.

And that was my very first client. I'll never forget that. And I think because of that, I treat my clients, generally, with a little more respect, a little more empathy, and I think that's why I've been in this business for so long. Sexually there's plenty of things I won't do. But it depends on the person. I let one guy restrain me – my legs and arms – which is a big deal for me, because I'm a big control freak. I could have been slashed up right there. This is a guy I'd seen a few times, so I felt comfortable with him enough to do that. So, that was pretty special. And I must say, it was pretty hot. There's a whole list of things I once said I would never do, including prostitution, and I've been crossing them off left and right. So, who knows?

People want different things. Some people want companionship, some people want a quickie. It's like some people ordering out pizza versus going to a fancy restaurant. It's different.

That's the kind of business I'm in. I'm in a service business. I believe the customer is number one. It's not like another job where I've gotta go and see the same asshole coworkers every day, week in, week out.

The weirdest thing I was ever paid to do was seduce this guy's lover while the guy was out of town. I had gotten this whole bike messenger outfit and my thing was to seduce him and do all these crazy things to him because when his lover got back, he'd have to confess out of guilt and then his lover would do all the same things that I did to him.

And I still wonder was that really the situation? I never met this guy who hired me. I had to get the money out of an envelope that was hidden outside somewhere. Was this whole thing some kind of fantasy that this person just made up? Maybe that was the guy who hired me. I don't know. I have no idea.

There wouldn't be any hookers if there weren't any customers. And I wouldn't be in business if I didn't have any customers. So there's definitely a supply and there's definitely a demand. I know so many guys who have done this stuff at one point in their life. Nobody forces me into prostitution. I've never chased clients down and made them pay for my services. It's all consensual. And why that's illegal is ridiculous.

They go about their business with an honesty based on not only knowing who they are, but also knowing who we are too. We made this film because we wanted to learn about hustlers, but we ended up learning more about ourselves.

OPPOSITE PAGE: Fenton and Randy holding Cable Ace Award for *Drop Dead Gorgeous*, November 17, 1997; *Drop Dead Gorgeous* title still

THIS PAGE: *The Fabulous Beekman Boys* title still; Lex Kyler was hustler #12 in *101 Rent Boys*

13
14
78
1
8
9
39
18
58
20
23
94
28
25
37
33
38
53
42
71
29
47
62
59
68
74
43
50
48
49
84

7
81
87
66
40
32
30
15
27
35
11
86
17
91
45
73
57
76
83
92
89
5
95
69
1
10
65
77
16
82
72
19

You might have thought that the only reason anyone ever hired a hustler was for sex, but that was often not the case. Often people just wanted companionship, to make a connection. People are so lonely and so starved for affection they need to be touched and feel that they are loved – even if they have to pay, and even if it is only for an hour. We don't think twice about going to a therapist, pouring out our problems (which often have something to do with sex) and paying at the end of the hour. So this is therapy with fewer words and no clothes. Why this would be illegal when every other aspect of our lives has been commodified made no sense to us.

The Fabulous Beekman Boys

How is this for a segue? We had known Josh way back when he was a drag queen named Aqua. You gotta have a gimmick, and his was fishbowl brassieres with live goldfish. Our paths crossed again after he wrote a poignant memoir, *I Am Not Myself These Days,* detailing his vodka-drenched love affair with a rent boy drug dealer crack addict. Amazingly, no one died. After that he met Brent, the straitlaced doctor working for Martha Stewart's Omnimedia. Their relationship was much more sustainable.

One weekend they went upstate apple picking together and – on a whim – bought an old farm. The Beekman 1802. Hilarity ensued as they bred goats ("who says gays can't have kids"), prettied up the barn, and made a go of Beekman as an organic brand. It might seem odd to swap high heels for Wellington boots, but drag queens know how to focus and make everything – even farming – fabulous.

We like to call Brent Ridge and Josh Kilmer-Purcell "the boys in the brand" because their business is their child, and they give it their undivided attention morning, noon, and night. Books, soap, iron bud vases, linens, heirloom seeds, T-shirts, cheese, cookbooks, candles, cajeta caramel sauce, flatware, placemats, napkins, scarves, and, pulling it all together, a TV show watching them do all this and more called *The Fabulous Beekman Boys*.

It's about more than the hard sell. At the core of their business is a heart – and that's their love for one another. Because Brent and Josh are a gay couple, the first gay couple to be the stars and focus of a reality show. In other words, that's so gay, but that's so normal. Viewers were shocked and stunned to see that the everyday life of a gay couple wasn't much different from their own lives. So shocked, in fact, that they were compelled to inundate Brent and Josh with a blizzard of e-mails:

"I have never been one to watch a gay show, but please I beg you don't take this the wrong way. You guys and farmer John have opened my eyes ... you are no different than me. You followed a dream and made it work and I just fell in love with you guys. Now I have most of my family watching it."

"I come from endless generations of farmers, and this world is bursting with homophobic males – I used to be one. I thank you for helping me get over that crap, and be accepting of all people."

"Last summer I 'accidentally' outed our only son. All the dreams of a big wedding, a daughter-in-law and tons of grandbabies were taken from me. Fast forward to a few weeks ago... My husband and I were watching your show and it was your birthday episode. It was such an emotional episode for me. Something about the look on your face, when you were upset because you thought you would be the first ones to be married on your farm, clicked. Right then I realized that no one, no religion, nothing should be allowed to decide that two people who love and respect each other cannot marry."

"I'm 16 and live somewhere not very diverse.... and I'm actually starting my own fowl hatchery! So far I have only a few birds but I love them!!! You guys are great and I want to be just like you when I'm older. One day

THIS PAGE: From left: Jeremy Simmons directed *Gay Hollywood*, documenting the lives of openly gay people in LA and including then-unknown screenwriter Dustin Lance Black, who would later win the Oscar for *Milk*; title still for the show whose working title was *Real Fag Hags of New York*

OPPOSITE PAGE: Title still for *Totally Gay*, a VHI doc directed by Wash Westmoreland, who would go on to win both the audience and jury award at Sundance for his film *La Quinceañera*; title still for the series of specials hosted by Perez Hilton and aired on VHI

I would love to come see your farm – it's like my dream house! I just want to know how I can deal with being gay. Where I live it's so hard trying to make everyone happy I don't even attend school anymore"

"On a personal note the two of you have made it very easy to show my children what it really means to be a same-sex couple – they watch your show with me and understand through your loving relationship with Josh – that everyone loves, laughs, and lives the same."

"My daughter and I had a field trip today to the State Park... At lunch two tables away were several fifth grade boys, one of them said 'Did you know the Beekman Boys are gay?' The one across from him said 'So' and another said 'Everybody knows that.' There were no laughs or nasty comments. The topic was dropped."

The reality of the postmodern family is finally here.

The Pink Fuhrer

In the fall of 2001, Gabriel Rotello came to us with a book written by German historian Lothar Machtan arguing that Hitler was gay. Thing about Hitler is that he is one of the most written-about figures of all time. Perhaps *the* most. If it really was the case that he was gay, how extraordinary that it had been ignored for so long.

No one was happy about the book. Critics were derisive, gay activists outraged, and historians suggested that the subject was not worthy of study.

It was all shaping up to be one giant shit storm.

Then 9/11 happened and there was no more gay-Hitler talk after that. Except we were intrigued. Why would historians be so opposed to this book? The saying goes that those who do not remember the past are condemned to repeat it. But perhaps it's more about understanding the past so we can make different choices in the present. And why would gays be opposed to it too? Gayness is not a moral force. We are no more saints and no less sinful than everyone else. Besides, truly, who would not be interested to know if Hitler was gay? It's hard to miss the streak of homoeroticism coursing through all Nazism: The uniforms! The buildings! The massive theatrical displays! And the book turned out to be a fascinating and compelling read, packed with anecdotes, gossip and, ultimately, what felt like an overwhelming body of evidence. So we acquired the rights to make a documentary based on it.

If Hitler was gay, who would not be interested? The uniforms! The buildings! The theatrics!

As we traveled around Europe interviewing the top historians and Hitler experts, it was fascinating to learn how little they seemed to know about homosexuality in particular and even sexuality in general. One historian found it impossible to buy the idea that a virtually homeless Hitler in Vienna turned to male hustling on the grounds that he talked too much and was not good-looking enough. As if that ever stopped anyone before.

In the countryside outside Vienna, we enacted the story Hitler's alleged boyfriend wrote in his memoir, in which a rustic ramble takes an unexpected turn when a thunderstorm forces them to take shelter in a barn:

"I took one of the big cloths, spread it out on the hay, and told Adolf to remove his wet shirt and underpants and wrap himself in the dry cloth...He lay down naked on the cloth. I folded the ends together and wrapped him up....He was highly amused by the whole venture, whose romantic conclusion pleased him greatly. Besides we were nice and warm by now..."

Well, huffed the historian, they were clearly wrapped in separate pieces of canvas, so how could there possibly have been any romantic entanglement?

They had problems with the evidence which, they said, was gossip. But just because something is gossip doesn't make it untrue. Even if the publicists con-

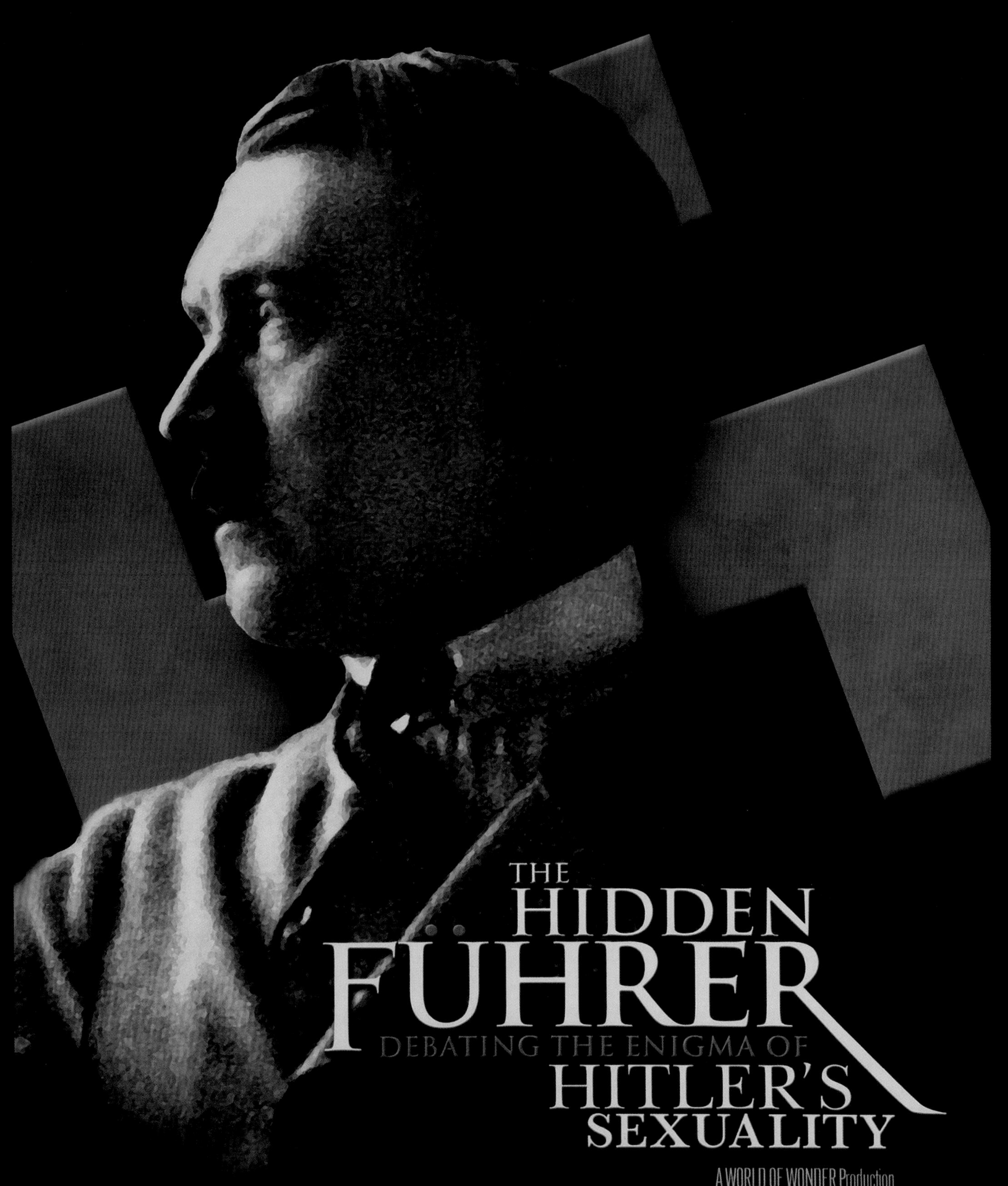
THE
HIDDEN
FÜHRER
DEBATING THE ENIGMA OF
HITLER'S
SEXUALITY
A WORLD OF WONDER Production
Directed by FENTON BAILEY and RANDY BARBATO
Produced by GABRIEL ROTELLO
For CINEMAX: Supervising Producer JOHN HOFFMAN
Executive Producer SHEILA NEVINS
PREMIERES TUESDAY
APRIL 20 AT 7PM

cinemax
reel
LIFE

demn it, we all know that a lot of what is in the *National Enquirer* is true. So why would historians refuse to consider the powerful body of evidence presented by gossip?

In Bremen, Lothar Machtan's old tutor angrily waved his finger at Lothar and said, "Unless someone stands up and says, 'I had sex with Hitler,' then the idea that he was gay could not be entertained."

It was the same everywhere we went; show me proof, they demanded.

What, semen-stained sheets?

According to Rochus Misch, Hitler's young telephone operator, the maids *did* indeed check the sheets at Hitler's country retreat. They came up with nothing. But maybe Hitler – like plenty of other people – had no interest in having sex in a bed. Or maybe he used a towel and cleaned up after himself.

Hitler was definitely good at covering things up. As soon as he came to power he used that power to eradicate his past and all possible evidence. The Brown Shirts – who it was known were disproportionately gay – were rounded up and shot, and the village he grew up in leveled and turned into a firing range. You don't have to be a brain surgeon to know that swishiness in those days would play even less well on the world stage than it does today.

Historians like to consider themselves above the scuttlebutt of sexuality. But sex *is* history: no sex, no people, no daisy chain of DNA to narrativize as history. Civilization – one group building on the advancements of another – depends upon sex. It is its engine. Without sexuality we would be fucked. Or not. No one would be around to care either way. Least of all write books about it.

Growing up gay, you quickly come to understand how our life's path is determined by sexuality. Yet we don't get to read in our history books about gay Florence Nightingale, gay Abraham Lincoln, gay Alexander the Great, gay Leonardo Da Vinci. When it comes to the history books, the gay label is reserved for fags getting their comeuppance like Edward II with the red-hot poker, or Alan Turing committing suicide.

So the whole experience of making the film proved to be a valuable lesson in what history is made of. We had always thought history was about truth and a neutral record of things. Instead, history is merely a reflection of the prejudices and preconceptions of those who write it.

If camp is the lie that tells the truth, history is the truth that lies.

If camp is the lie that tells the truth, history is the truth that lies

Oh, and we learned one other astonishing thing; at the end of the war, when the allied forces liberated the concentration camps, the gays didn't get to go free along with everyone else. The gays in the camps were sent straight back to prison. You can reasonably assume that it was the sort of thing that could only happen then, not now. And you would be dead wrong, as we learnt making *The Strange History of Don't Ask, Don't Tell.*

Don't Ask, Don't Tell, Don't Even Get Us Started

It's amazing that back in 1993, just a few months after Ru wowed the crowd in Washington DC (and vowed to paint the White House pink), that a law could have been passed forcing gays in the military to serve in secret. The law was called Don't Ask, Don't Tell. It superseded all previous regulations about gays in the military and, for the first time, made it against the law. If it seemed benign – hey, just don't tell us you are gay and we won't ask – it was a brilliant and sophisticated kind of persecution.

THIS PAGE: Stills from the Cinemax documentary *The Hidden Fuhrer.* Our film was based on Lothar Machtan's controversial book *The Hidden Hitler* that argued Hitler was gay

and told Adolf to remove his wet shirt and underpants...

-August Kubizek, "Adolf Hitler, Friend from My Youth," 1953

In the '90s there was a plan to build a gay bomb. The bomb would be dropped on the enemy turning them instantly gay

It was a new twist on the military and society's constant demonization of the queer ever since World War II. In the '40s, the gay was a sissy and femme, so limp-wristed he couldn't pick up a weapon. In the '50s, the gay was a communist spy, ready to betray democracy and freedom. In the '60s, the gay was mentally ill, suffering from psychosis that required psychiatric treatment. In the '70s, the gay was a decadent pleasure-seeker. In the '80s, a health risk, and carrier of plague. And come the '90s, having exhausted all the other possible stereotypes, the gay got a new gloss – being gay wasn't the problem, being open about it was. Because people so hated gays, just knowing they were in the vicinity of one would be enough to freak them out. Hence, the gay was required to hide his true self to protect national security, unit cohesion, combat readiness, etc etc. It was all for the greater good.

Well, asking someone not to tell was to put them in an impossible position. Because in a society, in a community, in the military people ask all the time. Questions like, "What did you do this weekend?" or "You went to the movies? Oh, with whom?" Such harmless chit-chat is the fabric of trust between people. Gagging gays not only excluded them from that basic circle of trust, it forced soldiers to betray their integrity, a key military value, by requiring them to lie. It created suspicion. Thus, it neatly created the very threat to unit cohesion the law had been created to protect.

And all this was done in full knowledge and defiance of three military funded studies conducted in the '50s, '80s, and '90s that all concluded gays could serve in the military just as well as straights.

You would have thought this self-evident insanity would either have prevented the law passing in the first place or led to its immediate repeal, but the reverse was true. In the mid-'90s there was a high-level plan to build a gay bomb. The idea was that the bomb would be dropped on the enemy, turning them instantly gay. So aroused by each other would the enemy become that they would be fucking in the foxholes instead of fighting. A righteous victory over anti-freedom faggots would be assured!

When America became embroiled in two wars and was faced with a shortfall of mission critical personnel (partly due to the discharge of gays under Don't Ask, Don't Tell), it introduced a moral waivers clause whereby criminals, prior drug addicts, high school dropouts, and even people making terroristic threats were admitted. This led to some predictably disastrous results when it came to war atrocities committed by the USA.

Not that Don't Ask, Don't Tell was ever enforced with any integrity or consistency; people were asked if they were gay and discharged even if they never told. And the military brass also knowingly sent gay people into combat.

Well, if they truly believed gays had a negative impact on combat readiness, unit cohesion, etc etc, they wouldn't do that. But they knew the unit cohesion thing was humbug. And, lest no indignity go unchecked, when the gay troops got home – assuming they survived after risking their lives for their country – the military did the honorable thing and discharged them.

The whole sorry episode of Don't Ask, Don't Tell was a sobering insight into hypocrisy and insanity at the heart of things. Barry Goldwater famously said, "You don't have to be straight to shoot straight," so why would you want a general who can't even think straight to wage a war on your behalf? Nathaniel Frank put it best: "This is bigger than just gay rights. It's something that cuts to the core of what America is, what America is fighting for, and is a reminder that when one group's rights are trampled upon, the entire culture is diminished."

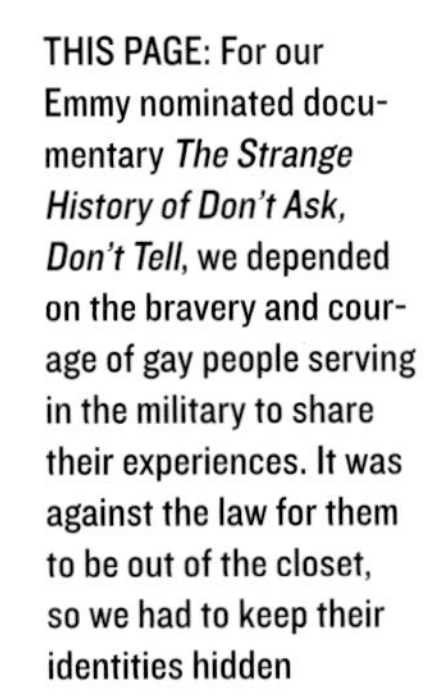

THIS PAGE: For our Emmy nominated documentary *The Strange History of Don't Ask, Don't Tell*, we depended on the bravery and courage of gay people serving in the military to share their experiences. It was against the law for them to be out of the closet, so we had to keep their identities hidden

HBO DOCUMENTARY FILMS® PRESENTS
THE STRANGE HISTORY OF DON'T ASK, DON'T TELL
INSIDE THE FIGHT TO SPEAK OUT.
HBO DOCUMENTARY FILMS® WORLD OF WONDER HBO DOCUMENTARY FILMS PRESENTS A WORLD OF WONDER PRODUCTION A FILM BY FENTON BAILEY RANDY BARBATO
"THE STRANGE HISTORY OF DON'T ASK, DON'T TELL" EDITED BY LANGDON F. PAGE CHRIS CONWAY ORIGINAL MUSIC BY DAVID BENJAMIN STEINBERG DIRECTOR OF PHOTOGRAPHY MICHAEL JACOB KERBER
ASSOCIATE PRODUCER JOHN BLAIR PRODUCED BY MONA CARD GABRIEL ROTELLO DIRECTED & PRODUCED BY FENTON BAILEY RANDY BARBATO FOR HBO: SUPERVISING PRODUCER JACQUELINE GLOVER EXECUTIVE PRODUCER SHEILA NEVINS
PREMIERES TUESDAY, SEPTEMBER 20, 8PM
SNEAK PREVIEW SEPTEMBER 19, MIDNIGHT
ONLY ON HBO®

Bruce Vilanch

COMEDIAN AND WRITER

Bruce is as famous for writing as he is for his collection of outrageous T-shirts. In the spring of 2005 we piloted a talk show which had a desk in the shape of a giant cheesecake with the show's host, Bruce Vilanch, sitting where several slices had been removed. Sadly, Bravo didn't bite

PHOTOGRAPHED BY IDRIS + TONY
AT HOME, HOLLYWOOD,
CALIFORNIA, NOVEMBER 15, 2009

Gabriel Rotello

PRODUCER, DIRECTOR, AUTHOR

Animal, vegetable, or gay? Gabriel has worked with us on countless projects: *Eyes of Tammy Faye, Party Monster, Hollywood Fashion Machine, Movies That Shook the World, The Strange History of Don't Ask Don't Tell.* He may be the only television producer and director who grows all his own vegetables

PHOTOGRAPHED BY IDRIS + TONY
AT HOME, LOS ANGELES, CALIFORNIA,
AUGUST 3, 2009

Paul Monroe

FASHION DESIGNER

Paul is deep in the background behind a doll portrait made by his longterm partner Greer Langton. Paul co-owned Einsteins with Julia Morton and was behind a brief "Men In Skirts" fashion moment

PHOTOGRAPHED BY IDRIS & TONY AT HOME, WEST HOLLYWOOD, CALIFORNIA, NOVEMBER 18, 2009

"It's all trompe l'oeil darling... embrace it!"

–PAUL MONROE

Micah McCain
ACTOR, COMEDIAN

At the very beginning of his career as a stand-up comic, Micah was a cast member of our series *Gay Hollywood* on AMC

PHOTOGRAPHED BY IDRIS + TONY
AT HOME, WEST HOLLYWOOD, CALIFORNIA, NOVEMBER 19, 2009

Brian Graden

FORMER TV EXECUTIVE

Brian was former president of programming at MTV, VH1, CMT, and Logo. He greenlit *South Park* and *RuPaul's Drag Race*

PHOTOGRAPHED BY IDRIS + TONY
AT HOME, LOS ANGELES, CALIFORNIA,
JULY 13, 2010

Perez Hilton

BLOGGER

We hope that one day he forgives us for not being able to get into our office party at Les Deux. The place was overcrowded and the fire marshal was on the door. Our hands were tied

PHOTOGRAPHED BY IDRIS + TONY
WEST HOLLYWOOD, CALIFORNIA,
NOVEMBER 14, 2009

Billy B
MAKEUP ARTIST

You could say he's our foundation. Although we have depended on Billy B's makeup genius almost as long as we have been in business, it was less known to us that he also buys and makes over houses in his hometown of Aberdeen, Mississippi. We told his story in our HGTV series *Hometown Renovation*

PHOTOGRAPHED BY IDRIS + TONY
HOLLYWOOD DELL, CALIFORNIA,
NOVEMBER 13, 2009

Simon Doonan

AUTHOR, BARNEYS NEW YORK CREATIVE DIRECTOR

Always a brilliant talker, we've interviewed him for our shows many times. But for years we tried in vain to persuade him and partner Jonathan Adler to let us follow them around with cameras. Everything out of their mouths is sheer genius, and to see it all go unrecorded is a crime against television

PHOTOGRAPHED BY IDRIS + TONY AT HOME, GREENWICH VILLAGE, NEW YORK CITY, JUNE 10, 2009

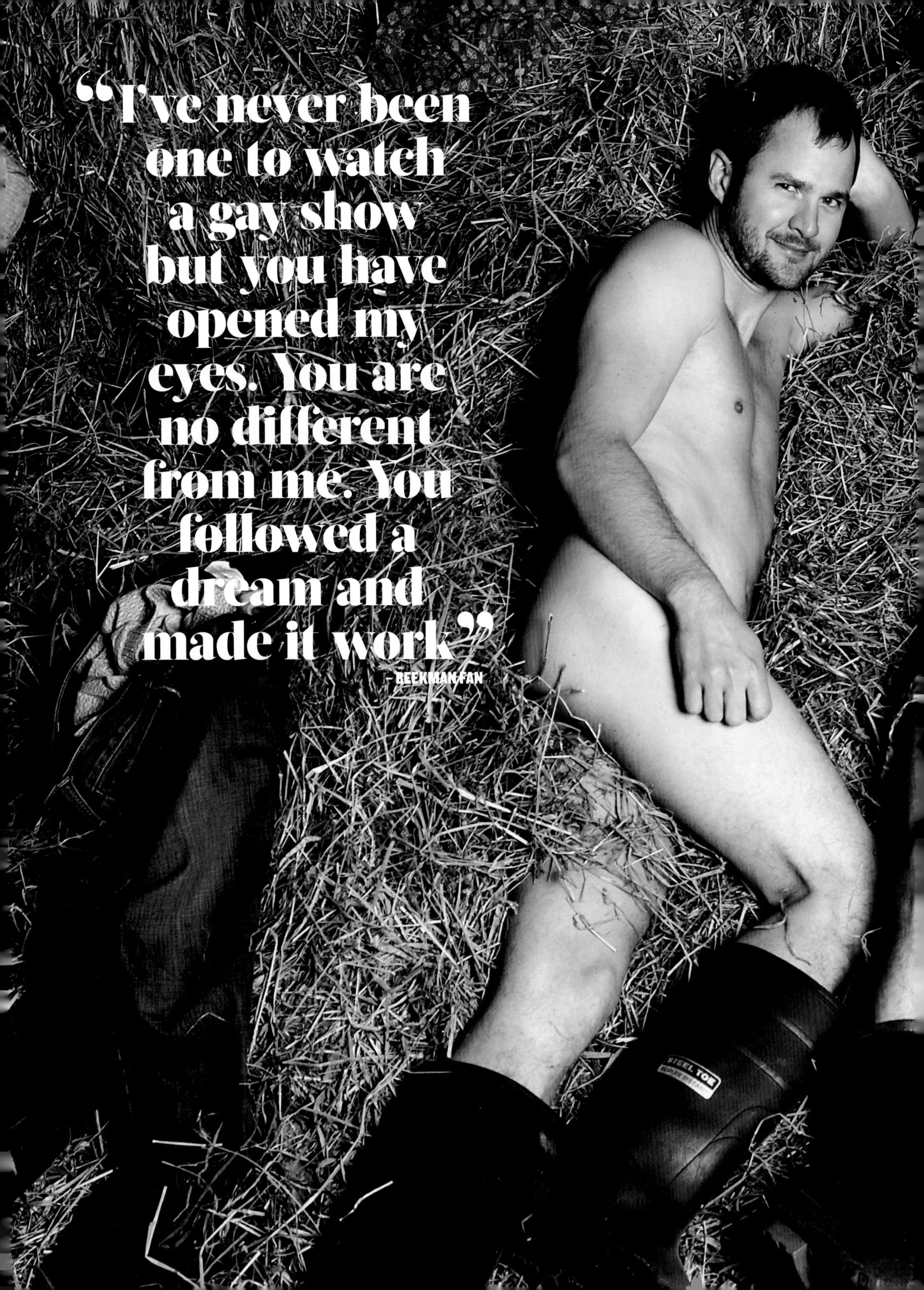
"I've never been one to watch a gay show but you have opened my eyes. You are no different from me. You followed a dream and made it work"
– BEEKMAN FAN
STEEL TOE

Josh Kilmer Purcell

AUTHOR, AD EXECUTIVE, FARMER

Brent Ridge

DOCTOR, FARMER

Two seasons of the series not only saw them transform their farm into a booming business, but also turn around the fortunes of neighboring village Sharon Springs. Make hay while the (gay) sunshines (even though a blizzard was raging outside)

PHOTOGRAPHED BY IDRIS + TONY
BEEKMAN FARM, SHARON SPRINGS, NEW YORK, JANUARY 29, 2010

David Munk
BLOGGER

Elisa Casas
VINTAGE STORE OWNER

One of the couples in the first season of our Sundance series *Girls Who Like Boys Who Like Boys*

PHOTOGRAPHED BY IDRIS + TONY
CHELSEA GIRL (ELISA'S VINTAGE CLOTHING STORE) SOHO, NEW YORK CITY, JULY 21, 2010

Rosebud Baker
ACTRESS, MUSICIAN

Sahil Farooqi
ACTOR, WAITER

Best friends from the first season of our Sundance series *Girls Who Like Boys Who Like Boys*

PHOTOGRAPHED BY IDRIS + TONY
THE HIGHLINE, NEW YORK CITY, JULY 21, 2010

Dustin Lance Black

SCREENWRITER

Since appearing in *Gay Hollywood*, Dustin has gone on to write the scripts for *Milk* and *J Edgar*. Oh, and win an Oscar too. Suppose one has to win one not to feel the slightest twinge of envy

PHOTOGRAPHED BY IDRIS + TONY
BROOKLYN, NEW YORK,
MARCH 25, 2010

Wayne Anderson
BLOGGER, ACTIVIST

His political rants added some friction to the WOW Report

PHOTOGRAPHED BY IDRIS + TONY
GREENWICH VILLAGE, NEW YORK CITY,
DECEMBER 18, 2009

Kristine W
SINGER

We managed her for a brief period and have never seen such a combination of pipes, chops, and sheer exuberance. An iPod without Kristine W is like pizza without cheese

PHOTOGRAPHED BY IDRIS + TONY
LAS VEGAS COUNTRY CLUB,
LAS VEGAS, NEVADA,
JULY 28, 2009

Ultra Naté

SINGER

We directed the video for her anthemic hit "Free" and set it in a hospital with straightjackets, gurneys, and IV drips. The record label hated it and made us lose the IV drips. Years later the song would become the signature tune for HSN

PHOTOGRAPHED BY IDRIS + TONY
BROOKLYN, NEW YORK,
OCTOBER 18, 2009

Angela Rae Berg

TV PRODUCER, DIRECTOR

Angela cut her teeth on *Showbiz Moms and Dads* before going on to showrun *The Fabulous Beekman Boys* and direct *All the Right Moves.* In real life she is a fabulous baker and amazing dancer

PHOTOGRAPHED BY IDRIS + TONY
BEEKMAN FARM, SHARON SPRINGS, NEW YORK, JANUARY 29, 2010

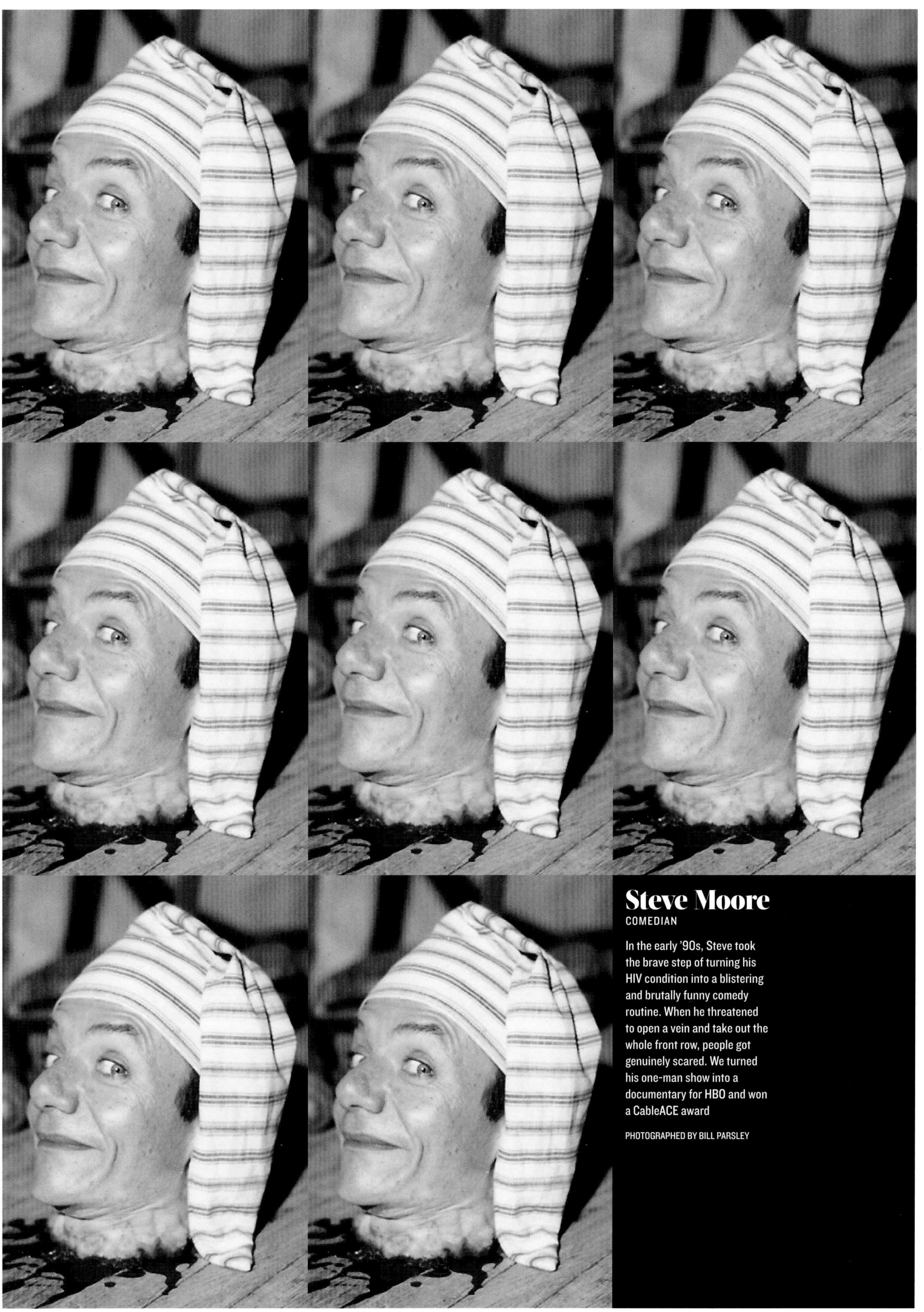

Steve Moore

COMEDIAN

In the early '90s, Steve took the brave step of turning his HIV condition into a blistering and brutally funny comedy routine. When he threatened to open a vein and take out the whole front row, people got genuinely scared. We turned his one-man show into a documentary for HBO and won a CableACE award

PHOTOGRAPHED BY BILL PARSLEY

Wash Westmoreland

DIRECTOR

Wash was inspired to make a documentary with us following the strange lives of gay Republicans, who to many people appear to be a contradiction in terms

PHOTOGRAPHED BY IDRIS + TONY
AT HOME, ECHO PARK, CALIFORNIA,
JULY 15, 2010

Aubrey Sarvis

EXECUTIVE DIRECTOR, SERVICE MEMBERS LEGAL DEFENSE NETWORK.

Aubrey's years long struggle to get Don't Ask, Don't Tell repealed is the central story in our HBO documentary *The Strange History of Don't Ask, Don't Tell*

PHOTOGRAPHED BY IDRIS + TONY
AT HOME, WASHINGTON, DC,
OCTOBER 29, 2011

"You don't have to be straight to shoot straight"

–SENATOR BARRY GOLDWATER

“I hadn’t come out to my family yet let alone told them I was getting thrown out of the military. I drop bombs for a living, but these were the biggest bombs I’ve ever dropped”

–VICTOR FEHRENBACH

Victor Fehrenbach

LIEUTENANT COLONEL (RETIRED), US AIR FORCE

Featured in our HBO documentary *The Strange History of Don't Ask, Don't Tell*

PHOTOGRAPHED BY IDRIS + TONY
AIR FORCE MEMORIAL, ARLINGTON, VIRGINIA, OCTOBER 30, 2011

Mike Almy
MAJOR, US AIR FORCE

Discharged under Don't Ask, Don't Tell and featured in our documentary

PHOTOGRAPHED BY IDRIS + TONY
THE DUPONT CIRCLE HOTEL,
WASHINGTON, DC, OCTOBER 30, 2011

Allan Brocka

DIRECTOR, SCREENWRITER

Glenn Gaylord

DIRECTOR, SCREENWRITER

Allan created *Rick & Steve: The Happiest Gay Couple in All the World* and Glenn wrote *Leave It on the Floor.* Together, at WOW, they produced and directed *Camp Michael Jackson*, a documentary about the Gloved One's loyal band of fans camped outside the courthouse during his 2005 trial. The sign behind them is from Neverland and was part of the preview exhibition for the aborted auction of Jackson memorabilia

PHOTOGRAPHED BY IDRIS + TONY
JULIEN'S AUCTION HOUSE, BEVERLY HILLS, CALIFORNIA, APRIL 14, 2009

BYE
GOOD-BYE
For Now
Julien's
NEVERLAND
Michael Jackson

Let's Talk About Sex

ERICA JONG ONCE TOLD US that because she wrote about sex she would never win big literary awards. She is most famous for inventing the "zipless fuck" in her novel *Fear of Flying*. People tend to think of the zipless fuck as sticking it in without disrobing. But after reading the book we were surprised to discover that the zipless fuck is actually an idea.

The theatrical poster for the Asian release of *Inside Deep Throat*

So why would poor Erica be so demonised just for thinking about sex? As we would come to understand, dealing with sex and sexuality in one's work is a high risk activity.

Consider this: The adult business is an $11 billion industry annually. It's regulated, excoriated, but virtually unexamined as an actual business. That was the thrust of a book called *Porn Gold* by David Hebditch and Nick Anning. They revealed that the industry was professionally run, on the cutting edge of technology, generating billions of dollars that benefited the bottom lines of such blue chip brands as Sony, Kodak, and even the Vatican. Who knew?

The book gave us the big idea to make a series about the history of pornography and call it *The Secret History of Civilization*. Our thesis (developed with Isabel Tang, who went on to write the book that accompanied the series) was that sexually explicit expression has been a vital civilizing force throughout history and, so far, more important than just being some smutty thing on the margins of society. Time and time again throughout history, pornography has been

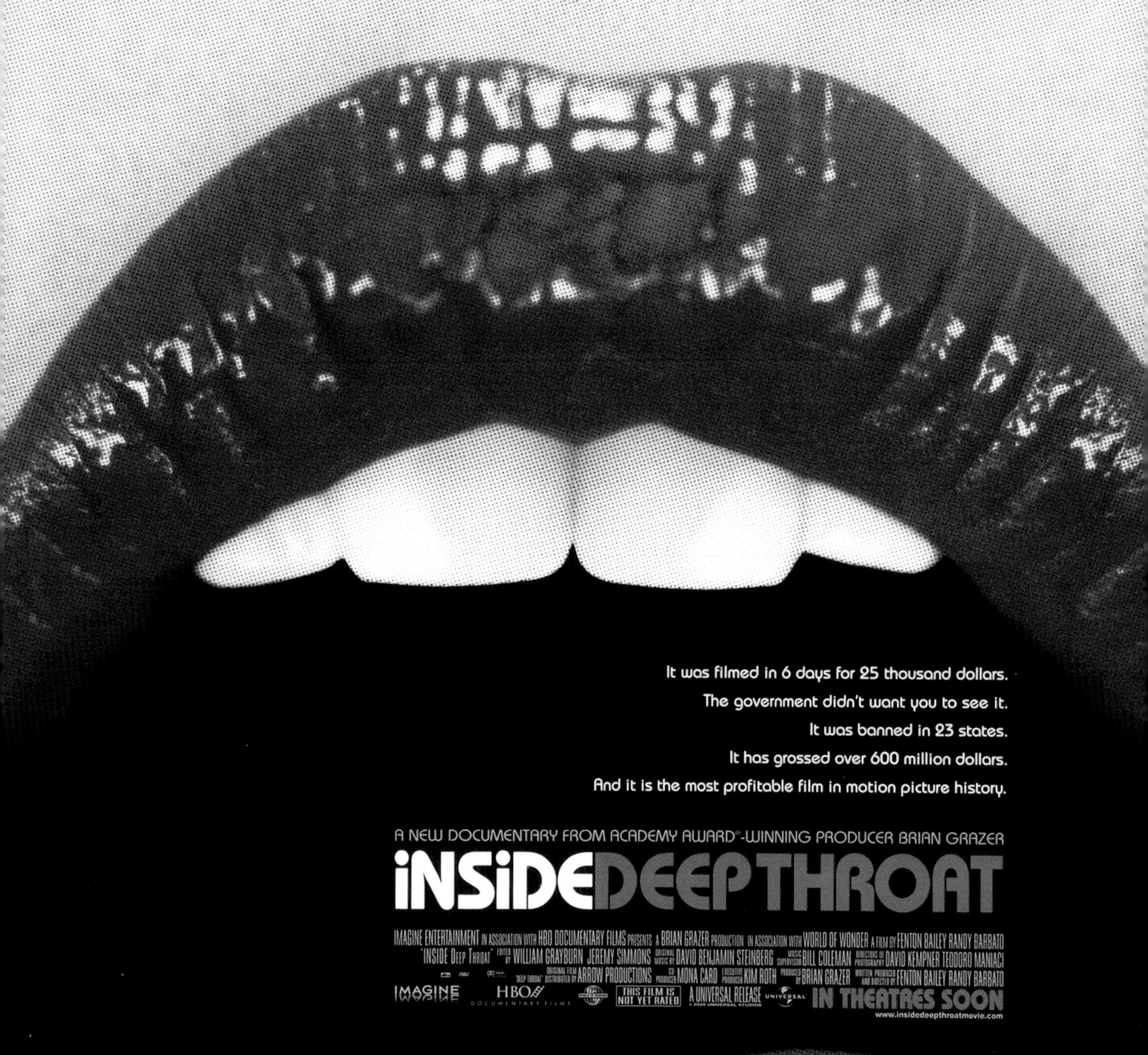
It was filmed in 6 days for 25 thousand dollars.
The government didn't want you to see it.
It was banned in 23 states.
It has grossed over 600 million dollars.
And it is the most profitable film in motion picture history.
A NEW DOCUMENTARY FROM ACADEMY AWARD®-WINNING PRODUCER BRIAN GRAZER
INSIDE DEEP THROAT
IMAGINE ENTERTAINMENT IN ASSOCIATION WITH HBO DOCUMENTARY FILMS PRESENTS A BRIAN GRAZER PRODUCTION IN ASSOCIATION WITH WORLD OF WONDER A FILM BY FENTON BAILEY RANDY BARBATO
"INSIDE Deep Throat" EDITED BY WILLIAM GRAYBURN JEREMY SIMMONS ORIGINAL MUSIC BY DAVID BENJAMIN STEINBERG MUSIC SUPERVISOR BILL COLEMAN DIRECTORS OF PHOTOGRAPHY DAVID KEMPNER TEODORO MANIACI
"DEEP THROAT" ORIGINAL FILM DISTRIBUTED BY ARROW PRODUCTIONS CO-PRODUCER MONA CARD EXECUTIVE PRODUCER KIM ROTH PRODUCED BY BRIAN GRAZER WRITTEN, PRODUCED AND DIRECTED BY FENTON BAILEY RANDY BARBATO
IMAGINE
HBO DOCUMENTARY FILMS
THIS FILM IS NOT YET RATED
A UNIVERSAL RELEASE
UNIVERSAL
IN THEATRES SOON
www.insidedeepthroatmovie.com
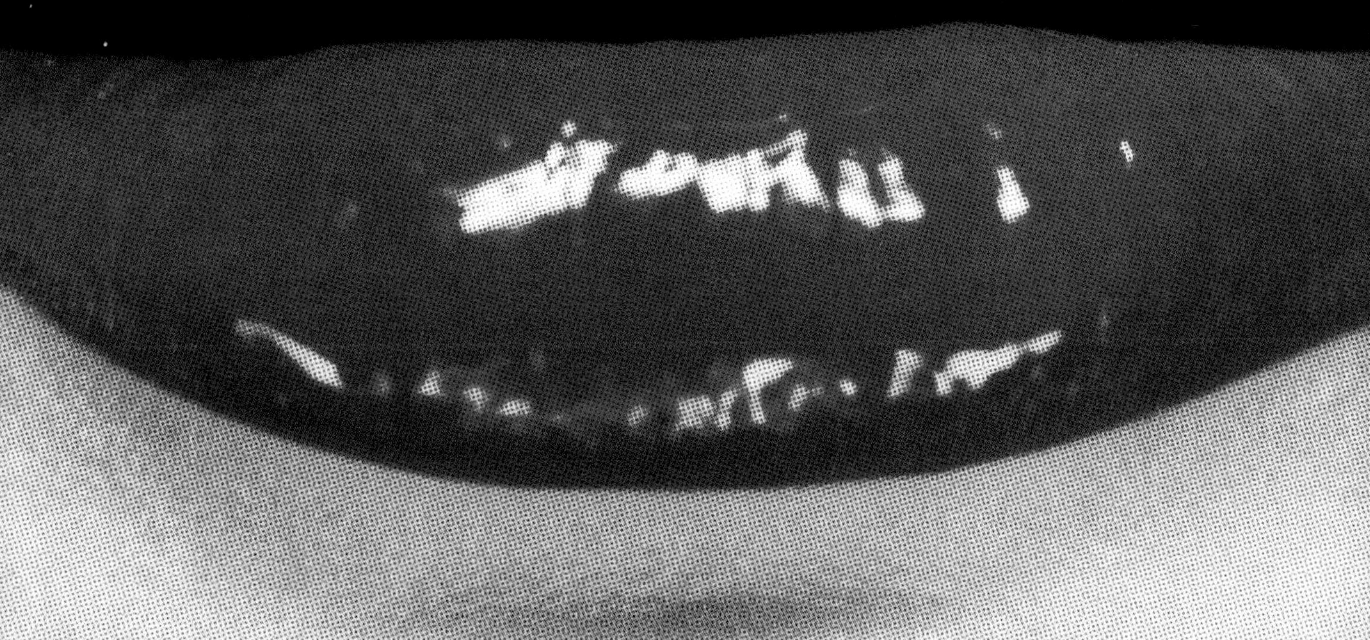

Throughout history pornography has been the initial and killer application for new media

the initial application and (as often as not) the killer application for new media. This, we found, was as true for the internet as it was for video, film, photography, and the printing press. Even cave paintings.

In the same way that bread needs yeast to rise, our series implied that pornography was the catalyst for the rise of media in our society. If only making it were as simple as baking bread. As Lynn Hunt wrote in *The Invention of Pornography,* "Pornography as a regulatory category was invented in response to the perceived menace of the democratization of culture." New media is always demonized as some kind of evil force that will lead to the collapse of society.

And so the project would take 10 years to get commissioned. It was first picked up at the BBC; however, a member of the board – the fabulously named Marmaduke Hussey – reportedly had a fit, and it was dropped like a hot potato. But when the idea's champion, Michael Jackson, moved from the BBC to Channel Four with Janey Walker, the idea got revived and finally green-lit. And it was a hit, a big one.

Of the six episodes, the one that was the most watched was all about video. Perhaps because at the time everyone in the audience had a VCR whose primary use – once the kids were in bed – was to watch porn. The episode was set predominantly in the San Fernando Valley where we met and became friends with Steve Hirsch, the co-owner of Vivid Entertainment, the most successful adult production company of all time – then and now.

Frankly, it was exciting meeting our first porn mogul. Vivid's headquarters were located in a nondescript warehouse on the outer edges of the Valley. A potted plant was dying in the overlit reception, with some vinyl chairs the worse for wear. Steve's office was a sort of inner temple with wood paneling, recessed lighting, and glass cabinets filled with awards. And then there was Steve himself – straightforward, likeable, and all business.

Out of that experience came the idea for a series going behind the scenes of the business. The concept was that porn stars were people too, with nine-to-fives like most everybody. It's just a job. So we followed Mercedes Bends as she took her kid to daycare and then off to work to do a double anal. We followed Sasha Grey home from a hard day of shagging to her boyfriend who wanted to talk about getting married. Or Savanna Samson, who on her day off would work with a Napa Valley vineyard that was launching her own wine label. No-brainer though this might have seemed, it took several years to set up. Everyone passed except Showtime, where it ran for three seasons.

And it might have been the reason we didn't produce one of the most successful doc-series of all time, *Keeping Up with the Kardashians*. They came in to meet us and it was a love fest. But we were passed over in favor of Ryan Seacrest. We later learned our ties to Vivid were "problematic." You see, it was Vivid who had distributed the Kardashian sex tape. The one that kind of put them on the map in the first place.

Maybe Erica Jong's dire warning about the impact of sex on a legitimate career could be put to rest when Brian Grazer approached us to produce and direct a documentary about *Deep Throat*. The little-reported fact was that *Deep Throat* was the most profitable movie of all time, measuring its $600-million take against its rock-bottom $25,000 cost. It was Brian Grazer's hope that the doc could win an Ocscar. We weren't so sure the Academy would go for it, but the opportunity to tell this story was too good to pass up – glittering prizes be damned.

Deep Throat Diary

2002

Monday, April 22

THIS PAGE AND OPPOSITE PAGE: Frame grabs from *Deeper Throat, Debbie Does Dallas Again,* and *Porno Valley,* all series we made for Showtime, going behind the scenes at Vivid Entertainment

NEW YORK – Linda Lovelace dies. Brian Grazer had a script for a biopic, but her death throws the life-rights issue into confusion. He begins to think about making a documentary.

2003

Saturday, January 11

LAS VEGAS – We fly to Vegas to cover the porn Oscars, officially known as the Adult Video News Awards. This is really the start of Hollywood's Awards Season. It's mind-boggling how huge the awards have become. Several ballrooms at the Venetian are joined to form one vast audience. The Golden Globes are rinky-dink in comparison. And nothing can beat someone thanking God for their award for Best Anal Performance.

Filming on the red carpet that stretches for perhaps a quarter of a mile through the lobby of the Venetian, it was surprising how so few of today's porn stars knew who Linda Lovelace was. So different from the previous night when we attended the Legends of Erotica awards, where Linda was remembered. A small crowd – maybe 50 porn diehards (and one very vocal drunk) – in one of Raymond Pistol's adult stores. Located far from the glittery part of the Strip, the cinderblock construction and harsh overhead lighting didn't afford much glamour. But it was touching that she should be remembered at all.

Sunday, January 12

Go to the adult trade show and talk with several legends of the business: Nina Hartley, Ron Jeremy, and Candida Royale.

Nina Hartley: *"I couldn't be here, happy and healthy and sane, had it not been for the '70s. The whole idea that women finally were able to have sex for their own purposes and not just to keep a man or to get pregnant was revolutionary. Today people don't understand that. So Deep Throat really opened up everything. The good and the bad. It opened up a Pandora's box. And so along with a sense of freedom comes sexual excess. And response to excess is conservatism. But the genie's out of the bottle. People want their sexual entertainment."*

Monday, March 3

Back in LA, we started off optimistically sending out hundreds of letters requesting interviews, but the stony silence that followed was disconcerting. Follow-up calls only yielded negatives. *New York Times* poo-bah Arthur Gelb wouldn't be interviewed – even though he led an entire editorial department from the paper to see the film when it opened. Gay Talese wouldn't be interviewed. He spent years writing *Thy Neighbor's Wife*, a completely un-put-downable account of the sexual experimentation that was to the '70s what *Bonfire of Vanities* was to the '80s. The judge in the New York trial wouldn't be interviewed. His verdict banning the film in New York blew the film up into a nationwide phenomenon, although he didn't even know what the missionary position was. The manager of the theater in New York that showed the film won't be interviewed – he's still wary of the mob connection.

Friday, May 16

PHOENIX – Our first interview is with Jeff Smith a reporter from the local paper who reviewed the film when it opened and then followed the trial. He lays the whole thing out for us.

"It's not the conservatives who've taken the fun out of American society now, it's the liberals. Because they've got money, they're driving Saabs and Volvos, they're sending their children to Montessori Schools. The very people who were behind 'Hey, let's get out and have a good time and sleep with everybody and we'll take any drug we can and get drunk and raise hell and make nasty films.' Uh-uh, they're not like that anymore. They've made a ton of money and they're locked away behind guarded gates. They know what you can get into by way

Measuring its $600 million take against its rock bottom cost of $25,000 makes Deep Throat the most profitable movie of all time

of mischief and fun and they don't want their kids to do it, and they don't want anybody else doing it, you know. Liberalism itself has changed. Liberalism doesn't mean anymore being independent and willing to embrace the new and willing to consider any point of view, no matter how outrageous or unpopular. Today's liberalism is so rigidly conformist. You gotta buy the whole package. You buy the lattes and Swedish cars and private schools and natural fiber clothing and the whole goddamn kit. You stray from that dogma and you'll be drummed out of the corps and called all sorts of nasty names at parties. And that's what's happened to me."

Wednesday, May 21
BOSTON – Interview legendary attorney Alan Dershowitz. When Harry Reems (co-star of *Deep Throat*) was convicted in Memphis, Dershowitz helped him on his appeal. He said the funny thing was that when Harry came to meet him at Harvard Law school, Harry was the one who looked like a lawyer, with short hair and in a suit. Alan, with long hair, jeans, and sneakers could have been mistaken for the porn star. He said that Harry would have made a fine lawyer.

Friday, May 23
NEW YORK – Shooting in Times Square. Susan Brownmiller is our tour guide, reprising the role she played taking people on Women Against Pornography tours in and around the sex shops of Times Square for $5. But today, Peepland and the rundown theaters are all gone, and in their place are the razzle-dazzle of America's favorite brand names, from Disney to McDonald's. It's so different, and yet. . . *"I don't know if we won anything,"* sighs Brownmiller, gazing up at the stories-high billboard of a naked Jenna Jameson.

From Brownmiller to Al Goldstein. Al Goldstein is a Rabelaisian character – fat, foul-mouthed, and unapologetic. He uses free speech to spew politically incorrect invective. For example, when we mentioned Susan Brownmiller's name, he exploded: *"You moron, dimwitted turd. You smelly little facsimile of a human being. First of all, some women have rape fantasies. Secondly, I want nothing more from a woman than to be her slave. I have told many women to own me. Use my tongue. Let me bring you off. I'm going to stay between your legs not for an hour, for days. I've taught her not to have one orgasm, but 20. . . ."* Etc.

Many find him repugnant, and he probably wouldn't disagree. He doesn't make the final cut of the film, even though he said one of the most important, truest things anyone would say: *"Our sexual freedom, your sexual freedom, it's very fucking important. And it's a war that's never won. So we need people like me who are either half-crazy or half self-destructive to keep the fight going. Because it's not going to stay won. You need nutcases like me to fight it."*

Thursday, June 26
SAN FRANCISCO – We are shooting at the Institute of Advanced Study for Human Sexuality, where Ted McIlvenna presides over an enormous collection of pornography (26 warehouses, three million items). Sexology seems a weird subject to have any academic status. But adult star Annie Sprinkle has a Ph.D in the subject from the Institute. We shoot an interview with her arranged on an array of cushions. It's *very* '70s. Turns out Annie's first job after leaving home was in the box office of a theater in Tucson where *Deep Throat* was playing.

"The first time I walked into the theater I looked up at the screen, and it was kind of an epiphany. It was really truly a religious experience... Little did I know that seeing Deep Throat *would impact the rest of my life. I then spent 30 years in the sex industry and studying sex and making sex films. So* Deep Throat, *I can honestly say, changed my life radically."*

When the Feds raided it, she received a subpoena to go on the witness stand. This otherwise unfortunate

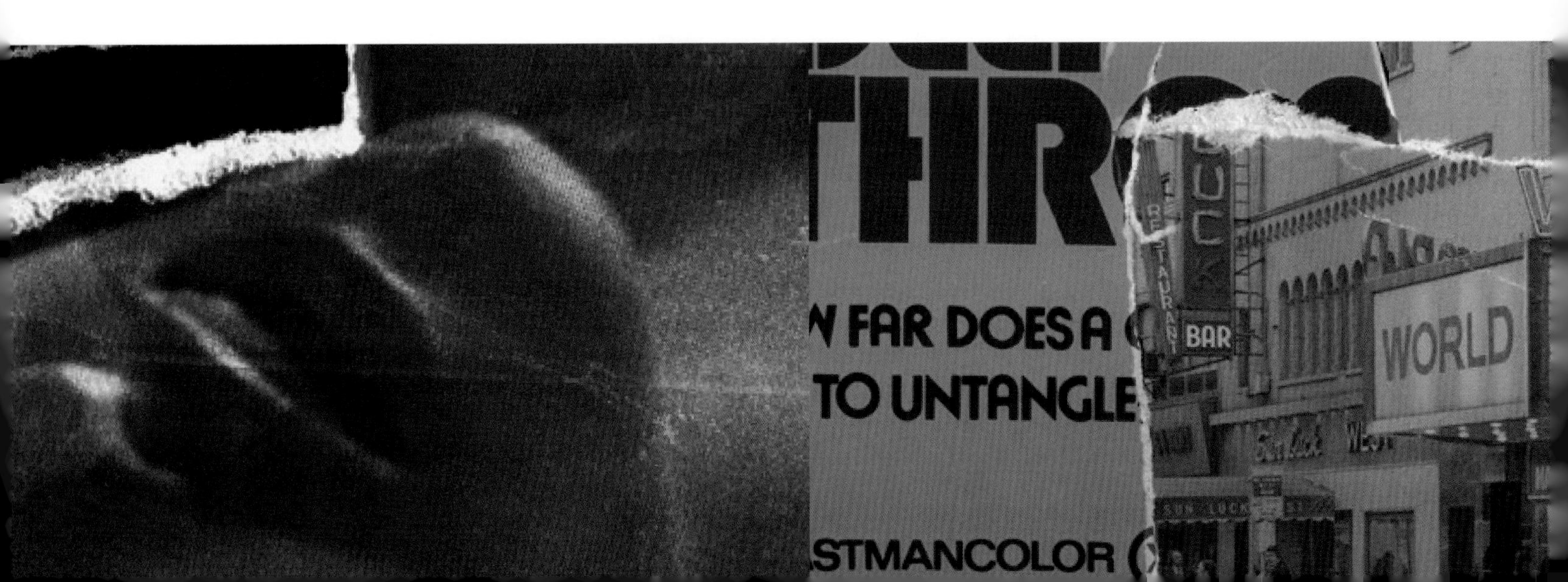

event had the benefit of introducing her to *Deep Throat* director Gerard Damiano.

"Sitting in the witness room, waiting for my turn to testify, I met Gerard Damiano and flirted with him shamelessly because, of course, to me it was like meeting Steven Spielberg. My in with Jerry was like, 'Oh, could you teach me to do Deep Throat?' So, he did."

Monday, June 30
LOS ANGELES – Interview legendary porn star #1, Marilyn Chambers. Marilyn was not in *Deep Throat*, but after Linda dumped her husband/manager, and the man who taught her how to deep throat, Chuck Traynor, it was Marilyn who took up with him. By her account, they had a happy and mutually beneficial relationship. She said Chuck also taught her to deep throat using the same technique of hypnosis that he had supposedly acquired as a Marine in Vietnam. Before Chuck, Marilyn had been married to a bagpipe player.

Tuesday, July 1
Interview legendary porn star #2, Georgina Spelvin. She was the star of Damiano's second big hit, the classic *The Devil in Miss Jones*. She has our hands-down favorite line of all time: *"Let's face it. There is no more sincere compliment in the world than an erection."*

Sunday, July 25
NEW YORK – Interview Erica Jong.
"We were very naive. We thought if everyone smoked hashish and marijuana there would be world peace. I mean, it was silly. Smoking dope did not bring about world peace. Instead, Nixon got re-elected after being declared politically dead. And the forces of repression came in, in a huge, huge way. And the forces of repression have been in control ever since. You'll probably cut all this out. But that's the real history of our times. What the '60s did in that brief six-year period, in which the sexual revolution went public, let's say, was to set up an excuse for the biggest backlash of all time."

Wednesday, July 28
MIAMI – Met the legendary Count Sepy Dobronyi, whose house was used as a location to shoot the original film. He came out to greet us in black leather shorts and explained that he designed and built his house to resemble a bull. We enter through the rear, so to speak, and find ourselves in the presence of a massive collection of erotic primitive art from Borneo. Overlooking the vast living room was a loft with the prow of a Viking boat that served as a bed, where the Count claimed to have been deep-throated by Linda Lovelace. Someone later referred to the boat as a canoe, but you refer to the count's prow as such at your peril. Just then, a pair of babes arrived in bikinis and an open-top sports car to go swimming. Turning down the offer of a skinny dip, we took our leave.

Saturday, July 30
FORT MYERS – Interview Gerard Damiano and his son and daughter at their home.
"I was asked a question by Oui magazine: What's better than sex? And a lot of people had given these flowery quotations of what they thought was better than sex. And I said better than sex is a good bowel movement. I always thought that sex was like water. It's all over the place. Water is only important if you don't have it. You die. Uh, sex, if you don't have it, that's when people go bananas. When you deny people the ability to be sexually free, if you take that away, then it's dangerous."

Wednesday, October 22
LOS ANGELES – Interview Gore Vidal, who mainly wants to talk about the boys in the war. It's all completely fascinating.

"There were 13 million of us, taken away from home in the Pacific Islands and same-sexuality flourished. And, uh, nobody questioned it. Yes, the authorities did. Officers were very strict. Not wanting us to have any fun. Just to be dead was their idea of a perfect, uh, military operation.

OPPOSITE PAGE AND THIS PAGE: Rick Morris' ripped and torn graphics for *Inside Deep Throat.* Rick has done many amazing title treatments for our shows

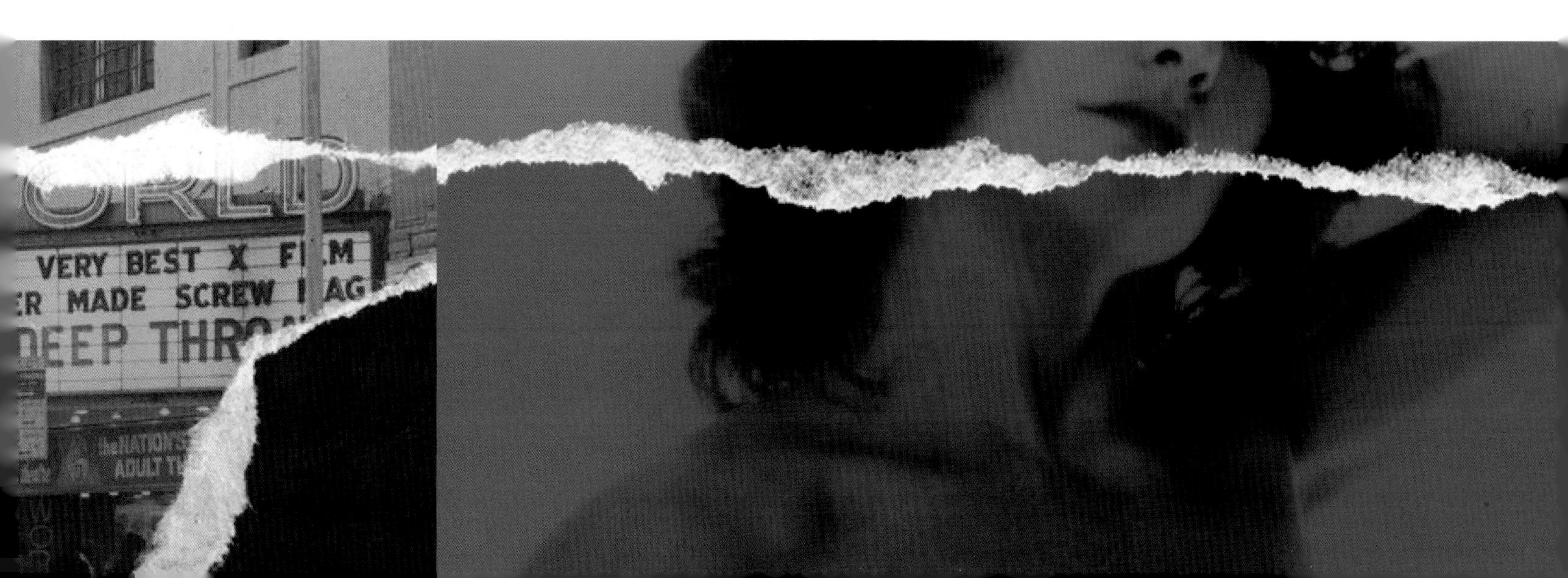

Let's face it. There's no more sincere compliment than an erection

About one entire island of Marines who just decided to pair off. They had this sort of buddy system. And everybody acquired a buddy. And it was the talk of the Pacific. The idea that our American boys who had just won the Second World War were involved in this sort of activity, sometimes to the point of obsession, sometimes to the point of falling in love, traumatized the whole country. Well, our boys were very busy winning the Second World War and also with one another. That was a fact. So, anybody that much younger than I, which practically everybody is, doesn't know what it's like to have had a free sex life."

Wednesday, November 5

Interview with Hugh Hefner. It's hard not to become slightly excited at going to the fabled Playboy mansion. Just as few nightclubs look magical in the cold light of day, a whiff of congealment hung in the air. It was less like a mansion, more like a boy's boarding school. Hugh Hefner was unusual in that he spoke in complete sentences and paragraphs without ums and ahs.

"When the subject is sex, don't expect a lot of reason. It isn't rational. Most of our views and values in terms of sex are based on religious views. And those have to do with superstition. They're not rational. Sex is a good thing, not a bad thing. This would be a very poor world without it. If we reproduced in some other way, it would be a colder, less worthwhile world. And the reality is that sex more than religion is the major civilizing force on this planet. It's the beginning of family and tribe and civilization itself. And it is the major motivating factor on this planet. I think on that note, I'm out of time."

Thursday, December 11

NEW YORK – Interview Richard Dreyfuss, you know, the guy from *Jaws*. After talking for more than an hour, the conversation turned to how the sexual revolution evolved into the mainstreaming of porn, at which point he said:

"You know, since you're not going to use this footage, could I…? The '60s was all about starting from an innocent point, and we can change the world, we can do the impossible, we can go back to Eden. We can put violets in gun barrels and things. And then someone went, Well, maybe we can make a pin about the flower in the gun and we'll sell it for 10 dollars. And then we get a T-shirt. And it inevitably became commercialized. That's the right's culpability – the worship of the business community.

The left's culpability is the celebration of individual rights to the point that it was madness. We have lost all the institutions that pin us down and give us our moral character. Our Andy Hardy small-town stuff. If the church is gone and the schools are gone and parenting is gone, we're just an amorphous blob of people manipulated by media and advertising. And pornography seeps into advertising and music and into the culture in every way. And it changes our atmosphere.

Am I saying pornography is the evil? No. But are we responsible for the destruction of our institutions so that you cannot defend pornography's affect anymore? Yes. It's not just a simple conservative, liberal thing. The sexual revolution was a good thing up to a point, and then it was a bad thing. Like democracy is a good thing, up to a point, and then it's a bad thing."

2004

Sunday, February 1

Thirty-two years ago, in 1972, *Deep Throat* was filmed during Super Bowl weekend. Janet Jackson flashes a bare breast during the Super Bowl and all hell breaks loose.

Tuesday, April 6

CAPE COD – Norman Mailer said he would give us half an hour. So that meant a red-eye to Boston and then a four-hour drive. For 30 minutes. We figured that if we went all that way, it shouldn't be too hard to keep him talking; he's bound to give us at least an hour, right?

He walks in, sits down, and everything out of his mouth is solid gold.

"One of the great differences between then and now is then people were into pornography – I hate that phrase – but it's that people were engaged in pornography, either by watching it or by actually filming it, because there was something exciting about it. It lived in some mid-world between crime and art, and it was adventurous.... I felt that there was something very exciting about porn films because it seemed to me that the actor was literally gambling with their soul. They are really a moral gamble; you didn't know if you were doing the right thing or the wrong thing by being interested in pornography, but it was exciting, it was viable. It was more than being turned on by it, it made you think, you thought about what the moral aspects were.

So Deep Throat's a silly movie. One of the reasons it was so popular, I think, is that it was the beginning of the downfall of taste in American life. You can say that in the '70s, it all began to collapse. The '60s had a craziness to it but, nonetheless, all sorts of vitality. People were experimenting all over the place. They were looking for new kinds of lives. They were looking to break out of all the old molds.

We felt in the '60s that sexual freedom was good, we were all ready to pursue it, because it would free us of all the locks and gates in our personality. Then, of course, a great many people began freaking out on drugs and such in the '60s. And people reacted back and said do we really want all of this?

Now pornography is a big money business. So it changed; you might say it changed the nature of pornographic sex from art to money. Well, money is not interested in the little alleys of artistic endeavor. It wants the main highway. And so what you've got now – my God, there must be thousands of video films made every year. They're all mediocre at best and the people in them are spiritless compared to the way these actors used to be good at the beginning of it. In other words, this is one art form that looked like it was going to burst itself into something, and instead it dwindled into a mediocre commodity. If pornography had ever become an art form, which was the potential, you might have had something incredible, absolutely incredible.

Things are going marvelously, and I'm half way through a question when he says, "I said I'd give you half an hour, but I'll let you finish this question since you've flown all this way to see me." And this is what he said:

"Sex is the last of the great mysteries. That and maybe war is another one of the mysteries. These elements are not to be abused, ideologically, intellectually, rationally speaking. You don't want them to make you comfortable. When you have every kind of sex there is, what do you do with your soul? And that, for me, is an open question to this day.... I'd say you really enter the mystery at that point."

Saturday, June 5
Ronald Reagan dies.

Sunday, September 12
As editing grinds on, there's a concern that the film fails to connect with the present. The remedy for this is to shoot frat boys, teen girls, and seniors talking about oral sex, try to show the shifting perspective from oral taboo to the "no biggie" it is today. We film at Brian Grazer's alma mater, the University of Southern California. Although we have permission, once the faculty gets wind of the subject matter they close down the shoot and attempt to confiscate our tape.

So it's OK to download porn in private – as all these kids do – but to have an intelligent open discussion

OPPOSITE PAGE AND THIS PAGE: Frame grabs from *Inside Deep Throat*. The controversial documentary included interviews with, from left, Erica Jong, Hugh Hefner, Helen Gurley Brown, Norman Mailer, and Al Goldstein

about it is verboten. Something of a paradox for a university to be afraid of the exchange of ideas.

Monday, November 1

The film is almost finished. We add the beginning of Supertramp's "Crime of the Century" at the top. The lyrics of the song are uncannily perfect:

Now they're planning the crime of the century / Well what will it be? / Read all about their schemes and adventuring / I'm sure it's well worth the fee

The crime of the century can be seen as either the work of the creators of the hard-core movie and the mob who controlled and distributed it, or the government that went after it, determined to exile sex not only from the cinematic experience but also from any adult consideration in the culture. That's what makes the second verse so perfect:

Who are these men of lust greed and glory? / Rip off the mask, and let's see! / But that's not right – oh no, what's the story? / But there's you, and there's me

The story connects to each of us. Directly.

Tuesday, November 2

Election day.

Wednesday, November 3

Bush wins. Again (if you count the first time as winning).

Friday, November 5

This year for our Christmas card we plan to dredge up an old Pop Tarts song, "Hot Christmas." Without boasting, it's a catchy ditty – in a completely toxic kind of way – with the chorus, "I'm dreaming of a hot Christmas, c'mon baby let's _____ this Christmas." Because no one is saying any rude words (there's just a silent pause where one might be), it's really very innocent. So we think, Who better to sing this song than Shane Klingensmith who sang "Hot Hot Hot" in our *Showbiz Moms and Dads* series? Everything is going just fine until Shane's manager intervenes:

"I'm pretty sure it implies having sex, but I think instead of putting the single beat in there (where the word would be) it should be changed to something like "Let's kiss this Christmas" or "Let's light a fire this Christmas." Hopefully you understand what I'm saying.

People are afraid even of innuendo, even of something unsaid.

We come up with the idea of asking Andrea True to do it instead. Andrea used to be an adult actress who had a big pop hit in the '70s with "More More More." We are interviewing her for the film anyway, and she readily agrees.

Monday, December 20

Record voiceover with Dennis Hopper. Perhaps it's no surprise to learn that one of the wildest children of the '60s is now a Republican. We are so used to the idea of Republicans as bible-bashing hate-mongering greed-obsessed trolls that we (airy wave of the hand to include all Hollywood) can hardly conceive of someone sane and intelligent being a Republican. But he is a joy to work with, and drinks Earl Grey tea from a cup, with saucer.

2005

Friday, January 14

We are with Tammy Faye at the Television Critics Association for WEtv's (Women's Entertainment) announcement of our film, *Tammy Faye: Death Defying*.

"Tammy Faye, are you going to Hell?"
"Why do you ask?"
"Well, you've lived in a house with Ron Jeremy, and got into bed with the people sitting beside you who have just made a film called Inside Deep Throat.*"*

THIS PAGE: In 1972, *Deep Throat* became a sensation and crowds lined up around the block to see it. The movie premiered in Los Angeles at the Pussycat Theater; Harry Reems' mug shot from his 1974 arrest on federal charges of conspiracy to distribute obscenity across state lines

"I don't get into bed with anyone."
"But as a Christian, how do you avoid judging these people?"
"I don't judge people because God doesn't judge people. God is God."

Oral Exam

In the run-up to the film's release, Universal's press department asked us to interview ourselves about the film for the press kit. So we did.

Does the original film have a message?
FENTON: We tend to dismiss Damiano's best idea – the ingenious MacGuffin of Linda's clitoris in the back of her throat – as a sexist faux pas. But at the time it was no such thing; it was a metaphor for every woman's – and every man's – unique sexual DNA. As a character says at one point, "Different strokes for different folks." Everybody's path to satisfaction, sexual or otherwise, is an individual path. *Deep Throat* is saying that there's nothing wrong with that, that sex in all its infinite variety is not only OK but also glorious. There's nothing to be ashamed of.

RANDY: Today from our vantage point or, rather, disadvantage point of fear – fear of everything from AIDS to terrorists – it's hard to connect with the film's exuberant message of experimentation.

Talk about the mob.
FENTON: Well, the mob produced and owned *Deep Throat*. But Lou Peraino Sr, the producer, was so much more than a mobster. He had a vision. With the money he made from *Deep Throat* he set up Bryanston distribution, a legitimate distribution and production company, and quickly scored with a succession of genre hits: *Enter The Dragon, Texas Chainsaw Massacre*, John Carpenter's *Dark Star*, and Andy Warhol's *Dracula* and *Frankenstein*. Martial arts, horror, science fiction, and art house – the Perainos were kings of the genre picture at a time when the Hollywood studios were struggling. It was a sort of prequel to Miramax.
RANDY: *Deep Throat* really is the quintessential independent film. Not just because it was made outside of the studio system but also because it was independently distributed. And very effectively too. At one point, according to an informant working in the counting office, there was so much money they couldn't even count it anymore. So they weighed it. As effective as their method of distribution was, it was also extremely porous. Everything was in cash. And the people hired to do the job weren't necessarily the most reliable.

So where did all the money go?
RANDY: Well it certainly didn't go into Damiano's pocket, and it didn't go into Harry Reem's or Linda Lovelace's pocket. It all just disappeared. Fatal subtraction!

Did these guys know what they were doing?
RANDY: No. Add it all together and you've got the gang that couldn't shoot straight. It's more than ironic that *Deep Throat* would end up seeding a multi-billion-dollar adult porn industry.

FENTON: The film's message was to do your thing and find yourself. But you can't watch any of the 12,000 adult titles released last year and find in any of them even a trace of that ideology. So porn today is a very different experience from the porn of yesterday.

RANDY: Pornography was a frontier of expression, a place for people "to boldly go." And, believe it or not, a lot of people who are successful in Hollywood and the media today were part of that scene – though not that many of them are prepared to talk about it.

What are we to make of Linda Lovelace?
RANDY: Linda Lovelace is an enigma. She was an ordinary girl with ordinary dreams, who found herself in extraordinary circumstances, and her life

Everybody involved with Deep Throat paid a very, very high price

THIS PAGE: Randy and Fenton with Gerard Damiano, director and writer of *Deep Throat*; Fenton and Randy with Harry Reems at the premiere party for *Inside Deep Throat* at Sundance Film Festival, January 21, 2005

was transformed. Not necessarily because of her ability to deep throat, but from stepping in that world of fame, from becoming a celebrity.

FENTON: 1972, the year *Deep Throat* was released, was also the year that the Loud family was on television. It was the very beginning of ordinary people becoming stars, and she was one of the first reality stars. If it happened today, we'd say, Oh sure, porn star crossing over. Jenna Jameson. Write a book, do some movies, launch a fragrance, star in your own reality show. Or think of Kim Kardashian with her sex tape. We're all used to that now, but at the time people didn't know how to treat her and she didn't quite know what to do with herself either.

RANDY: In the end, the girl next door did find some contentment as the grandma next door; spending time with her grandchildren, her cats, and decorating for Halloween and Christmas.

And Harry Reems?
FENTON: Harry Reems' best performance was arguably not in *Deep Throat*, but in the role he played subsequently, defending himself against an unprecedented government assault on his constitutional rights. It was the first and only time that an actor has been charged for merely playing a part.

Convicted of what?
RANDY: Conspiracy to distribute obscene materials across state lines.

And why did Harry suffer most of the brunt of the legal action? It seems so arbitrary.
FENTON: They arrested Gerard Damiano very early on, and made him cop a plea. So he – reluctantly – became a cooperating witness, and this also meant that in return he got immunity. So they couldn't prosecute him, much as they would have liked to. They did the same with Linda Lovelace, although there was also a feeling in the South that it was unseemly to prosecute a woman. So that just left Harry Reems. The strategy was quite deliberate: Harry Reems was a high-profile actor, so if you make an example out of him and send him to jail that's going to discourage other young people from following in his footsteps.

RANDY: But they underestimated Harry Reems, who turned his conviction into a cause célèbre.

FENTON: The extent of the government's desire to stop not just *Deep Throat* but all pornography was so blatantly an attempt to curb freedom of expression. Because pornography was the one thing that most people are least likely to defend. No politician wants to stand up and say, "I'm for pornography." So it was a great political move. And you can trace today's culture wars and that bitter divisiveness to *Deep Throat*.

So Harry got off?
RANDY: Ha ha. Harry got off. Very funny.

What about Gerard Damiano?
FENTON: Damiano saw himself as an auteur filmmaker, and the outlaw medium of sex was the way for him to express himself. Because there was no independent film business to speak of at the time, and Hollywood was a closed shop. *Deep Throat* really is a keystone of independent film, because it showed people, perhaps for the first time, that there was a way to make movies that made money outside of the studio system.

What was it about Deep Throat that appealed to you as documentarians?
RANDY: I think it was the blowjob, really. As a society, America is obsessed with blowjobs. To an OCD degree. After making *Monica in Black and White,* it seemed to us that sex is such a divisive, problematic

THIS PAGE: Title still of our six-part documentary series telling the history of pornography and showing how it has been a vital civilizing force; Gerard Damiano behind the camera for Deep Throat

OPPOSITE PAGE: Randy and Fenton, shooting in Times Square, pay homage to Damiano

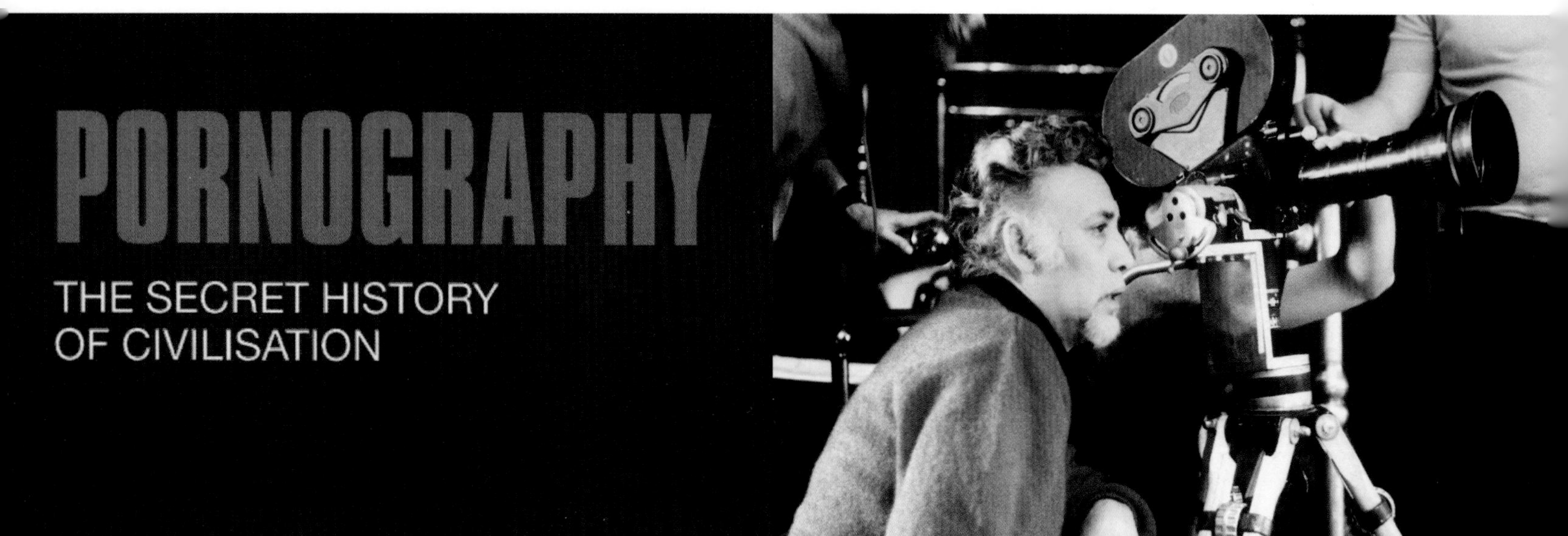

force in our society today. It was the furor surrounding a blowjob that all but destroyed a presidency.

FENTON : We love to tell the stories of people or things that the mainstream considers unfit, or dismisses as marginal. And we love to do that because we've always had a keen sense of our own marginality. So whether it's rent boys, Tammy Faye, Monica Lewinsky, or club kids, we love to show just how mainstream the marginal is, how critical to the fabric of our lives. And everybody involved in this film paid a very, very high price.

What was the secret of the film's success?
RANDY: Although the film is a hard-core film, first and foremost it was a comedy. A comedy about sex. Hard-core + humor = box office! The comedy element gives people permission to see it and talk about something they've been curious about for so long.

FENTON: But, perhaps above all, the government's attempt to shut down *Deep Throat* made it a hit. The more they tried to shut it down, the more attention it generated.

Who went to see Deep Throat?
RANDY: Everyone. Previously, pornography had been for dirty old men only. But with *Deep Throat,* hard-core jumped demographics. Ordinary middle-class men and women who wouldn't be seen dead in a porn theater openly went to see *Deep Throat*. Hard to imagine today how openly popular it was. It was chic.

So what did you learn personally?
RANDY: In 1972, the culture war was about a hard-core pornographic movie. Today it's about things that aren't even hard-core: Janet Jackson's nipple. We've come a long way baby – in reverse!

FENTON: And if you don't want people thinking about what the real issues at hand are, i.e., a war in the Middle East, well then, let's get everyone in a lather about Janet Jackson's nipple. It's a weapon of mass distraction.

RANDY: And Erica Jong is probably right. We won't get nominated for an Oscar.

FENTON: But we do have a number of AVN awards.

RANDY: Like the Academy Award, they are gold.

FENTON: But made out of plastic.

Steve & Laurie Hirsch

FOUNDER AND CO-CHAIRMAN OF VIVID ENTERTAINMENT

Everyone has some idea of what a porn baron must be like. But Steve is polite, smart, professional, and fair

PHOTOGRAPHED BY IDRIS + TONY
AT HOME, CHATSWORTH, CALIFORNIA,
JULY 15, 2009

The pornography business is an $11 billion dollar business

Larry Flynt
FOUNDER AND PUBLISHER OF HUSTLER

Larry was a valuable contributor to our *History of Pornography* series and also our *OJ Mania* piece for the BBC

PHOTOGRAPHED BY IDRIS + TONY
HUSTLER OFFICE, BEVERLY HILLS, CALIFORNIA, JULY 29, 2009

John Waters
DIRECTOR, AUTHOR

The hilarious, notoriously camp filmmaker with the pencil moustache was an invaluable contributor to *Inside Deep Throat*; however he drew the line at narrating an episode of *Shock Video*

PHOTOGRAPHED BY IDRIS + TONY
BROOKLYN, NEW YORK,
NOVEMBER 10, 2010

Harry Reems

ADULT FILM ACTOR, RETIRED

The funny goofy star of *Deep Throat* became its scapegoat when the authorities clamped down on the film. In later life, Harry became a devout Christian and a real estate agent in Park City, Utah

PHOTOGRAPHED BY IDRIS + TONY
AT HOME, MIDWAY, UTAH,
JANUARY 24, 2011

Top left clockwise:

Georgina Spelvin

ADULT FILM ACTRESS, RETIRED

"Let's face it, there is no greater compliment than an erection." That's what she said

PHOTOGRAPHED BY IDRIS + TONY
AT HOME, HOLLYWOOD HILLS, CALIFORNIA,
JANUARY 24, 2010

Marci Hirsch

ADULT FILM EXECUTIVE

Marci is not only Steve's right-hand man at Vivid, she is also his sister

PHOTOGRAPHED BY IDRIS + TONY
VIVID'S OFFICES, BURBANK, CALIFORNIA,
JULY 17, 2009

Kim Roth

EXECUTIVE PRODUCER AND PRESIDENT OF PRODUCTION AT IMAGINE ENTERTAINMENT

Kim was our executive producer on *Inside Deep Throat* and never once lost her cool

PHOTOGRAPHED BY IDRIS + TONY
BEVERLY HILLS, CALIFORNIA,
JULY 27, 2009

Brian Grazer

PRODUCER AND CO-FOUNDER OF IMAGINE ENTERTAINMENT

It was the Academy Award winner's idea to produce a documentary telling the story of the film *Deep Throat*

PHOTOGRAPHED BY IDRIS + TONY. BEVERLY HILLS, CALIFORNIA, APRIL 22, 2010

Savanna Samson

ADULT FILM ACTRESS

In addition to her esteemed work in the adult-film industry, Savanna also heads up her very own respectable wine label

PHOTOGRAPHED BY IDRIS + TONY
BOTEGA DEL VINO, NEW YORK CITY,
JULY 29, 2010

Paul "PT" Thomas

ADULT FILM DIRECTOR

PT became a virtual in-house director for Vivid. The former choreographer brought imagination and ambition to his movies that often led to conflict with the more bottom-line oriented Steve Hirsch

PHOTOGRAPHED BY IDRIS + TONY
CANOGA PARK, CALIFORNIA,
JULY 15, 2010

Dr Annie Sprinkle
PERFORMANCE ARTIST

Beth Stephens
ECOSEXUAL ART PROFESSOR

This shoot was inspired by their love affair with all things trees. You might say they got wood

PHOTOGRAPHED BY IDRIS + TONY
HOLLYWOOD HILLS, LOS ANGELES,
JULY 5, 2010

Simon "Horse" Morley

PERFORMER

As co-founder and one half of the wildly popular show *Puppetry of the Penis*, Simon has twisted his penis into so many original origami shapes it's a wonder it still works. We put his dick tricks on film for HBO

PHOTOGRAPHED BY IDRIS + TONY
CHINATOWN, NEW YORK CITY,
JUNE 24, 2010

> "When the subject is sex, don't expect a lot of reason"
>
> –HUGH HEFNER

But Seriously...

IT HAS NOT BEEN ALL hookers, trannies, porn stars, and drag queens. Not that there is anything wrong with that. But it is hard to make single documentaries and make them pay. On the other hand they have often rewarded us in some other way. In *Ghetto Ballet*, director Jeremy Simmons followed the path of Sibahle, a young dancer who was part of a program that trains kids from South Africa's townships, offering them a once-in-a-lifetime shot at going professional with a spot in the prestigious South African Ballet Theatre. The film tracked her as she trained for her audition. We felt sure she would win the golden ticket to a new life. She was smart, committed, and, living in incredible poverty, just deserved it so much. How could they deny her?

They did. They said she was too fat. Devastated, she returned to her mother's shack. Soon afterwards she was pregnant.

"You followed the wrong person," sighed Sheila Nevins. She was right, of course. The short film didn't get nominated for an Academy Award. Attention and awards rarely go to characters who fail to triumph over the odds against them. So the film screened on HBO2 and we thought no more about it. However, someone was watching TV that night. Someone who was so moved by the story that she placed a call to the Atlanta Ballet. The ballet company offered to fly Sibahle to America to train with them. She had never left South Africa before, let alone been on a plane. Her golden ticket had arrived.

In this case all the blood, sweat, and tears that went into making a single short documentay paid off in spades. Sibahle flew to Atlanta and had a life-changing experience. Now other US ballet compaines are offering her places. Sometimes you just have to close your eyes and take the risk. *Party Monster* (the documentary), *101 Rent Boys*, and *The Eyes of Tammy Faye* were all either initially funded by us or, in the case of *Becoming Chaz*, completely self-financed. The risks are high, but the high of not having to do anyone's notes is just too good to be passed up.

Another completely self-financed feature came about when we started reading that the honeybees were disappearing. They were becoming disoriented, losing their hive instinct, and flying off randomly to die; it was not only heartbreaking but a metaphor

THIS PAGE: Sibahle, the main character of *Ghetto Ballet*, dances outside her shack. Photographed by director Jeremy Simmons, Khayelitsha Township, South Africa, October 5, 2008

HBO DOCUMENTARY FILMS.
presents
GHETTO
Ballet
FOR A WAY OUT, THEY HAD TO STAY ON THEIR TOES
PREMIERES WEDNESDAY, DECEMBER 30 AT 8PM/7C
HBO2
HBO DOCUMENTARY FILMS PRESENTS A WORLD OF WONDER PRODUCTION DIRECTED BY JEREMY SIMMONS
PRODUCED BY FENTON BAILEY & RANDY BARBATO CO-PRODUCER MONA CARD EDITOR MIKE RYSAVY
COMPOSER DAVID BENJAMIN STEINBERG FOR HBO: SUPERVISING PRODUCER SARA BERNSTEIN EXECUTIVE PRODUCER SHEILA NEVINS

the last beekeeper

WORLD OF WONDER PRESENTS "THE LAST BEEKEEPER"
DIRECTED AND EDITED BY JEREMY SIMMONS ORIGINAL MUSIC BY DAVID BENJAMIN STEINBERG
CO-PRODUCER MONA CARD FIELD PRODUCER ANGELA RAE BERG PRODUCED BY FENTON BAILEY & RANDY BARBATO
A WORLD OF WONDER PRODUCTION

for our social atomization and the madness of consumer society.

It came as a serious shock to know that bees spend much of their lives on the back of flatbed trucks, being transported hither and thither. Arriving at their destination, they are woken up, sent out to pollinate, then packed up again to be shipped off somewhere else. Somehow they have survived this life on the road. Until now.

Jeremy Simmons did a beautiful job directing the film, interweaving the narrative of four beekeepers each challenged by the mass disappearance. But the real stars were the bees, and audiences gasped watching them crawling along the ground, shaking and unsteady, unable to fly, before finally dying.

Although Laura Michalchyshyn came in and snapped up the film for Planet Green, we still haven't made our money back. On the other hand, when *The Last Beekeeper* won the Emmy for Outstanding Nature Program it all turned out to have been more than worthwhile.

When Billy Luther came to us with an idea to make a film about the Miss Navajo beauty pageant we thought we knew what to expect. Glitter! Gowns! Crowns! We could not have been more wrong. There was no swimsuit competition; instead, the pageant's categories included traditional dress, governance, and live sheep butchering. That's right: Each contestant must kill, prepare, and serve a sheep. Held on the Navajo reservation, this pageant is a very low-key affair with a dwindling number of entrants (just five the year the film was made). One of them is a young woman named Crystal, who doesn't take the whole thing seriously and ends up coming in second place. Was it another case of following the wrong person? In the following year, Crystal came to embrace many of the customs and traditions that she had previously dismissed, and to her and her family this proves to be a prize far greater than any crown or trophy. That said, Michael Moore did award Billy Luther his founder's prize at the Traverse City Film Festival. So it won in the end.

At the Sundance premiere of *Miss Navajo*, Billy gave such a generous and moving account of how seeing *The Eyes of Tammy Faye* inspired him to become a filmmaker, that we couldn't help but contribute to funding his next feature about the Laguna Pueblo Indians.

Grab tells the story of a very specific feast day. "Each year residents of the Laguna Pueblo in New Mexico honor individual family members by throwing food, water, and gifts from the rooftops of their homes to the community that gathers below," says Bird Runningwater, director of Sundance Institute's Native American and Indigenous Program. Preparing for this event can take all year as families purchase thousands of dollars of stuff to throw. In some respect it's like Christmas, except that the giving at Christmas is based on the idea of receiving in return. But on Grab day the families just give and invite strangers into their houses to feast. The film's tagline is *Indian Giver, Redefined.*

As Bird Runningwater explained, "For many Native Americans today, generosity and giving are as much core cultural values of contemporary life ... Contrast this reality with the phrase 'Indian giver,' which is a common phrase within American culture although its etymology is not fully known. In a consumer-driven and capitalistic culture such as the USA, very few citizens can name examples beyond typical holidays such as birthdays and Christmas where gifts are given and individuals are honored, but for many Native peoples the culture of generosity has withstood the test of time and is in full practice daily."

Tony and Idris – the principle photographers of this book – were invited (along with Cybelle Codish) to take pictures that came to be a Smithsonian exhibition at New York's National Museum of the American Indian. Bird Runningwater said, "These

There was no swimsuit competion; instead, the pageant's categories included traditional dress, governance, and live sheep butchering. Each contestant had to kill, prepare, and serve a sheep

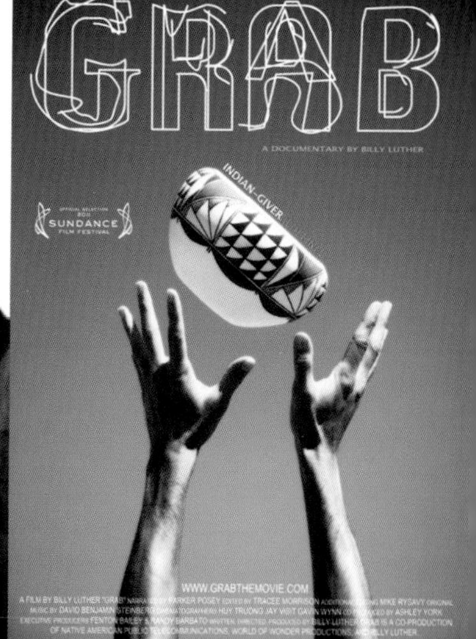

THIS PAGE: The poster for *Miss Navajo*; crowds wait for the grab to begin – the climactic scene of Billy Luther's *Grab*, photographed by Idris + Tony in Seama, New Mexico, July 26, 2009, along with the poster they designed for the movie.

photographers make an offering themselves, as highly prized as any gift given during Grab Day. In this offering they too become part of the cycle of generosity."

Y UK

The truth is that if it weren't for British television we would not even be in business. Thanks to Channel 4 especially, we got a number of amazing opportunities to make the kind of programs that we would never have been able to make elsewhere.

For example, we made a film about our friend and inspiration Nelson Sullivan, stitching together his videos into a portrait of his life and work. No network in the States would have greenlit such a project.

One of the first films we ever made, edited by fellow NYU film school student Laurie Weltz, *Nelson Sullivan's World of Wonder*, planted the seed that we could actually get paid for making films we were passionate about.

And we also owe it to C4 for allowing us a few spectacular failures. Like *Ring My Bell*, a live phone-in show with five celebrity guests on different phone lines taking viewers' calls. The show consisted of cutting between the calls, (eaves)dropping in and out of conversations. We billed it as the first live interactive talk show and booked Boy George, Joey Ramone, Margaret Thatcher's daughter Carol, and RuPaul, natch, prompting Michael Attwell to issue a No More Drag Queens edict. The whole affair was hosted by Laurie Pike as a traffic cop. And we even did live commercials. I think the idea was knocked on the head after the first one, in which a topless stud named Max got gloriously and gratuitously covered in suds while selling washing powder.

It was a grueling white-knuckle ride of live television and, when it was all over, we'd head back to the green room and the drinks would flow. These afterparties were actually fabulous. Perhaps we should have taped them. The show, however, was not a success. Critics hated it. So we brought it to the States where we made two pilots. Although the show didn't get picked up, it did give us the opportunity to meet two of our lifetime heros, Adam West (Batman) and Burt Ward (Robin). And it was also the first time we met Tammy Faye Bakker. Occasionally, we run into our first agent Mark Itkin from William Morris Endeavor and he says he still believes in it. So do we.

In *Video Killed the Radio Star* (a co-production between Channel 4 and VH1) we had the opportunity to tell the story of the rise – and demise – of the music video. When MTV first launched, no one had seen anything like it. Dire Straits even wrote a song about it, "Money for Nothing," perhaps the first and only song ever written about a TV channel. MTV was essentially a 24/7 commercial for the American way: cars, babes, French fries, and Coke. Who knew that it all began with Michael Nesmith, a former Monkee, with his show Pop Clips. When he sold the rights he envisioned a channel that was a free speech frontier and video art space. Well, that didn't last too long, although MTV's impact would prove to be revolutionary on a global scale. When the Berlin Wall came down and the people streamed from East to West, the kind of freedom they wanted was their MTV. So video didn't just kill the radio star, it ended the Cold War.

British TV also gave us the opportunity to make the kind of ideas-based documentary series that would be inconceivable in the USA. *Pornography: The Secret History of Civilization* was followed by *Surveillance*. What struck us as so remarkable was that George Orwell's doomsday vision in *1984* – a society controlled by a totalitarian all-seeing Big Brother – never came to be. Yes, we are watched. We are on CCTV hundreds of times a day. And not only do we not care, we actually *want* to be watched.

Take Times Square, which today is one of the most surveilled places on the planet. It wasn't always that way. Back in the '70s, Times Square was the rotten core of the Big Apple. Porn central. It was considered to be among the most dangerous places on Earth. A succession of mayors had tried and failed to clean up the place. In 1972, when *Deep Throat* came out, the installation of CCTV cameras met with such fierce opposition that they were removed.

And so it was assumed that Times Square would never be cleaned up because it could never be cleaned up. That is until an architect named Jon Jerde came up with a plan NOT to make Times Square classy, but to make it flashy and Vegasized with giant screens and electronic billboards. And this time when the cameras came back to Times Square there were no protests. The feeling was that this was a space in which we are all players. And it worked.

As with Times Square, so with the culture. The whole feeling about surveillance has been flipped on its head. Professor Thomas Levin at Princeton University told us about a group of kids who went out shooting passersby with paint balls. "When they got caught, they got caught with the videotape that they had shot of themselves doing this. Now, this is a radical transformation of the classic logic of surveillance. It used to be that you tried to avoid being seen by the eye of power because you were going to get into some kind of trouble. But now it's something you want, something you desire. And it's something the bourgeoisie desires as much as punk delinquents."

Specifically for the bourgeoisie, avant-garde architects Diller Scofidio + Renfro designed a restaurant not far from Times Square where a camera positioned above the entrance shows everyone entering the restaurant on a row of monitors above the bar. As they told us, "Yesterday's paranoia is today's health; once we were nervous about being watched, now we are nervous if we are *not* being watched. You can start to see the fear of unwatched spaces paralleling the fear of electricity collapse or the fear of not being on the telephone."

It's as if they were talking about The Eye, London's central and pre-eminent landmark. A giant Ferris wheel, anyone who takes a ride in one of the giant pods gets a complete view of London.

As Levin stepped onto the wheel, he looked around and said, "The London Eye is an example of happyveillance, where surveillance becomes a form of distraction and spectacle that is completely emptied of its scariness, becomes something that one enjoys. It's not accidental that the pod structure of the London Eye is somewhat womblike. There's something enveloping about happyveillance. It's a womb with a view. By allowing you to occupy the position of the surveyor, literally inside the Eye here, you are being given the thrill of the surveillant position. The world becomes a studio. And people might say we're losing that space of privacy, but I think we're moving beyond that."

The point is simply that television is taking over not only our downtime but also our architecture. It is reconfiguring the spaces around us. The good old-fashioned brick, the basic building block for thousands of years, is being replaced by the television screen. Surrounded by screens and cameras – being both watched and watching 24/7 – traditional ideas about privacy are slipping away.

Welcome to the Screen Age!

Crazy Rulers of the World

It's as if the lens were a rabbit hole through which we have gone, emerging into an electronic wonderland on the other side. And who is there to greet us? None other than mad hatter Jon Ronson. Jon Ronson is a strange creature. He has a way of peering at you from behind his glasses as if *you* were the

OPPOSITE PAGE: Frame grabs from *Ring My Bell* with Boy George and Joey Ramone

THIS PAGE: Frame grabs from *For the Love of...*, hosted by Jon Ronson, featuring enthusiasts talking about their passions – trainspotting, trees, transmitter towers, etc

Jon is Jewish. Seeing him pal around with Klansmen at one of their gatherings and even trying on a hood was one of those indelible moments of television

specimen. It could have been creepy were it not so completely endearing. Jon speaks in a slow deliberate way with some words absurdly elongated as if he were ET. We bonded over moments of near-miss pop stardom. Jon was the keyboardist for an act called Frank Sidebottom, whose signature look was wearing a giant head.

He occasionally likes to let it be known that as a child he was found so annoying by his friends that they threw him in a lake and left him to drown. To be sure, there is something tenacious about him. But what can seem like gum stuck to your shoe makes him a highly effective gumshoe.

The first time we met he wanted to make a film about the Klu Klux Klan, *New Klan*. Jon is Jewish. Seeing him pal around with Klansmen at one of their gatherings and even trying on a hood was one of those indelible moments of television. In the last film we made together, *Stanley Kubrick's Boxes*, he managed to gain exclusive access to the reclusive filmmaker's archive.

But we did our best work together on two series: *Secret Rulers of the World* and *Crazy Rulers of the World*. In the first, Jon went on a journey to sort out the paranoid conspiracy theories swirling about the New World Order, the Illuminati, and the international elite. Were the Jews really shape-shifting lizards who came from outer space?

With a character called Alex Jones, he infiltrated Bohemian Grove, an annual retreat deep in the woods north of San Francisco, where presidents and other heavy hitters of government allegedly wore women's clothes, peed in public, and engaged in a sacrificial ceremony before a giant owl.

The second series picked up where the first left off, continuing to explore the notion that oftentimes the most conservative and avowedly rational of people embrace the craziest beliefs. For example, the government had run a remote viewing campaign, hiring people to sit in a room somewhere in America and search for weapons of mass destruction in Iraq by travelling the astral plane. Jon Ronson's longtime researcher and producer, John Sergeant, unearthed something called the "First Earth Battalion," an army of soldiers who would march into battle blasting beautiful love music. He also found a Black Ops initiative tasked with walking through walls and killing goats by staring at them.

This led to *The Men Who Stare at Goats,* a movie version of the book that was based on the series. In the film, Jon's character was played by Ewan McGregor, while John Sergeant claimed he had been airbrushed out. But that's Hollywood. Though the film made much ado about being based on a true story, the truth is really stranger than the fiction. We all know that Hollywood can't handle the truth.

The most fun we had together was a series called *For the Love Of...*, a talk-show series in which Jon conversed with an assortment of very specific enthusiasts. Transmitter tower spotters. Lunar landing conspiracy theorists. Scientologists. Subterraneasts. Cryptozoologists. Pet communicators. Time travellers. Grouse shooters. Aetherians. And – a personal favorite – tree lovers. Instead of rushing along like most talk shows *For the Love Of...* moved at a treacly pace. Slumped in his armchair in ragged cardigan and a cloud of cigarette smoke, Jon would gently probe. It was very much the un-chat show. There was no audience, no laugh-track, no blue cards, no tightly produced segments. It was shaggy-dog in a way that television rarely, if ever, is.

The Little Channel That Could

It was often said that these were the kinds of shows that could never be made in America. And Trio was the exception that proved the rule. Trio was a

small Canadian arts channel that somehow found its way into Barry Diller's hands and became part of Universal. At Trio, Michael Jackson, Lauren Zalaznick, and Andy Cohen all came together in an orgasmic moment of televisual brilliance.

And they did buy our shows – lots of them. *Secret Rulers of the World* and *Pornography: The Secret History of Civilization,* which aired as the tentpole of their Banned Season. It was somewhat shorn of its bare-all glory. Giant red dots were slapped over all the nudity, which both threw back to the days of censoring things and made the point that it was all completely absurd.

We did, however, manage to add a twist with *Good Clean Porn*, in which we took adult films and cut all the naughty bits out. *Time* columnist Joel Stein narrated these from an overstuffed leather club chair, *Masterpiece Theatre* style.

Among the other high-concept and specials that followed was *Brilliant But Cancelled*, which unearthed un-aired pilot and series cancelled before their prime. There was the *Awards Show Awards Show*, handing out awards for the best awards shows, and the *Blockbuster Imperative*, deconstructing the formula for how to make a big fuck-off Hollywood film.

If it seemed too good to be true, it was. The channel got bought by NBC, who then shuttered it. Trio joined its own line-up as brilliant but cancelled.

The days for a channel like Trio were inevitably numbered. Cue more handwringing about the decline of civilization, but the simple truth is that TV is a medium not yet even a hundred years old. As it enters its adolescence, it's still finding itself. Reality TV is just the hormonally raging teen.

And it is at this point that one cannot but observe an epistemological shift: TV used to be about things, but now it was becoming more about character, story, relationships. Just look at Andy Cohen. He went from being the executive behind a desk commissioning programs about art and culture to the guy on TV with his own talk show, *Watch What Happens Live*. We were pitching him the other day and it took us back to the first-ever time we met with him, at Trio. He sat behind his desk and seemed to yawn in our faces. I guess Matt Collins' series examining the shifting ideas of representation in self-portraiture was not for him. We remained good friends. Cut to years later and Andy looks younger than ever. He's got a fabulous new office and the walls are papered with memorabilia and pictures of himself with famous people. Life is good. He is on the face of every bus, every billboard, and every cab. He sits in a chair, feet up, holding his trademark tumbler. He's not yawning now. And when he tossed out a question it was as if he was interviewing us on his TV show. It was so exciting.

The Nothing Special

Perhaps it's no surprise that we were always obsessed with Warhol. He was a fixture on New York's downtown scene in the '80s. He was its pontiff. Hanging with Keith Haring. Collaborating with Basquiat. Out at every club every night. Not quite a drag queen, but with his shocking white frightwig, almost. Artistically, he was considered something of a burnout even though the '80s were perhaps his most interesting and insanely productive phase.

Ever since his sudden death in 1987, we had wanted to make a series about him. But the feeling was very much that he was overrated, overexposed. While we couldn't disagree more and felt that Warhol truly was the architect of the times we live in – or at least its seer – there wasn't much we could do about it. And then something magical happened.

OPPOSITE PAGE: Jon Ronson puts on the infamous white hood in our Channel 4 UK documentary *The New Klan*

THIS PAGE: Title stills from shows we made for Trio, a brilliant if short-lived Arts channel where we got to make funny, smart Arts-adjacent programs with our long-term colleagues and good friends Lauren Zalaznick and Andy Cohen

Andy Warhol had a Kardashian-like ubiquity. His life and work foreshadowed the lives of today's reality stars

We were sitting in Janice Hadlow's office at Channel 4 UK pitching various arts ideas. None had stuck and we were out of pitches and she was cueing that the meeting was almost over. I looked down, glum, and happened to see written on a piece of paper on her desk – and with a big circle around it – the word "Warhol."

"We've always wanted to make a series about Andy Warhol," I said.

She lit up like a Christmas tree.

The result was *Andy Warhol: The Complete Picture*.

Why was Andy Warhol so important? He did everything. He mass-produced his work and he also produced masses of it, not just in one discipline but in every area – paintings, films, photographs, books, TV shows, music, magazines, and nightclubs. And he was also his own work of art. He endorsed products in commercials, appeared in TV shows, and went out all the time and got his photograph taken by paparazzi. He had a Kardashian-like ubiquity. His life and work foreshadowed the lives of today's reality stars. In fact, he probably invented the medium. He once talked about a show called *Nothing Special*, in which people hung around and did nothing. Hello, what is *Big Brother*?

He was nothing if not prescient. It's such a cliché that you are almost reluctant to repeat it for what must be the sextrillionth time, but "In the future everyone will be famous for 15 minutes" kind of sums it all up. A quarter of a century after his death Andy's Theory of Relatability proves to be as immuteable as Einstein's.

Back then it must have seemed such an outrageous idea. Remember, this was the heyday of authentic macho artists like Pollock, and here was this fay faggot called Andy who did commercial art and then opened a factory where he didn't drip, didn't even paint – at least not by hand. Instead, he and his assistants churned out screen prints of soup cans, Brillo boxes, and Coke bottles by the hundreds. Eventually he did do drip paintings: He got some canvases, coated them with copper oxide and then pissed all over them. That's what he thought of the abstract expressionists. The paintings, by the way, are stunning. Revenge is a piece of piss.

Everybody was in the series and it filmed all over. But one of the most memorable experiences we had was the trip behind the (former) Iron Curtain to the small village of Medzalaborje in Slovakia, not far from where Andy's parents had lived before moving to Pittsburgh. "Meat with 3 germs," was on the menu at the local restaurant. The former Soviet-built gymnasium, a hulking building right in the middle of town, had been converted into a museum. They xeroxed Andy's cow wallpaper and put up a few posters. Behind a glass case was one of his leather jackets – perhaps the only original Warhol in the place. And all this for a man who never came to visit. The English teacher from the local school happened to be one of the extended Warhola clan. He likes to wander around the town wearing a platinum wig and shades. The resemblance was uncanny.

From there, we traveled to Moscow, where Warhol had finally – 15 years posthumously – been given his own exhibition. It was a milestone in how pop culture had won the Cold War. Everything Warhol championed made the Cold War hot and smashed the Iron Curtain. He had never been allowed to exhibit here before, but as we walked around the city we could see that Warhol had been in Russia for years – in ads, billboards, and street art. He was all around us.

And so, as producer/director Chris Rodley summarized, "How can we ever miss you if you have never gone away?"

Andy would have loved it.

THIS PAGE: Title still from our Andy Warhol series; filming in Medzalaborje, Slovakia, with DP Doug Harrington, Fenton, series director Chris Rodley, the local teacher (dressed as Andy Warhol), Sarah Mortimer, and soundman Tony Burke

OPPOSITE PAGE: Poster for the World of Wonder Storefront Gallery's 2009 show commemorating the 21st anniversary of Warhol's death

Warhol
DEAD AT 21
GROUP
ART
SHOW
WORLD
OF
WONDER

SAVAGE
PORT-A-STAND

Jeremy Simmons

DIRECTOR, PRODUCER

For World of Wonder Jeremy has directed and produced such serious series and celebrated documentaries as *The Last Beekeeper*, *Ghetto Ballet*, *Transgeneration*, and *One Punk Under God*

PHOTOGRAPHED BY IDRIS + TONY
WESTERN AND HOLLYWOOD SUBWAY STATION, LOS ANGELES, CALIFORNIA, JANUARY 21, 2010

Tim Hancock
PRODUCER

Tim headed up development in our UK office and was also one of the creators and a frequent contributor to our cult online show *This Is a Knife*

PHOTOGRAPHED BY ALEX GRACE
AT HOME, ISLINGTON, LONDON,
FEBRUARY 9, 2010

Matthew Collins

ART CRITIC, AUTHOR

With Matthew writing and hosting, we produced a number of UK Arts series including *Matt's Old Masters*, *Impressionism: Revenge of the Nice*, and *Generation Me*, about the tradition of self-portraiture

PHOTOGRAPHED BY ALEX GRACE
AT HOME, HOLLOWAY, LONDON,
FEBRUARY 24, 2010

Noah Thomson

DIRECTOR

Noah directed the HBO documentary *Children of God* based on his personal experience growing up in the Christian cult The Family. The film premiered at Slamdance in 2007

PHOTOGRAPHED BY IDRIS + TONY
LOS ANGELES, CALIFORNIA,
JANUARY 25, 2010

Thad Russell

AUTHOR, PROFESSOR

History tells us that the United States of America, was forged by the Roosevelts, Kennedys, Rockefellers etc etc. Not a bit of it, argues history professor Thaddeus Russell in his radical book *A Renegade History of the United States*. Instead, he gives the credit to gays, drag queens, gangsters, drunks, and prostitutes. We optioned the book to make a bold history series

PHOTOGRAPHED BY IDRIS + TONY
LOS ANGELES, CALIFORNIA,
JULY 16, 2010

Vuyelwa & Nkosinathi

BALLET DANCERS

Cast members of *Ghetto Ballet*, a documentary following several young South Africans from the townships vying for a single place in a professional ballet company

PHOTOGRAPHED BY JEREMY SIMMONS
GUGULETU TOWNSHIP, OUTSIDE CAPE TOWN, SOUTH AFRICA, 2009

John Sergeant
PRODUCER

John was our key researcher and producer on such series as *Crazy Rulers of the World* and *Secret Rulers of the World*. He also directed our series *Aircrash*, about what it's like to be in a plane crash. The good news is you have a 50% chance of survival

PHOTOGRAPHED BY ALEX GRACE AT HOME, BRIXTON, LONDON, FEBRUARY 3, 2010

Jon Ronson

AUTHOR, BROADCASTER

The first episode of our series *Crazy Rulers of the World* got made into the George Clooney film *The Men Who Stare at Goats*

PHOTOGRAPHED BY ALEX GRACE
AT HOME, ISLINGTON, LONDON,
FEBRUARY 9, 2010

Top left clockwise:

John Cooper

DIRECTOR, SUNDANCE FILM FESTIVAL

Thanks to Sundance's support, seven World of Wonder films have premiered at the Sundance Film Fetival. *Grab, Miss Navajo, Becoming Chaz, Inside Deep Throat, Party Monster* (the doc), *Party Monster* (the movie), and *The Eyes of Tammy Faye*

PHOTOGRAPHED BY IDRIS + TONY
AT HOME, LOS FELIZ, CALIFORNIA, JULY 7, 2010

Robert Farrar

WRITER

Robert wrote much of *RuPaul's Christmas Ball* for Channel 4 UK

PHOTOGRAPHED BY ALEX GRACE
AT HOME, HIGHBURY, LONDON, MARCH 18, 2010

Michael Jackson

TELEVISION EXECUTIVE

At Channel 4 UK, he championed our documentary series on Andy Warhol and *The History of Pornography* before moving to the US, where he molded Trio, an arts channel, into a serious and provocative network

PHOTOGRAPHED BY IDRIS + TONY
AT HOME, NEW YORK CITY, JULY 29, 2010

David Keeps

JOURNALIST AND TV HOST

David traveled to the world's art capitals where he schmoozed artists, hoteliers, gallery owners, and the local glitterati as the host of our series *Art and the City* for the start-up arts channel Ovation

PHOTOGRAPHED BY IDRIS + TONY
ELYSIAN PARK, LOS ANGELES,
CALIFORNIA, APRIL 9, 2009

Video didn't just kill the radio star, it ended the Cold War

Michael Nesmith

FORMER MONKEE

One of the visionary founders of MTV, Michael told us his story in *Video Killed the Radio Star*, our 1999 eight-hour definitive history of the music video for VH1 and Channel 4 UK

PHOTOGRAPHED BY IDRIS + TONY AT HOME, CARMEL VALLEY, CALIFORNIA, APRIL 20, 2011

Sarah Luther

MISS NAVAJO, 1966

Billy Luther was inspired by his mom's experience as a pageant queen to make *Miss Navajo*, which premiered at the Sundance Film Festival 2007 and aired on the PBS series Independent Lens

PHOTOGRAPHED BY IDRIS + TONY
HOLLYWOOD, CALIFORNIA,
APRIL 21, 2010

Bird Runningwater

DIRECTOR OF THE NATIVE AMERICAN AND INDIGENOUS PROGRAM AT THE SUNDANCE INSTITUTE

Gold is his favorite color

PHOTOGRAPHED BY IDRIS + TONY
WORLD OF WONDER PRODUCTIONS,
HOLLYWOOD, CALIFORNIA, JULY 17, 2010

Billy Luther

DIRECTOR

In addition to directing *Miss Navajo* and *Grab*, Billy gets credit for thinking up the idea for this book

PHOTOGRAPHED BY IDRIS + TONY
WORLD OF WONDER PRODUCTIONS,
HOLLYWOOD, CALIFORNIA,
JANUARY 22, 2010

No Fixed Agender

AS THE YEARS WENT BY, it became clear to us that people are always full of surprises. None of us truly fit the demographic or social boxes constructed for us by society. Gay straight, black white, male female. No one sticks to their particular corner. ♦ Ralph Lauren made clothes to appeal to the WASP elite. But they were snapped up by hip-hop kids. So gangbangers were cross-dressers too? Not that there's anything sissy about a cross-dresser. Quite the reverse. Take for example David Hoyle aka The Divine David, star of *Takeover TV* and for whom we created a spin-off show, *The Divine David Presents*. Words cannot begin to describe the kind of mandrogynous terror he brings to the stage. It's psychodelia and sickadelic, disturbia of the most archetypal kind. He is quite simply of no fixed agender. The Brits seem to have a flair for this.

RuPaul and Pete Burns backstage at *The RuPaul Show*, VH1 Studio, July 19, 1997

Spin Me Around

"I've got one word for you."

It was the London opening of *Party Monster*. The voice was a thick northern accent that could cut like glass. But the person speaking looked like a Geisha from *Blade Runner*. Amanda Lepore lips, Vivienne Westwood platforms, some piercings and tattoos meant that this could be none other than Pete Burns. As in Dead or Alive Pete Burns. The "You-spin-me-round-baby-right-round-like-a-record-baby-right-round-round-round" Pete Burns.

"I've got one word for you: Management."

And then he was gone.

We never did get to manage him. Instead, he went to jail.

Allegedly, he'd harassed and threatened his ex-boyfriend (and then husband) after becoming unhinged by his appearance on the UK's *Celebrity Big Brother*. So the next time we would speak would be when he emerged from the gates of Wandsworth prison after being incarcerated for six weeks.

Our cameras were rolling as Pete got in the van to be greeted by his lawyer; we had persuaded a UK cable

A Film by Fenton Bailey and Randy Barbato

BECOMING CHAZ

A WORLD OF WONDER PRODUCTION "BECOMING CHAZ" A FILM BY FENTON BAILEY RANDY BARBATO PRODUCER CHAZ BONO CO-PRODUCER MONA CARD ASSOCIATE PRODUCERS HOWARD BRAGMAN DINA LAPOLT EDITED BY CAMERON TEISHER MUSIC BY DAVID BENJAMIN STEINBERG DIRECTORS OF PHOTOGRAPHY MARIO PANAGIOTOPOULOS HUY TRUONG FIELD PRODUCERS THAIRIN SMOTHERS ASHLEY YORK DIRECTED AND PRODUCED BY FENTON BAILEY RANDY BARBATO

FOUND IN TRANSITION

WORLD OF WONDER

The ideal body of a supermodel is that of a teenage boy. Trans fat that!

channel to let us make a film about this pop legend. That grey day in London it was hard to tell who was more disgruntled, the unhappy-looking man in the raincoat hugging a briefcase or Pete in a ratty old dressing gown and pajamas.

"Who the fuck are you?"

The man in the raincoat explained that he was Pete's lawyer, which set Pete off on an expletive-laden rant. Ten minutes later, the lawyer was unceremoniously dumped at a roundabout somewhere near the prison.

Perhaps the lawyer had it coming. Pete, after all, had been in prison for over a month on charges his boyfriend had dropped weeks ago. It was hard not to sympathize with him when he said his case was a travesty of justice.

But this was only the beginning of our trip down the rabbit hole.

By order of Her Majesty's court, Pete had to leave London and go into the custody and care of the person who paid his bail. A man named Peter Quint. He claimed to be Pete's number-one fan.

When we arrived at the house in Plymouth several hours later, the fan at first was nowhere to be found, but then rather suddenly and creepily appeared and prostrated himself before his idol.

BURNS: Oh, for fuck's sake, pull yourself together.

QUINT: You are being pilloried for your beauty.

BURNS: People aren't pilloried for their beauty. Angelina Jolie is not pilloried for her beauty.

QUINT: Angelina's not beautiful. Somewhere Hemingway said, "If you are very brave or very beautiful or very clever the world will try to kill you."

[*Begins to cry*]

BURNS: Don't cry on camera.

QUINT: Why not?

BURNS: It'll make your mascara run.

Quint composed himself and, taking a seat next to his idol, began to read aloud one of his poems:

If that skirt were any shorter you could kiss her anal sphincter
Never mind her arse!
That's not a mouth that's a suction pad.
Head? She'll suck your face off!

"This is like fucking *Misery*, this is," Pete muttered under his breath to the camera. Which actually was something of an understatement.

If you think Pete is freakish, he is perfectly ordinary compared to the man to whose home he had been legally committed. And what of the judge who saw fit to send him there in the first place? Sensibly defying the court order, he went to a hotel for the night and then headed back to London.

Not long after making the film *Pete Burns: Unspun*, we got to work with Pete again on a series called *Pete's PA*, in which a number of would-be personal assistants lived together and competed in a series of challenges and eliminations for the chance to be his personal assistant.

"I'm only doing it because I need the money," he grumbled at the press conference. The network wasn't happy about that, but we were relieved just to have gotten him to the press conference at all. In the weeks leading up to production, Pete had gone missing. The rumor was that he was getting face work done in Milan. So Johnni Javier, the showrunner, was dispatched to find him and bring him back to England.

Johnni finally caught up with Pete – and boyfriend Michael – in a small pensioni in Milan's suburbs. After a lovely dinner and couple of glasses of red wine, it was agreed that they would all return to England together the next morning.

Then something happened and all Hell broke loose. Tables were overturned, bottles thrown as Pete and Michael got into the mother of all brawls. Johnni remembered Pete at one point shimmying down a drainpipe outside the building to escape Michael who was running from room to room brandishing a pair of scissors.

The next morning everyone got up, had a civilized breakfast, and left together as planned. As if nothing had happened.

The shoot went smoothly. Pete chose his PA and got married to Michael. His ex-wife was best man. While it might not be entirely true to say that they all lived happily ever after, they are all still very much alive.

Transvision: Gen XY

Trans tales were present at the very beginning of our working relationship. We were both graduate film students at NYU and for his first-year film Randy had written a script called *Such a Nice Neighborhood.* It told the story of a trans woman coming to live in a suburban New Jersey community and discovering that the neighborhood really isn't so nice after all.

The twist was that Robin – the trans lead – was based on a real-life Robin who played herself. Randy and Robin had been dormmates back at Emerson College. Randy also enlisted the neighbors to play themselves too. Everything went fine until we had to shoot the final scene in which they confront Robin and try to drive her out of town by roughing her up.

They just couldn't do it. They were more shy than hostile, more curious than bigoted. And that could just be why transgendered shows really rate on television. Because we are all a little bit trans. None of us is 100% male or 100% female. To varying degrees we all contain a little bit of the opposite sex. That's not to say we are all transgendered, just trans curious enough to watch shows about it on TV.

The only thing is, the advertisers don't like it. It's not the right image for their products which – let's be frank – trade on crude ideas about what it means to be a man or a woman. Often these gender stereotypes are a complete lie. Even the fashion and advertising perpetrators know this – the ideal body of a super-model is that of a teenage boy. Trans fat that!

This is as good a time as any to share the story of Mike, a 19-year-old who had had a bit of a weight problem but, after shedding the pounds, knew what he wanted to be when he grew up – a coyote!

Plushies and Furries was the title of a film we made that Rick Castro directed for the MTV series *Sex 2K*. We also made plushie films for Channel Five and HBO's *Real Sex* series. Who can resist people who dress up as animals and attend con*fur*ences?

In a way it all makes total sense. We were all raised on Disney and, while many little girls grow up wanting to be a princess bride, don't some of us grow up wanting to be Donald Duck? Or a coyote?

Parents might look at it differently, of course. The scene in which Mike aka Yote (short for Coyote) comes out to his mother is priceless. Instead of sitting her down and telling her, he just appears in the living room in full coyote drag. Surprise! And his mother is so sweet because she doesn't know whether to laugh or cry. And so she does a little of both. Then she gets up, walks over to him, and gives him a big hug. Not quite a bear hug, more like a coyote hug. Not a dry eye in the house.

OPPOSITE PAGE: Frame grabs from our documentary *Unspun* about the legendary Pete Burns, lead singer of Dead or Alive

THIS PAGE: Title still for *Transamerican Love Story* (on Logo) and *TransGeneration* (on Sundance)

TRANSAMERICAN LOVE STORY

"I'm going to have a sex change and I want you to film it," Chaz said

Man, woman, or mascot, love transcends all.

Over the years, trans subjects are something we have returned to again and again. In *Transgeneration,* director Jeremy Simmons followed four college students for a year as they transitioned. By observing the mundane details of these trans students' lives, viewers could connect on a profound level with the subjects and their stories. One of the students had reassignment surgery during production, which was where we first met Dr Marci Bowers, one of the world's pre-eminent gender reassignment surgeons. Transgendered herself, she ran a surgery in the former mining town of Trinidad, Colorado.

That led organically to the series *Sex Change Hospital*, directed by Chris McKim, in which we followed Dr Bowers through the working week as she performed up to two operations a day.

In each episode we tracked two patients, from the eve of their surgeries to their release from the hospital. In between, we would tell the stories of their journeys to transition, which were so powerful. Often these were straight, married people with kids. They had done everything they could to avoid making the transition and to crush the feeling they had of living in the wrong body. They didn't want to hurt their family and loved ones or be rejected. So they lived a lie for fear of what might happen if they lived their truth. In the end they realized they simply had to have the operation or life was not worth living. It was truly a life-or-death decision. Jim Howley, for example, had tried to commit suicide before he transitioned to a man.

We had no inkling of any possible connection to Jim when Calpernia Addams came into our lives. Calpernia's story is famous because of the film *Soldier's Girl* that tells the story of her relationship with Private First Class Barry Winchell. Soldiers on the base found out about the relationship and began to harass Winchell. Under Don't Ask, Don't Tell – the law banning gays from serving openly in the military – Barry was afraid of reporting this for fear of being discharged. Tragically, he was beaten to death as he slept in his barracks.

Now, years later, Calpernia wanted to start afresh. It was producer Joe Del Hierro's idea to suggest that Logo do a house-based competition elimination show to find Calpernia a man, a man willing to date a trans woman. *Transamerican Love Story* was hosted by the hilarious Alec Mapa, and Andrea James played Calpernia's best friend and advisor (just like she does in real life). The competition elimination dating show is a staple of reality television, but no one had ever done one before where the contestants were vying for the hand of someone they knew was trans. The set-up might have been extraordinary, but as the series unfolded, it became clear that everyone's desires were as ordinary as the next person's. And it was as much about what makes a woman a woman as it was about what makes a man a man. Indeed, one of the male suitors was Jim Howley from *Sex Change Hospital*. Although he didn't win the competition, he made it to the final episode.

Found In Transition

We had no idea what Cher's daughter wanted when she walked into our office a couple of years ago. She was with Howard Bragman, who over the years had become well known as an advisor to celebrities coming out of the closet.

"I'm going to have a sex change, and I want you to film it."

For a while after Chaz went public about his intentions, it looked like we would be making the film for HBO. But then they dropped out just a few days before Chaz was due to have his double mastectomy.

What to do?

We decided to go it alone and make the film anyway. Not that we were sure we would find a home for it. Chastity was already being Chaz. Dressed in jeans, a wifebeater, and with cropped hair, he already looked like a man. After breast surgery he had no plans to have bottom surgery. So what would the difference really be? As it turned out we were in for a change that none of us expected – least of all his girlfriend Jennifer or even Chaz himself. Because the physical transformation was the least of it. Instead, Chaz and everyone around him went through profound psychological changes. And the fact that he looked more or less the same only underscored the depth of the drama.

It was not our intention at the outset to interview Cher. Chaz was pretty clear with us that this was his story, and that after a childhood growing up in the shadow of his megawatt parents, now it was his turn. Not that he had any interest in celebrity; the spotlight had always made him feel uncomfortable. However, he saw this occasion as an opportunity to show all sorts of people the reality of being transgendered. Because, unlike other trans stories, the audience already felt they knew Chaz. They had seen him as a little girl in those cute-as-a-button appearances on *The Sonny and Cher Show.* They felt they had grown up with this kid. He was one of the family. Chaz knew this could perhaps get people to think about transgenderedness in a whole new light.

At first we were quite happy not interviewing Cher. But then, as filming went on, it became apparent that we were kidding ourselves. For many trans people the struggle is not with who they are. They already know that, and have known it for years. What can take far longer – decades – is for them to act on it. So they sit tight. And wait. Perhaps they wait for their kids to grow up, perhaps they wait for their parents to pass away.

In other words transitioning is so much about the people around the person undergoing the sex change. But Cher hadn't spoken publicly about Chaz's decision beyond issuing a minimal statement saying that she was trying to understand. Would she even speak about it now? Reluctantly, Chaz put in the request for his mom to sit down with us and off we went to New York (where we were filming another project) thinking it would be a few weeks, months even, before we heard anything. The next morning at lunchtime the phone rang.

Cher would do the interview. There was just one catch: it would be in Vegas, and it would be that night.

There was just enough time to get to the airport, buy a ticket, and get on a plane. It would be tight but we would land in Vegas in sufficient time to interview Cher right after her show at Caesar's Palace.

And then the unimaginable happened – a summer storm rolled in at the precise moment the plane taxied onto the runway. And so we sat. And sat. At first it was just the runway that had been shut down. But then it was the entire airport.

Sometimes you just want to scream.

But the storm passed and by midnight we were set up in the basement of the Colosseum ready for Cher. This was no freewheeling interview. The questions were pre-screened and there was a strict time limit. The manager stood nearby. He could not have been nicer, but it was also clear that one false move and he would reach out and grab us by the scruff of our necks. No pressure then. Oh, and it's Cher, by the way, only one of the most famous people on the planet.

Everything went fine. Until Cher said, "Well, it's not how I would like to do it," referring to the way Chaz had been so public about his sex change. So, feeling all cosy and conversational, the next question could

OPPOSITE PAGE: Title still of *Becoming Chaz*; Chaz with his mom Cher at the premiere of *Burlesque* at Mann's Chinese Theatre, Hollywood, California, November 15, 2010. There can perhaps be no more complex relationship than that between a mom and a daughter-turned-son

THIS PAGE: Fenton and Randy before and after the world premiere of *Becoming Chaz*, (also in the picture: Thairin Smothers far left; Mona Card and Robert Farrar near left) photographed by Idris + Tony at the Sundance Film Festival, Park City, Utah, January 23, 2011

> **"I like being a woman so much that if I woke up tomorrow in a different body I couldn't get through the change fast enough"**
> **–Cher**

only be, "Well, how would you do it? How would you go about having a sex change?"

This was not a preapproved question.

Oh shit!

There was a pause.

"Well, I wouldn't do it," she said kindly. (Translation: "Duh.")

And then for the first time she shifted in her chair and said, "This is the thing that makes me know how important it is. I like being a woman so much that if I woke up tomorrow and I looked down and I was in a different body, I would be like 'Get me out of here.' I couldn't get through the change fast enough."

This was not Cher the superstar talking. This was a mother speaking about her own transition from confusion to enlightenment. And there really is no clearer, simpler, more direct way of putting it than that. And this is perhaps how everyone else can understand it. After all, what would you do, what would any of us do, if we woke up one morning in the body of the opposite sex? Most of us like being who we are. When we don't take that for granted, it becomes easier to imagine the trauma of being trapped in the wrong body.

So when someone transitions it isn't just about the person having the gender reassignment, it's also about the family, friends, and loved ones. They may not have to change their gender, but they do have to change their agenda. And the effect continues outwards. We the filmmakers had to change our thinking, and the audience watching has to change its thinking too. Cintra Wilson wrote a piece in the *New York Times* about the film and realized that early on she had wondered if Chaz was doing all this in some twisted Oedipal manifestation to spite his mom. And as she came to see the craziness of that idea, she also came to terms with her own transphobia.

Sometimes the title comes first, and sometimes it comes last. Even as the film was being finished we didn't have a title. Finally, we had settled on a title and sat Chaz down to tell him. We told him we would call the film *All That Chaz*.

"That's shit. You guys can do better than that."

But we had been racking our brains for months. Nothing seemed better. And even *Becoming Chaz* with the tag line "Found in Transition" seemed kind of ho-hum. But after the Sundance world premiere we realized it was perfect. It said it all. The audience leapt to their feet and gave Chaz and Jennifer a standing ovation.

"Wow, I guess when you are true to yourself good things happen," Chaz said, beaming.

Indeed. Shortly before heading to the festival, we signed a deal licensing the film to OWN, the Oprah Winfrey Network. *Becoming Chaz* would be the first-ever film in her documentary club curated by Rosie O'Donnell.

We couldn't quite believe it ourselves. When we went to the taping of Chaz' appearance on *The Oprah Winfrey Show* (one of the last episodes), Oprah stayed behind to take questions from the audience. Someone asked her why she chose *Becoming Chaz* as the film to launch her documentary club. We had often wondered the same thing ourselves because, after all, there are only an estimated 700,000 transsexuals in the States today. It's the most minor of minorities. But Oprah essentially said that she chose the film because Chaz had had the courage to find out who he was and then lead an authentic life. Trans or not, all of us face the exact same challenge.

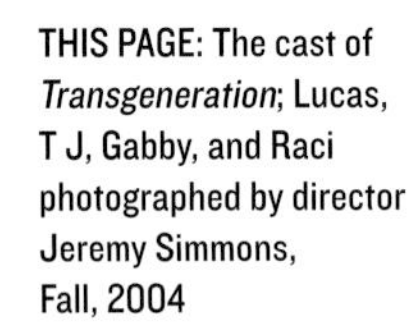

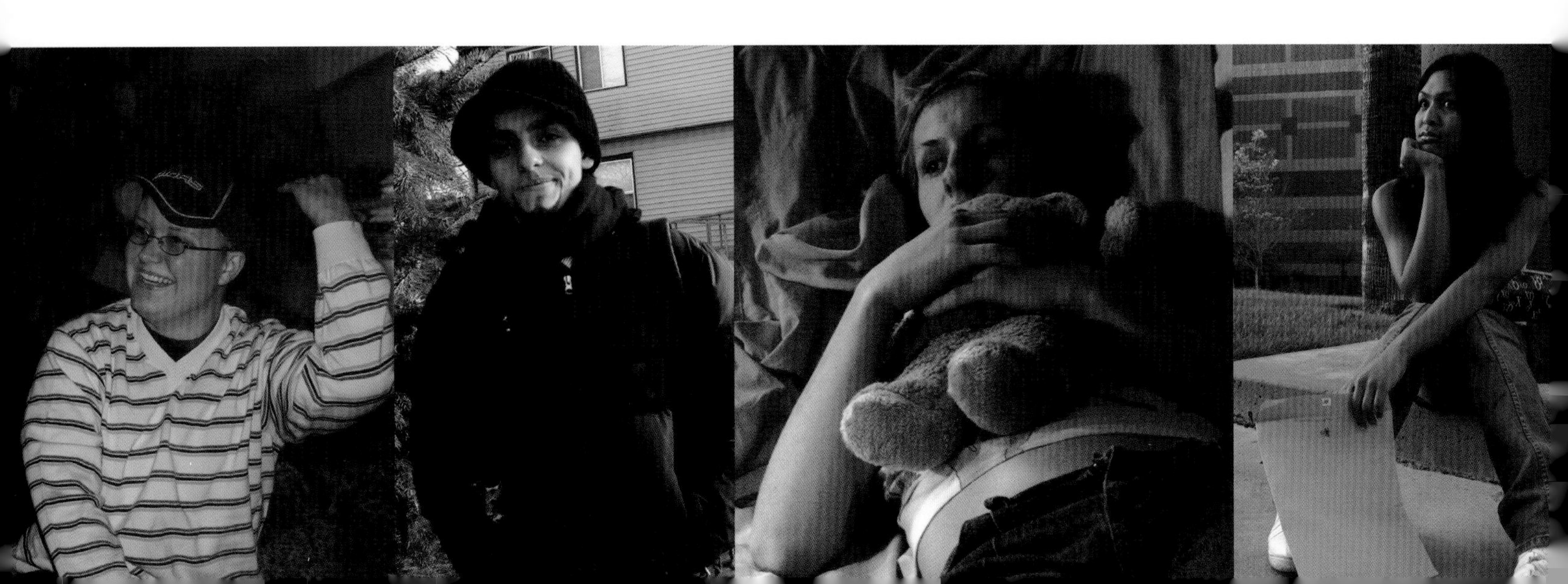

THIS PAGE: The cast of *Transgeneration*; Lucas, T J, Gabby, and Raci photographed by director Jeremy Simmons, Fall, 2004

A SUNDANCE CHANNEL PRODUCTION IN ASSOCIATION WITH LOGO™

✓ Hang Poster
✓ Buy Textbooks
✓ Drop Calculus
☆ SEX Change

TRANS GENERATION

FOUR COLLEGE STUDENTS SWITCHING MORE THAN THEIR MAJORS

SERIES PREMIERE SEPT 20

sundance
CHANNEL

SUNDANCECHANNEL.COM

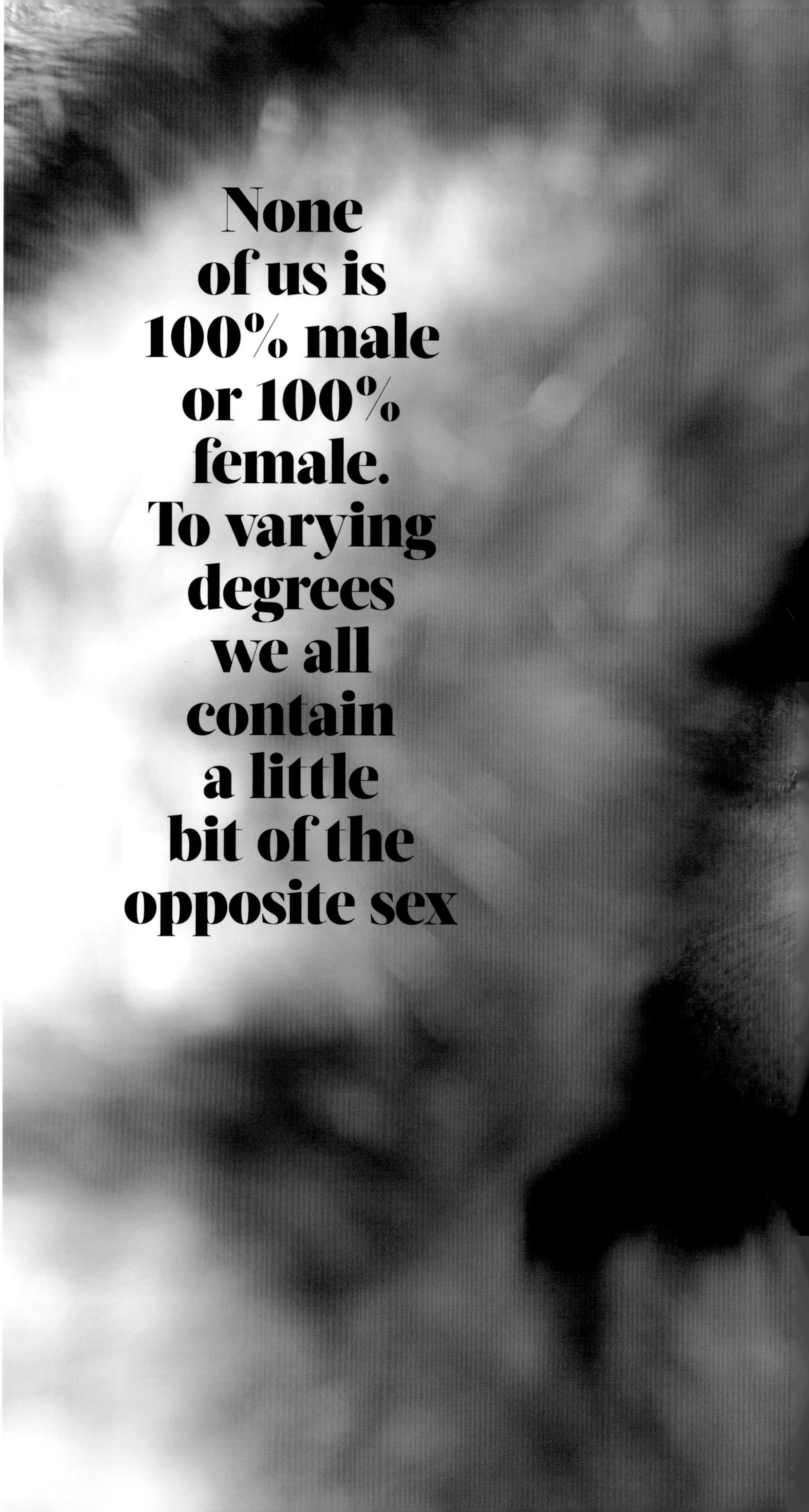

None of us is 100% male or 100% female. To varying degrees we all contain a little bit of the opposite sex

Johnni Javier

PRODUCER, DIRECTOR

Johnni headed the UK office for a number of years and also produced and directed *Unspun*

PHOTOGRAPHED BY ALEX GRACE
COLUMBIA ROAD, LONDON,
MARCH 4, 2010

David Hoyle aka The Divine David
PERFORMANCE ARTIST

To this day, our show *The Divine David Presents* remains one of the most creative and out-there shows we have ever made

Pete Burns

SINGER

Pete was reluctant to do a show following his search for a personal assistant. "I am only doing it because I need the money," he grumbled at the press launch. But he was a pro throughout the entire production

PHOTOGRAPHED BY JIM MARKS
EAST LONDON, 2007

Holly Woodlawn

PERFORMER, AUTHOR, WARHOL SUPERSTAR

Holly's autobiography *Low Life In High Heels* has been an inspirational text when it comes to the basic human right of "if you want something, just go out and grab it by the balls." She is featured in our documentary series on Andy Warhol

PHOTOGRAPHED BY IDRIS + TONY AT HOME, WEST HOLLYWOOD, CALIFORNIA, NOVEMBER 19, 2009

Andrea James

ACTRESS, LGBT ACTIVIST

Calpernia Addams

ACTRESS, LGBT ACTIVIST

Calpernia Addams' search for love was the spark for our series *Transamerican Love Story*. Her best friend Andrea co-starred on the show. Before that, Calpernia's true-life story was the basis for the film *Soldier's Girl*

PHOTOGRAPHED BY IDRIS + TONY
WORLD OF WONDER PRODUCTIONS,
HOLLYWOOD, CALIFORNIA, APRIL 15, 2009

Raci Ignacio
STUDENT

Raci was featured in *Transgeneration*. She poses here at Skooby's, amazing tenants of World of Wonder who always pay their rent on time

PHOTOGRAPHED BY IDRIS + TONY
SKOOBY'S HOT DOGS,
HOLLYWOOD, CALIFORNIA,
JULY 29, 2009

Transgender Law Center

FROM LEFT: Mila Pavlin, Jesse Welz, Matt Wood, Masen Davis, Jason Tescher, Kristina Wertz, Vikram Swaruup, Danny Kirchoff, and Maceo Persson

PHOTOGRAPHED BY IDRIS + TONY
SAN FRANCISCO, CALIFORNIA, JULY 6, 2010

Man, woman, or mascot,
love transcends all

Robert Hill
ARTIST, ILLUSTRATOR

Robert was featured in our MTV True Life documentary *Plushies and Furries*

PHOTOGRAPHED BY IDRIS + TONY
AT HOME, IRVINE, CALIFORNIA,
NOVEMBER 12, 2009

Rick Castro

GALLERY OWNER, FINE ART PHOTOGRAPHER

Rick directed our popular documentary *Plushies and Furries* for MTV, and is our neighbor in Hollywood. He owns and runs the Antebellum art gallery around the corner from our office

PHOTOGRAPHED BY IDRIS + TONY
ANTEBELLUM GALLERY,
HOLLYWOOD, CALIFORNIA,
NOVEMBER 11, 2009

Alec Mapa
ACTOR, COMEDIAN

Alec was the host of *Transamerican Love Story* and is also much-loved for his appearances on *Desperate Housewives* and *RuPaul's Drag Race*

PHOTOGRAPHED BY IDRIS + TONY
HOLLYWOOD HILLS, CALIFORNIA,
NOVEMBER 13, 2009

"I guess when you are true to yourself, good things happen"
– CHAZ BONO
breaking dawn
eclipse
NORMAN MAILER
JAMES PATTERSON
PURSUIT
LISA SCOTTOLINE
LONDON BRIDGES
JAMES PATTERSON
THE LAKE HOUSE
TESS GERRITSEN
APPRENTICE
JAMES PATTERSON
THE DA VINCI CODE
DAN BROWN
ANGELA'S ASHES

Chaz Bono
AUTHOR, ACTIVIST

Jennifer Elia
ACTRESS

Chaz and Jen and their relationship were the focus of our documentaries *Becoming Chaz* and the sequel *Being Chaz*, both of which aired on OWN. While they are no longer a couple they remain great friends

PHOTOGRAPHED BY IDRIS + TONY
AT HOME, WEST HOLLYWOOD, CALIFORNIA, JANUARY 27, 2010

Stars in our Eyes

"ALL RIGHT, MR DEMILLE, I'M READY FOR MY close-up." And with that, legend of the silver screen Norma Desmond begins her long, slow descent toward the camera at the end of the movie *Sunset Boulevard*. She thinks she's back on set filming her triumphant return to the movies. In reality she's performing for the news cameras, there to film her arrest for murder. And in that instant, in 1950, the writing was on the wall. Hollywood would give way to Reality. Goodbye Norma Desmond and MGM, hello Lindsay Lohan and TMZ.

Pamela Anderson on the set shooting *Pam: Girl on the Loose*, body painting by Marcus Suarez. Photographed by Thairin Smothers, April 22, 2008

How ironic that one of the most famous lines in all of moviedom is actually about its demise.

Not that Hollywood has embraced television, much less reality television. "I am big, it's the pictures that got small," spat Desmond. A-list movie stars' contempt for the small screen still lingers, yet every day they seem a little more like Marie Antoinette on her pseudo farm at Versailles. They play their roles, pretend to be real people, while acting like royalty and hand out awards. Meanwhile, beyond the palace gates, real people doing real things are proving much more compelling than any performance.

Those are the stars in our eyes.

Take, for example, The Nutters in *Showbiz Moms and Dads*, a soap doc that we produced with David Perler, tracking the lives of parents pushing their kids onto the stage. Attempting to get his seven kids to make it as actors, Duncan Nutter moved his entire family from a Vermont farmhouse to a cramped New York apartment. But only Duncan, it seemed, truly wanted this fame. The rest of the family's lack of desire was matched by their lack of aptitude. Yet they were more entertaining, more convincing than Hollywood's A-list stars. His family were stars in his eyes, and that was all that mattered. Same with Debbie Klingensmith. Her son Shane's rendition of "Hot Hot Hot" was pitchier than a roller coaster, but had an iconicity foreshadowing

SO, YOU **KNOW** THEY CAN DANCE.
NOW, CAN THEY SUCCEED?

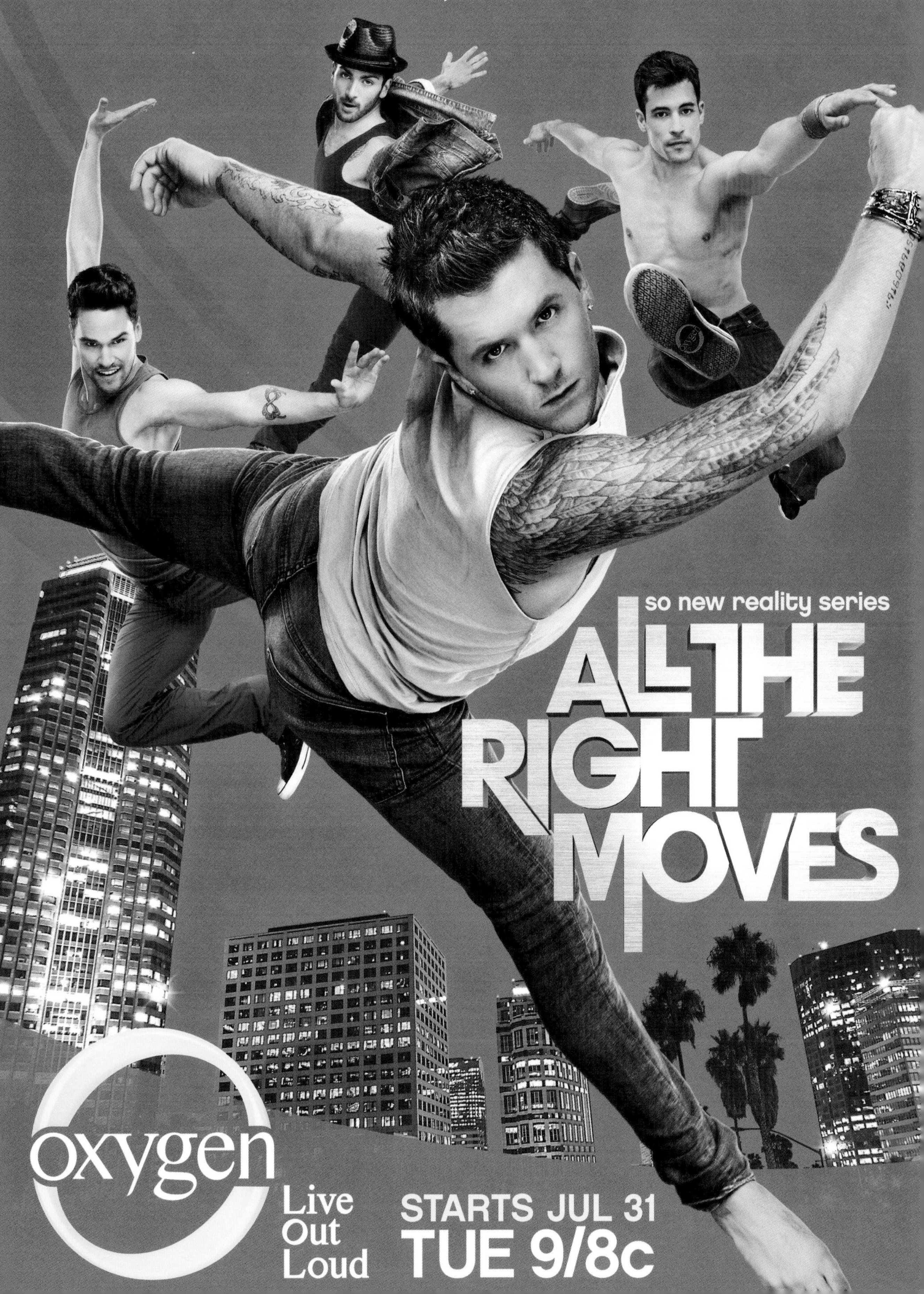

They don't just tell it, they sell it. Watching them work is like having a backstage pass to the American Dream

William Hung's *American Idol* audition. You couldn't help but fall in love with this plucky kid and pushy mom.

Meanwhile, we still had a thing for real estate agents. Debbie Berg was our real estate agent when we moved to LA. She was tiny, yet drove a big gold Mercedes the size of a boat and had to sit on the Yellow Pages to be able to see over the dashboard. What she lacked in stature she made up in fierceness. So one day we thought, "What about a series following high-end real estate agents?"

We began looking around, and one of the people who came to the fore was Elaine Young. She had sold OJ Simpson his Brentwood house and was famous for selling celebrity homes. She was also famous for her plastic surgery. It was said that her eyes leaked tears of silicon, the way crude oozes from the La Brea Tar Pits. We had featured her in our *OJ Mania* documentary and then began talking to her about the possibility of doing a series just as she was in the process of setting up her own firm. She lived life as we all should, playing the starring role in her own movie to the hilt. Bravo was intrigued by the idea, but also a little scared. Was she too much, they asked? Of course she was! That was the point!

In the end, the matter resolved itself when Elaine passed away. But *Million Dollar Listing* would eventually launch with a rotating cast of agents, beginning with Dia and Ray Schuldenfrei. In the second season, we landed our dream team of three guys, Josh Flagg, Madison Hildebrand, and Chad Rogers (yup, the guy with the hair). After three seasons Chad bowed out and was replaced by Josh Altman, affectionately reviewed in the press as "douchey but charming." And the series has branched out with a New York cast: heartthrob Ryan, adorable Michael, and Swedish bully Fredrik.

Why would anyone be interested? The secret of their appeal is that they are marketeers. They don't just tell it, they sell it. Watching them spin, work, and (hopefully) close the deal is like having a backstage pass to the American Dream. Not to mention all the delicious property porn!

Celebrity 2.0

While we patiently wait for the Brad and Angelina clan to do a reality series, Hollywood has been gradually coming around.

When Cher did an infomercial back in the early '90s it was as if she had made a sex tape. She was excoriated. Why would a music legend and Oscar-winner demean herself by doing an infomercial for Aquasentials? There was even talk that her career was over. Cher can only have laughed all the way to the bank. Jack LaLanne fitness videos. Lori Davis hair care products. Equal sweetener. Even a home gothware catalogue of her incense, sconces, candles, crucifixes, and overstuffed chairs. She was a pioneer.

Fast forward to Tori Spelling, the quintessential rich girl. After her megarich dad died her inheritance turned out to be only a reported few hundred thousand. So it was time for this poor little rich girl to roll up her sleeves and go to work. That was the pitch in the room, and it was perfect.

Season one of *Tori & Dean: Inn Love* followed them opening a bed and breakfast in Temecula. They soon returned to Hollywood, but didn't stop working. A bestselling jewelry line on the Home Shopping Network, a series of bestselling books, a line of children's clothing, a wedding-event business, and even a store called InvenTORI. What's in a name? An entire brand! *CelebraTori* is the title of her party planning book (and let's not forget *sTORI Telling* and *Uncharted TerriTORI*), *sTORIbook Weddings,* the name of her show, and ediTORIal, the name of her social networking site. It could be irritating, but it's brilliant merchandising savvy.

She is a TORInado, and working with her – and this is said with love – is TORIture because while she's the talent, she's also the producer with an eye for detail, total recall, and a relentless drive for perfection. And if she spares no one, she spares herself least of all. For a privileged girl mocked for never having to work a day in her life, she works incredibly hard.

More than that, she is the pioneer of a new kind of celebrity: Celebrity 2.0.

Sure, there were stars and people were famous before the movies, but for our purposes celebrity begins with Hollywood. It is here that the rules about what makes you a star and how to behave like a star were forged. Just like the Olympian Gods of Ancient Greece they were put on a pedestal, worshipped from afar. Then came television, the great destroyer. For a while they held on, but gradually their privacy was eroded. Today we know where they live. We know what they look like with no makeup on their morning Starbucks runs. If they're male stars, most likely James St James has blogged their peen print as they leave the gym in sweats.

To some extent the old model was unsustainable anyway – "Fame puts you there where things are hollow," David Bowie sang in "Fame." The unbearable loneliness at the center of stardom is perhaps celebrity's best-kept secret, protected by a kind of omertà. It's the price to pay for access to the Gifting Suites.

Well, it doesn't have to be that way anymore. You don't have to go all crackerjack alone in your Sunset Boulevard mansion. 2.0 celebrities place themselves right in the middle of things. When Tori schlepps to Starbucks, she raises the bar by taking the pet goat. They live it, breathe it, eat it, and tweet it 24/7. The accompanying reality show is just another window on their world. They are the American dream live, and in action.

The notion that the star is something to be protected and shrouded in mystery is old hat. If we can't see it and touch it we don't want it.

We learned this lesson, surprisingly, with Pamela Anderson. The *Baywatch* pin-up is famous for being mostly naked but she is smart, curious, and self-deprecating. And she didn't really want to do a reality show. Indeed, the idea was so abhorrent to her that we were forbidden from even using the word in her presence. Instead, it was to be called "an observational documentary series."

"Er, what's that?" an E! executive asked us one day.

The first meeting was a hoot. She rapid-fired her vision of what she wanted this show to be: Faster Pussycat – European – layered – textural – Faster Pussycat – gauzy – swirling – artsy – avant garde – experimental – Faster Pussycat!!! Every time she invoked Faster Pussycat, she thrust her breasts out across the boardroom table. She certainly was very persuasive, if mammary serves. And she also did the splits. We were rapt.

Vincent Gallo, that take-no-prisoners provocateur, sat beside her, cool as a cucumber. Inscrutable. He was to direct this great work. The E! execs gathered around the table were every bit the cool customers as Vincent. Still, the blood drained from their faces as her vision was revealed. She wanted to find ways to subvert the medium and make the boob tube smart. She wanted to abandon traditional story-telling devices: sit down interviews? Who needs sit-down interviews! Oh, and it just *had* to be shot on film. Video was yuk. Reality shows were shot on video. It just *had* to be film.

Was the audience ready for a post-modern deconstructionist film? On E!?

We felt it would be a challenge, but even if all she did

OPPOSITE PAGE: Title frame grab from *Showbiz Moms and Dads*, the series that spawned *Showdog Moms and Dads* and *Sports Kids Moms and Dads*; poster for *Million Dollar Listing*

THIS PAGE: Title still for *Tori and Dean: Inn Love;* Dean McDermott flashes a victory sign after his near-fatal motorcyle accident in season five

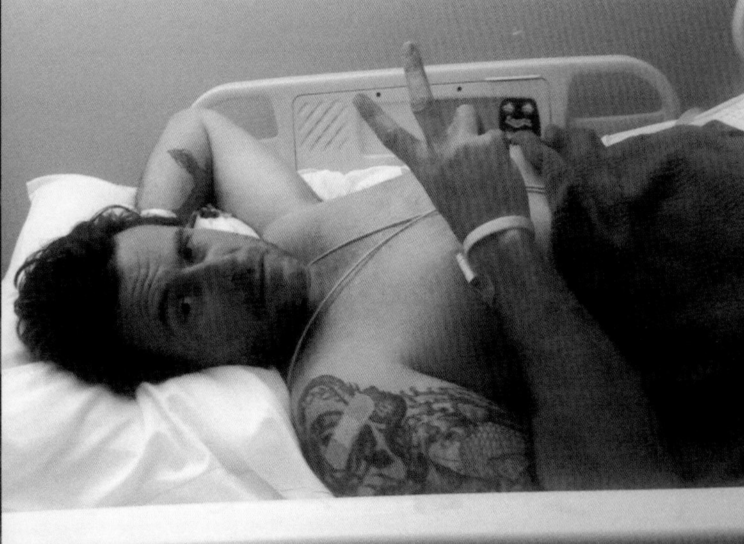

"Why on earth am I doing this?" The Duchess asked. "Just embrace the fear and walk right on through it," said Oprah

was read from the phone book the show would work. Pam was just so compelling.

Vincent was one of the first casualties. In spite of many fascinating and lengthy late-night calls with him, we could not make a deal. He needed complete creative control. So ways were parted. Amicably. Legendary music video director Nigel Dick signed up for the roller coaster ride that would become *Pam: Girl on the Loose*. We would start to shoot scenes and Pam would relent and decide we needed to turn the camera off. So we got a lot of great but incomplete scenes. Or she would let us shoot as long as she was far away from the camera or off to the side. You see, she really didn't want to be prominently featured – in her own show! When it came time to edit together our fragments, Pam was in the edit bay. She persuaded the editors – remember, Pam can be very persuasive – to add layers, grain, and other effects. She was there so much that we renamed the edit bay "edit bay watch." But the one thing she wouldn't do was a sit-down interview to string it all together.

The end product was a visual extravaganza, unlike anything else out there. Less of a reality show and more like a chopped salad. But there's a reason why you don't re-invent the wheel. The takeaway is that whether you call it a reality show or an observational documentary series, it's probably not worth making if you don't plan on revealing yourself some way some how. The audience can sense they are being held at arm's length and leave to watch something else. But Pam is brilliant, make no mistake, and has more to give the medium than *Baywatch*.

Vogue!

Like the universe, celebrity is ever-expanding, and annexing new areas. Ultimately everyone will be, you know, famous for etc etc. In her decades at *Vogue*, Anna Wintour has both witnessed this and herself become the queen of cool. Wherever she goes, paparazzi flock. Like it or not, she is a star. And under her watch we have seen models become supermodels, we have seen designers become rock stars, photographers become world famous. Traditionally behind the scenes, it is now the turn of the fashion editors to embrace their fifteen minutes. To coincide with the publication of a book about their work, HBO approached us to make a film about them.

Although extremely used to being around shoots and working with celebrities, they seemed disinclined and even reluctant to go in front of the camera. After all, fashion is something easily made fun of. The purpose and seriousness of it is less easily expressed – especially on film. And although we found nothing remotely resembling *Zoolander* or *Devil Wears Prada*, we did find a family of unique and fantastic characters, who could not have been more sincere, more disciplined, more hard-working. Grace Coddington, Tonne Goodman, Camilla Nickerson, Phyllis Posnick, Susan Train, Vera Wang all shared the most profound insights from this supposedly most superficial of all professions.

Had we drunk the Kool-Aid? After all, who really cares about fashion? But the fact is that we are all born naked. And whether the rest is drag or fashion is splitting hairs; everyone has to get dressed in the morning. And we put on our clothes, our drag, our armor, with intent; to look better, perhaps. To feel better, certainly. So everytime we get dressed, it's not about dressing the body, it's about expressing the soul.

Royalty To Reality

The great thing about reality is that it can show us people as they really are. And reveal how different that reality is to what we were brought up to believe.

Case in point, *Finding Sarah*, the series we made for OWN. Thanks to fairy tales we believe that a girl

marries her prince and lives happily ever after. And that princess myth of the fairy tale princess – as all the hoopla over the William and Kate wedding demonstrated – is hard-wired into our consciousness.

Finding Sarah: From Royalty to the Real World is the story of how someone trapped by that princess myth strives to re-connect with reality. The stakes could not have been higher. In August we had our first phone call with her. She was still reeling from the scandal in which she had been caught on tape taking money for supposedly selling access to Prince Andrew. We now know of course that the *News of the World*, the paper responsible for this sting, was shut down by its owners in the wake of an ever-expanding ethics scandal. Not that that has brought the Duchess any respite. The UK press relentlessly and sadistically torment her. The unhappy result is that the public appears to have been happily brainwashed into assuming that she is every bit as bad as they read and hear.

Long before the scandal, we had wanted to work with her. Setting a meeting wasn't the easiest thing but finally, after about a year of back and forth, the date, time, and location were set. We left the meeting in love with her indomitable spirit and energy. She was a firework. A whole box of fireworks.

However, fate intervened with the *News of the World* sting. We could not imagine her ever trusting anyone in the media again, so we assumed that this would just be one of those ideas that got away. But when we heard she had pacted with OWN to make a series, we volunteered ourselves.

"Why on earth am I doing this?" the Duchess would ask from time to time, anxious that this latest television outing would lead to yet another drubbing. She feared it would appear self-obsessed and self-indulgent. As she set out on the journey, Oprah called her with a pep talk.

We are not doing this to be a television show. We are filming it, it's being documented, but I'm not interested in a television show. What I'm interested in is your process. Being so pure so strong and so authentic. That every single person who sees that, feels not just your pain but they feel his or her own. They feel your triumph and therefore feel the possibility of their own. They feel your struggle, they feel your journey and they feel their own. I find my story in your story. I get to see myself. And so in order to do that you've got to be willing to do what you are doing. So take the risk and embrace the fear. Just embrace the fear. And just walk right on through it.

Oprah was right. If it was about Sarah, it was also about ourselves. As we listened to what Dr Phil, Suze Orman, Martha Beck, and occasionally Oprah herself said about her, all of us on the crew found ourselves thinking about our own mistakes, our own regrets and our own issues. For example:

- That we generate the results in life that we believe we deserve.

- That when you know better you do better.

- That "Am I good enough?" is the thing that gnaws at most of us.

- That it is none of my business what other people think of me.

- That I am addicted to the approval of others.

- That just being myself is enough to be loved.

- That forgiveness is giving up the hope that the past could have been any different.

- That life is something to be managed, not fixed.

There were more, many more, but just one of these

OPPOSITE PAGE: Poster for *Man Shops Globe*. Host Keith Johnson, photographed by Jeremy Simmons, March 13, 2010; poster for *Fantasia for Real* on VH1

THIS PAGE: Sarah Ferguson and Suze Orman chat with Oprah Winfrey at the launch of OWN on January 1, 2011; Oprah poses for a snapshot with Fenton and Elise Duran

The idea of the star shrouded in mystery is old hat. If we can't see it, touch it, and tweet it we don't want it

would have been enough.

It was kind of unbelievable that all these people – Dr Phil, Suze Orman, and the others – would give of themselves so freely and with such generosity. But such is the magic of royalty that when a Duchess shows up people want to do their best and to give their best. And we would chuckle about it because no matter who went in there guns a-blazing (I don't care who she is! I don't want to be her friend!), they would come out Duchified. There's no other word to describe it.

But there was another dynamic at work here too. Here was a member of the royal family coming not just to television, but to reality television. It's a significant shift. And one that sends a message that perhaps some don't want to hear – that the Duchess of York is just an ordinary person.

Getting ready to interview Sarah at the end of the production, Oprah asked Elise Duran, the amazeballs showrunner, what she thought Sarah feared about doing the series. Elise said it was fear of the series itself. Oprah replied that she could relate to that because that was her fear too.

Really? Oprah, the Queen of all media, afraid? She said she would wake up in the middle of the night afraid that people would judge her; why should she think that just because she has a successful show she can have her own network?

Every queen – from the Queen of England to the drag queen getting ready to lip-sync for her life – gets nervous. We are all the same. We might not have a title, but it's not about that. It's about finding what's royal within. Because we are each and every bit as royal and as special as the royal family.

Of course there were some negative reviews when the series aired and the Duchess got another Fleet Street bashing. But, hopefully her newfound fortitude protected her. Regardless, it will not diminish the achievement of helping so many other people. And so our hope is that everyone who watches the show will not judge her, but instead will see themselves in her.

Just as we saw ourselves.

THIS PAGE: Fantasia strikes a pose for Jeremy Simmons in the World of Wonder studio, February 8, 2010

THIS BOMBSHELL IS ABOUT TO GO OFF.

PAM GIRL ON THE LOOSE™

PREMIERE EVENT
SUNDAY
AUGUST 3
@10/9c

E!

EONLINE.COM

Dean McDermott
ACTOR

Tori Spelling
ACTRESS, AUTHOR

With their oldest two children, Liam and Stella

PHOTOGRAPHED BY IDRIS + TONY
AT HOME, MALIBU, CALIFORNIA,
JULY 17, 2009

What's in a name? An entire brand! CelebraTORI, sTORItelling, ediTORIal. Tori and her family are a TORInado

Mehran Farhat
FASHION DESIGNER

Mehran is known as Tori's gusband, a portmanteau of gay and husband. He is also her creative partner on her jewelry and clothing lines

PHOTOGRAPHED BY IDRIS + TONY AT HOME, WEST HOLLYWOOD, CALIFORNIA, JANUARY 26, 2010

Richard Courtney

PRODUCER

Richard is the longtime showrunner of *Tori and Dean*

PHOTOGRAPHED BY IDRIS + TONY
FORMER PUSSYCAT THEATRE (NOW A BRAZILIAN CHURCH), HOLLYWOOD, CALIFORNIA, JULY 14, 2010

Patsy Lemmer

NANNY

Patsy has been the Nanny to all of Tori and Dean's children and a breakout star on the series

PHOTOGRAPHED BY MATHU ANDERSEN
ENCINO, CALIFORNIA, MARCH 3, 2010

Scout Masterson

ENTREPRENEUR

Bill Horne

ENTREPRENEUR

Scout and Bill are known as The Guncles on *Tori and Dean*. They were married on the show May 23, 2009, and in 2010 adopted their own baby, Simone

PPHOTOGRAPHED BY IDRIS + TONY
AT HOME, WOODLAND HILLS,
CALIFORNIA, APRIL 24, 2010

Dia & Ray Schuldenfrei
REAL ESTATE AGENTS

Chase Campen
REAL ESTATE AGENT

Dia and Ray and their protégé Chase were featured in the first season of *Million Dollar Listing*

PHOTOGRAPHED BY IDRIS + TONY
BEVERLY HILLS, CALIFORNIA,
JANUARY 25, 2010

Linda Evangelista

MODEL

"Oh God, no supermodel questions, please!" she sighed when the inevitable moment came. She couldn't have been nicer, funnier, and – it goes with saying – breathtaking. She was even kind enough to let us interview her on her birthday

PHOTOGRAPHED BY RUSS GELTMAN
THE STANDARD HOTEL, NEW YORK CITY, MAY 10, 2012

Carnie Wilson

SINGER

Carnie along with her husband Rob, manager Mickey, gay best friends Daniel and Brian, and Aunt Dee Dee starred in *Carnie: Unstapled* for GSN

PHOTOGRAPHED BY IDRIS + TONY AT HOME, WOODLAND HILLS, CALIFORNIA, NOVEMBER 16, 2009

Aunt Dee Dee

CARNIE WILSON'S AUNT

PHOTOGRAPHED BY IDRIS + TONY
WOODLAND HILLS, CALIFORNIA,
NOVEMBER 16, 2009

Todd Radnitz

TV PRODUCER

Todd was showrunner on the hit show (and cult classic) *Showbiz Moms and Dads* and has worked with us ever since, overseeing the last two seasons of *Million Dollar Listing* for Bravo. On the side, he's a master property flipper and cookie fanatic! He has never competed in a beauty pageant

PHOTOGRAPHED BY IDRIS + TONY
HOLLYWOOD DELL, CALIFORNIA,
JULY 16, 2010

Kyra Sundance

DOG TRAINER

Kyra and her hounds starred in *Showdog Moms and Dads*

PHOTOGRAPHED BY IDRIS + TONY
AT HOME, NORTH ANTELOPE VALLEY,
CALIFORNIA, JANUARY 23, 2010

Shareen Mitchell

DESIGNER, FASHION RETAILER

Shareen was the star of *Dresscue Me*, a series that aired on Planet Green and followed the vintage clothing business she operates out of an unmarked warehouse in downtown Los Angeles

PHOTOGRAPHED BY IDRIS + TONY
LOS ANGELES, CALIFORNIA,
APRIL 28, 2010

Andy Cohen

TV EXECUTIVE, TALK SHOW HOST

Andy is the host of the wildly successful Bravo promo talk show *Watch What Happens Live*. The set of his show so closely resembles his apartment it's hard to tell them apart

PHOTOGRAPHED BY IDRIS + TONY
TRIBECA, NEW YORK CITY,
OCTOBER 15, 2009

Josh Altman

REAL ESTATE AGENT

When Chad Rogers decided he no longer wanted to do *Million Dollar Listing* after three seasons, Josh stepped into the breach, bless him

PHOTOGRAPHED BY IDRIS + TONY
THE GRAND HAVANA ROOM, BEVERLY HILLS, CALIFORNIA, JULY 13, 2010

We've always had a thing for real estate agents

Madison Hildebrand

REAL ESTATE AGENT

Madison is not only one of the nicest agents you will ever meet (if you're lucky), he is also the original *Million Dollar Listing* cast member who has been in every season

PHOTOGRAPHED BY IDRIS + TONY
MALIBU, CALIFORNIA, JUNE 17, 2009

Chad Rogers
REAL ESTATE AGENT

The dude with the hair from *Million Dollar Listing*. He brought a whole new meaning to hair-raising when viewers became completely obsessed with his

PHOTOGRAPHED BY IDRIS + TONY
HOLLYWOOD HILLS, CALIFORNIA, JANUARY 27, 2010

Edith Flagg
FASHION DESIGNER, PHILANTHROPIST

Josh Flagg
REAL ESTATE AGENT

Edith is a holocaust survivor and was the first to import polyester into the US. Well, somebody had to. Her grandson Josh is a star on *Million Dollar Listing*, and they love each other to bits

PHOTOGRAPHED BY IDRIS + TONY AT HOME, LOS ANGELES, CALIFORNIA, NOVEMBER 18, 2009

Gigi Levangie Grazer

AUTHOR

The bestselling novelist (*Maneater*, *The Starter Wife*) hosted our competition floral elimination show *The Arrangement*. She has also been a frequent and popular guest judge on *RuPaul's Drag Race*

PHOTOGRAPHED BY IDRIS + TONY AT HOME, BEVERLY HILLS, CALIFORNIA, JANUARY 24, 2010

Travis Wall
Mischa Gabriel
Nick Lazzarini
Teddy Forance

DANCERS

The boys are charter members of Shaping Sound Dance Company and subject of our series *All the Right Moves.* When this shot was taken they had just performed an interpretive dance about World of Wonder as part of Randy and Fenton's acceptance speech as recipients of Outfest's Outstanding Achievement Award

PHOTOGRAPHED BY MATHU ANDERSEN
THE ORPHEUM THEATRE, LOS ANGELES, CALIFORNIA, JULY 7, 2011

Paul Reubens

CREATOR OF PEE-WEE HERMAN

We've always had big plans to work with Paul and interviewed him for our Trio show *The Christmas Special Christmas Special*

DOLL BY EMILIE ODEILE
PHOTOGRAPHED BY IDRIS + TONY
MCKIBBIN PLAYGROUND, BROOKLYN, NEW YORK, NOVEMBER 18, 2011

Pamela Anderson

ACTRESS

Star of her own show, *Pam: Girl on the Loose* on E! and guest judge on *RuPaul's Drag Race*

PHOTOGRAPHED BY MATHU ANDERSEN
CULVER CITY, CALIFORNIA, AUGUST 29, 2011

Eric Buterbaugh
FLORIST

The legendary florist was the resident judge on our competition floral elimination show *The Arrangement*

PHOTOGRAPHED BY IDRIS + TONY
WORLD OF WONDER PRODUCTIONS,
HOLLYWOOD, CALIFORNIA, JULY 7, 2010

Fredrik Eklund
Ryan Serhant
Michael Lorber

REAL ESTATE AGENTS

Michael, Ryan, and Fredrik are the stars of *Million Dollar Listing New York*

PHOTOGRAPHED BY IDRIS + TONY
CHELSEA, NEW YORK CITY, NOVEMBER 4, 2011

Fantasia

SINGER

Although diminutive in person, Fantasia is a larger-than-life presence. Superman. "Yeah, but even Superman gets tired," she likes to say in her lovely husky little-girl voice

PHOTOGRAPHED BY IDRIS + TONY
KMA RECORDING STUDIOS, TIMES SQUARE, NEW YORK CITY, DECEMBER 16, 2009

Carlyne Cerf de Dudzeele

FORMER FASHION EDITOR, *VOGUE*

Hamish Bowles described her to us as a "flamboyant french aristocrat with a mouth like a trouper." One of her claims to fame was pairing a Christian Lacroix couture top with blue jeans on a cover shoot for *Vogue*. It was so against precedent that the printers called up the offices convinced it was a mistake

PHOTOGRAPHED BY TIM WALKER
CHELSEA, NEW YORK CITY, NOVEMBER 4, 2011

“I used to be called the spoiled brat of the fashion world, and I was”

–POLLY MELLEN

Polly Mellen

FORMER FASHION EDITOR, *VOGUE*

Polly's first production as a fashion editor was The Great Fur Caravan, a five week expedition to the snowy wilds of Japan with Richard Avdeon and Veruschka. She travelled with 13 coffins of specially made furs and no assistant. No wonder she set off as a brunette and returned with white hair

PHOTOGRAPHED BY TIM WALKER
CHELSEA, NEW YORK CITY, NOVEMBER 4, 2011

Sarah Ferguson Duchess of York

WRITER, DUCHESS OF YORK

In the final episode of the series we travelled with the Duchess to her childhood home in the British countryside. She brought along a delicious picnic lunch for the entire crew

PHOTOGRAPHED BY ROBIN LAYTON
DUMMER, ENGLAND.
MARCH 10, 2011

> "Forgiveness is giving up the hope that the past could have been anything different"
>
> – OPRAH WINFREY

It Takes a Village, People!

IN 2000, WE MOVED INTO OUR OWN BUILDING on Hollywood Boulevard. It would take a long time, but we would eventually revamp the offices (thanks to A J Bernard's amazing design work), renovate and restore the exterior of the building to its former art deco glory years, build a studio in the basement, build a state-of-the-art post department with 40 edit bays, and open an art gallery in one of the storefronts. The building came with a rich history. It was the first headquarters of the Screen Actors Guild, and presumably where Ronald Reagan might have come to work as its president. Attached to the building is a theater, which although currently a church, is where *Deep Throat* played for a number of years in the '70s. In 1977, the now-legendary punk club, The Masque, opened in the basement of the building and bands such as Joan Jett and The Runaways, The Go-Go's, The Germs, Darby Crash, and other punk pioneers made their debuts.

WOW Report contributor Brian Heinberg found a stash of ceramic owls, by an unknown artist, online. They were made, we think, in the '60s and used to hide cans of hairspray

But when we moved in, the buzzy thing was the digital space, and in 2000 we launched the WOW Report, a monthly list of 10 things we liked, links to check out. A few years later we re-launched the WOW Report as a blog, built by Tom Wolf and edited by Stephen Saban who had relocated to LA from New York after writing his famous nightlife column in *The Soho News* and *Details* magazine for a couple of decades. Meanwhile, James St James had been in and out of the office more or less constantly since *Party Monster's* various iterations and he later started contributing as well. The two of them had known each other forever. Putting them both in one office was as potentially explosive as pairing Joan Jett with Ronald Reagan, but together they now (more or less) happily co-edit the WOW Report.

On the ground floor, we rented out the retail space to a store called Touch of Romance that euphemistically claimed to be selling essential oils and candles, it was

Fenton as all six Village People, photographed by Idris + Tony, World of Wonder Productions, Hollywood, California, April 19, 2010

One of the first shows in our World of Wonder Storefront Gallery, "Golden Gals Gone Wild," was curated by Lenora Claire and featured a topless Bea Arthur

a porn store, basically. Often, people coming to meet with us at World of Wonder would wander into the store, unaware that the entrance to our office was actually around the corner on Cherokee. It was always a good ice-breaker. Bette Midler loved it, Courteney Cox not so much.

But then the recession came, and perhaps we were in a position to know about this ahead of the mortgage meltdown because Touch of Romance came to us asking for a big reduction in rent. It is said that the adult business is the canary in the coal mine when it comes to the economy; if guys stop buying essential oils and things of that nature (porn), then rest assured, the shit will hit the fan.

Once they vacated the premises why not, we thought, turn the place into an art gallery. Fun idea, but who would run it? We thought James would make the perfect curator and with Thairin Smothers and Steven Corfe the three ran the place. One of our first shows, curated by Lenora Claire, was called "Golden Gals Gone Wild" and featured a topless Bea Arthur. The rest of the show went along the same lines and we had a kick-ass opening-night reception. In fact, all our opening nights were spectacles. "The Drag Show" – coinciding with the launch of *RuPaul's Drag Race* – was so packed that Ru himself could not get in and held court in the parking lot. We held a show to celebrate Vivid's 25th anniversary with a porn summit discussing the recession in the adult business. We celebrated the 21st anniversary of Andy Warhol's death with a tribute exhibit entitled "Dead at 21. "

With Michael Lucid, James next launched the *Daily Freak Show*, a digital report from the boîtes, dives, and red carpets of LA's nightlife. The moment he arrived at an opening to record a segment for the *Daily Freak Show*, the event would go into high gear: drinks were spilled, underwear thrown, and a good time had by all. But at some point it dawned on us that having a kick-ass opening was not the same as running a viable art gallery.

Fortunately, the guys who had put together the Bettie Page group show wanted to take over the lease of the place as a permanent store. And so, after 24 memorable months, the World of Wonder Storefront Gallery closed its doors.

On November 6, 2010, Thairin Smothers taped this conversation between James St James and Stephen Saban.

JAMES ST JAMES: This is 21 years of World of Wonder. Can you imagine? We've known Randy and Fenton for about 25 years.

STEPHEN SABAN: Yes, since the '80s.

J SJ: Do you remember the first time you met them?

S S: I think it might have been backstage at the Limelight.

J SJ: When they were doing –

S S: The Fabulous Pop Tarts.

J SJ: Yeah, and we used to get dragged to their shows every week. (*laughs*)

S S: And every year they made promotional items. They would record a Christmas single and send it out to people.

J SJ: Oh, I remember that! They really understood merchandizing very early.

S S: They inundated me at *Details* with merch. And I never wrote about them.

J SJ: (*laughs*) But they were very cute back then. They would be "twinks" now. Nelson Sullivan became one

THIS PAGE: Steven Corfe and Thairin Smothers at work, October 23, 2007; invitation to the opening of Clancy Cavnar's solo "Owls" show at the World of Wonder Storefront Gallery, November 13, 2008; Sham of Hollywood self-portrait from his one-man show that inaugurated the gallery; Britney Spears by Clancy Cavnar from the exhibition "Just Britney"

of their first subjects. Remember him? He was a really amazing person. And he had one of those old-fashioned video cameras that was just clunky.

S S: It was always literally attached to him.

J S J: Right, and it had a big honking light on it.

S S: He was the only one documenting the scene. My greatest regret was that I avoided him.

J S J: I did too! I think I was always coked out of my mind, and I think you had said to him don't take my picture.

S S: I did. I sooooo regret that now.

J S J: The nightclub scene was just kind of full of natural-born performers. So I was like a duck to water.

S S: He died at the end of the '80s. There's footage of his last moments.

J S J: Oh my God, there is?

S S: On the dock by the Hudson, and it's sundown. He was just saying what a wonderful day it had been. And how wonderful everything was. He died that night.

J S J: Then along came RuPaul. I was in a gay bar in Charlevoix, Michigan – one of those tiny little tragic ones way up in the middle of nowhere – and there was a monitor and all of a sudden I saw RuPaul, and skrinkle skrodel "Supermodel" came on.

S S: Was this the skanky RuPaul?

J S J: No, this was "Supermodel," and I was like, "That Bitch is a star, I cannot believe she made it!"

S S: The first time I met RuPaul it was at the New Music Seminar in 1985, and he came up to Musto and me and he was wearing a pair of rubber waders and football shoulder pads with mylar streamers coming off of them and a pink mohawk and a daisy on his cheek. He was just the nicest thing. But he had that hank of hair all on one side and looked like street trash. Unbelievable. And always saying, "Everybody say love."

J S J: Remember when "Supermodel" came out? It was right after Kier and Deee-lite, so there was this sort of downtown explosion that was happening in New York.

S S: Did downtown ever stop exploding?

J S J: After Andy Warhol died things did slow down. But then the Club Kids came along and, um...

S S: Infested –

J S J: – the whole scene.... You know, World of Wonder really has always been on the forefront of gay culture for 21 years now.

S S: They've taken things that were previously untapped, this underbelly of gay culture and celebrated it, like drag. Like...

THAIRIN SMOTHERS: Club kids?

J S J: Exactly! Things that were considered a little seamy and inappropriate. They made them warm and cuddly! And Ms Monica Lewinsky, dear God in heaven, don't you just want to hug that woman? And just tell her it's gonna be OK, and cradle her in your arms?

S S: No, I don't. I've always liked her but I never wanted to hug her.

J S J: Don't you remember when she was on *Saturday*

THIS PAGE: For "Dead At 21" we turned the gallery into a re-creation of Andy Warhol's factory, lining the walls with foil, January 11, 2008; a packed house at one of the first World of Wonder Storefront Gallery openings, 2007

Some of Thairin Smothers' candid shots taken over the years. Can you spot Amy Winehouse, Dolly Parton, Elvira, Pee-wee Herman, Monica Lewinsky, and Bobby Trendy?

Universal Studios Hollywood
HALLOWEEN HORROR NIGHTS
October 29, 2009
WOW TV
glaad
FROM IN CROWD to INNKEEPER
CBS

Stephen and James had known each other forever. Putting them both in one office was as potentially explosive as pairing Joan Jett with Ronald Reagan

Night Live and you were like, "Good for you, Monica Lewinsky!"

S S: I didn't think she did anything wrong. But I didn't want to hug her. Although the other day, I was in the elevator here with her and it was all I could do NOT to hug her!

J S J: The Duchess of York. She was in the office the other day. And she is just a star, just royalty. She's fabulous. I'm so excited about this. So I mean World of Wonder has a history of taking –

S S: Well, you know their theory –

J S J: That people who are on their way up are not that interesting because they are all about the career and too absorbed in themselves. It's only after they have been around the block a few times and they're desperate again. That's when they're fun.

S S: And so much easier to get.

J S J: OK, moving along! Anna Nicole Smith? Let me just say this: If you're gonna succeed spectacularly you're gonna fail spectacularly too, and that Anna Nicole Smith doc I thought was offensive and upsetting.

S S: You thought that the vomiting toothless relative was offensive?

J S J: It felt exploitative. Like we were making fun of the girl.

T S: You've watched it?

J S J: Don't tell me that I did not see it because I did see it! I went to the premiere at the Castro. They've had a few missteps and that was one of 'em. I'll tell you what the other one was, because you got me started now.

T S: *The Daily Freak Show*?

J S J: *Vinyl Justice*. Do you remember *Vinyl Justice*?

S S: I loved that show.

J S J: (*laughs*) Oh my God! OK, the point of *Vinyl Justice* was that they were cops who would break into your house and go through your record collection. And you would get tickets written up, right?

S S: Somebody had to break into people's houses and check their music, what they're listening to, because there is some bad stuff out there.

J S J: There is! (*laughs*) I remember the opening night party for that. It was at 360 on Vine and Sunset. And it was like a real la-di-dah party. At one point they brought out the monitors and the party stopped and we all watched it. Everyone let out a gay gasp and ran from the building as soon as it was over.

T S: OK, so what about the highlights?

J S J: One of the best was the *101 Rent Boys*. Thairin and I would go out every single night to Spotlight, a hustler bar here in Los Angeles, and we would find hustlers for them to film. And they would just talk. It's so real it makes you uncomfortable, but it's something that you've never seen before. Some of the guys are hot and some of the guys are not hot. Some of them you think it's gonna be sexy and it's so not sexy.

S S: Well, they were rent boys.

J S J: Yeah, but there's a fantasy in your head of getting prostitutes, you know, *Pretty Woman* and stuff, and what you see is the reality and it's very sad and upsetting.

T S: It was right before the internet hit. It was like the last of the Santa Monica Boulevard scene.

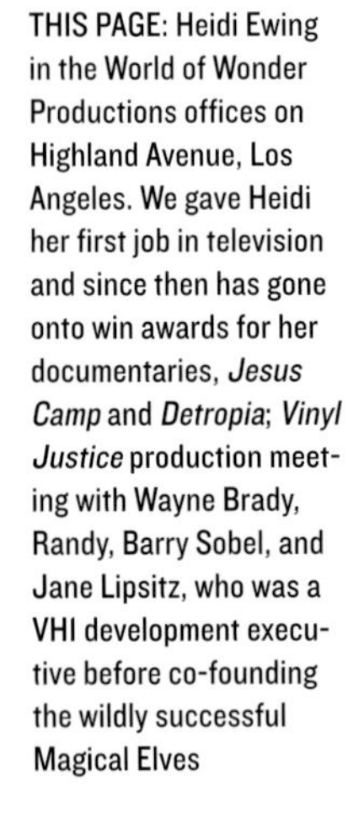

THIS PAGE: Heidi Ewing in the World of Wonder Productions offices on Highland Avenue, Los Angeles. We gave Heidi her first job in television and since then has gone onto win awards for her documentaries, *Jesus Camp* and *Detropia*; *Vinyl Justice* production meeting with Wayne Brady, Randy, Barry Sobel, and Jane Lipsitz, who was a VHI development executive before co-founding the wildly successful Magical Elves

TOP ROW: Get your group on! Wash Westmorland, Wilson Cruz, Gregg Araki, Randy, Lauren Zalaznick, Andy Cohen
FRONT ROW: Marcus Hu, James St James, Fenton, Thairin Smothers, and Jim Galasso, who was our long-suffering assistant before going off to write for Lost

BACK ROW:
Fenton, Garth Roberts, Jeff Hasler, Randy, Doug Plummer, Laura Michalchyshyn
FRONT ROW:
Angela Berg, Brent Ridge, Josh Kilmer- Purcell, Tracy Kachtick-Anders, Rosie O'Donnell, photographed by Chris Wrobleski at the American Hotel in Sharon Springs on Saturday, September 18, 2009

All the gallery's opening nights were spectacles. The moment James arrived with camera in tow, things went into high gear – drinks were spilled, underwear thrown

S S: The dregs.

T S: I just want to go back to Calpernia's *Transamerican Love Story.*

S S: That was fun to watch.

T S: *The Bachelorette*, but with a transsexual.

J S J: We love Calpernia. Oh my God!

S S: She's lovely and, of course, she's the woman from *Soldier's Girl.*

J S J: Oh! With Jane Fonda's son!

S S: Yes, as her boyfriend who got murdered.

J S J: I did not know that.

S S: Bashed to death.

J S J: Stop *it!*

S S: I've never watched *TransGeneration* but apparently it was a huge monster hit. For pre-ops.

J S J: That pre-op demographic, you know, it's getting bigger.

S S: Oh, *The Last Beekeeper*. What a beautiful movie that is.

J S J: I never saw it. Tell me about it.

T S: It won an Emmy.

J S J: It did?

T S: Jeremy Simmons directed it. He started out as an editor. He worked on the Billy Haines doc *Out of the Closet, Off the Screen.*

S S: It's about four beekeepers and how their bee colonies were depleted and how they built them back up. But it was visually so beautiful. They had closeups of bees with mites; you could actually see the mites on the bees.

J S J: That close?

S S: And you sort of began to know each bee.

J S J: And they had personalities?

S S: Yes. And you ended up loving them.

J S J: That's nasty.

S S: They were cuddly. I knew it would win.

J S J: What was *Ghetto Ballet?*

T S: That was a short that Jeremy did, it's about the Dance for All ballet company in South Africa. But it's very – did you see *District 9*?

J S J: Yeah!

T S: With the kids in the township.

J S J: They are like the aliens?

T S: Well, they live in the slums and then they try and get into this ballet school.

J S J: So it's like *Billy Elliot* meets *District 9*, is that what you are saying?

S S: They don't have prehensile proboscises do they?

J S J: They don't spit slime?

T S: No. But they are from the slums and they want to get into a prestigious ballet school and there is this one girl who is too heavyset and isn't gonna make it. And so you get sad.

S S: (*Whispers*) Heavy set. Euphemism.

J S J: The blog. Stephen, you started it in 2004, am I correct?

S S: Yes. And the first month I just wrote and wrote. But I didn't post anything because I was terrified of having people read it. They were gonna have a huge launch party, and I wouldn't let them do that either. It's crazy. Like I wouldn't allow Nelson to photograph me. I'm just insane like that.

J S J: When I first started on the blog, I was doing the "St James Version" and once a week I would write something.

S S: It was mainly "Phone Call from a Felon," your conversations with imprisoned Michael Alig.

J S J: But my point is that I would work and work and work on it and then I would rewrite it and rewrite. But the thing about blogs is that they're instantly forgotten. It's popcorn. Styrofoam peanuts.

S S: I know that now.

J S J: And how quickly you adapt to the fact that you don't have to slave over each post. You just have to get your thought out there and move on to the next one. It's very fast!

S S: But I'll send you an email later saying you forgot an apostrophe.

J S J: Twenty times a day. But it's funny that in 2004 it really was like the Wild West of the internet. There weren't that many bloggers out there. There really weren't the tropes and the clichés of blogging and the way there's a structure now to it. Back then you could just sort of do whatever you wanted. At the time, I was working with Thairin at the World of Wonder Storefront Gallery, which was a delight, let me tell you.

S S: (*Laughs*) Oh, the stories I heard.

T S: I'm sure you could hear them upstairs from all the way down in the gallery.

J S J: Ohhhh, we argued, but the gallery really was fabulous when all was said and done.

T S: I definitely miss it now.

J S J: It's weird how it's missed and loved when you take it away and it's in the past; whereas at the time let me tell you –

S S: No, no, no. I loved it at the time actually.

J S J: It was a great excuse to have a party every month and –

S S: And they were packed. More people came to the parties than read the blog.

J S J: It wasn't about art with a capital A, it was about whimsy, it was about the artists we knew and giving people a platform to show their stuff. Every month we had themes.

T S: "Dial M for Madonna," "Just Britney."

J S J: And we would change up the gallery every time. We tin-foiled the walls for Warhol.

S S: I had something in the Warhol one. That was great.

OPPOSITE PAGE: Exterior of World of Wonder's first West Coast office, Koreatown, Los Angeles; interior of the same office after the Northridge Earthquake, January 14, 1994; exterior of our office (with Randy's lighthouse) at Crossroads of the World, which we moved to in September, 1996

THIS PAGE: Before and after construction on our current offices on Hollywood Boulevard, where we moved in 2000. The design was done by A J Bernard

ARRESTING SMILES
Left to right, second row;
BEAU GENOT
LIZ DAWSON
BRYAN RABIN
KIANA MOORE
RODNEY ASCHER
NISA AHMAD

TAKING THE FIFTH
Left to right, bottom row;
DREW FORNI
M'DAYA MELIANI
FRED DECHOW
LISA FANCHER
CHERYL JOHNSON
MARK ISLAM

WOWLUMNI MUGSHOTS
Left to right, top row;
ANGEL JONES
SEBASTIAN JUNGWIRTH
DEVON SCHNEIDER
JASON BRYAN
JUSTIN HROBUCHAK

COPPING A PLEA
Left to right, third row;
TIM ATZINGER
ADRIENNE WADE
DANIEL BLAU
MICHELE MILLS (aka MEESH)
NICOLE FLOWERS

Volume 1, December 2000

The Wow Report from World of Wonder is a monthly list of things we like. Simple as that.

BOOK

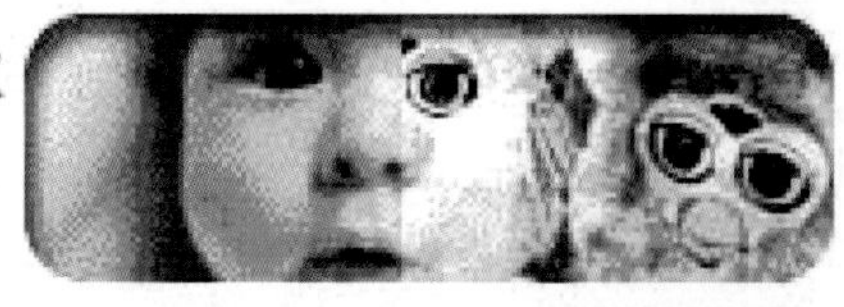

01

THE PLAYFUL WORLD
by MARK PESCE

http://www.playfulworld.com

02

SURVEILLANCE
CAMERA PLAYERS

WEBCAM

http://www.notbored.org/the-scp.html

COMMUNITY

03

CITIZENX.COM

http://www.citizenx.com

04

NEST

MAGAZINE

http://www.nestmagazine.com

PHOTOGRAPHY

05

ANTHONY
GOICOLEA

http://www.anthonygoicolea.com

06

POPBITCH.COM

GOSSIP

http://www.popbitch.com

PERVERSION

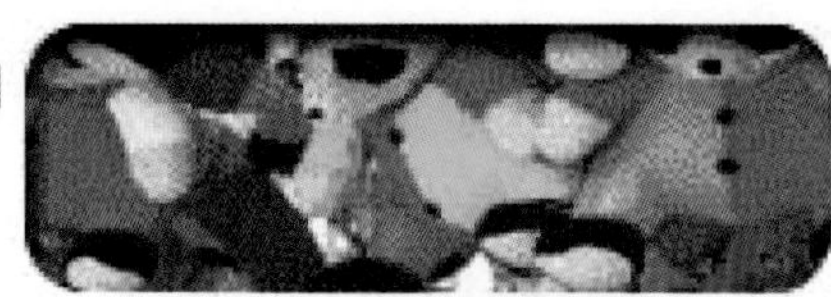

07
ADULT CONTENT

PLUSHIES

http://www.plushies.com

08

AIRSTREAM
CLUB

RETRO

http://www.airstream.net

To learn more about World of Wonder, click here

To **subscribe** to the WoW Report and receive via html e-mail, click here

To **unsubscribe** to the WoW Report, click here

THIS PAGE: The original WOW Report, launched in January 2000 and designed by David Littleton and edited by Lucien James, was a monthly email blast of 10 things

OPPOSITE PAGE: The current WOW Report, edited by Stephen Saban and James St James and designed by Tom Wolf, is among the top-20 celebrity blogs according to Wikio, and in 2011 won an LA Weekly Award for Best Counterculture Blog

THE WOW REPORT

The content on this site does not necessarily reflect the views and opinions of World of Wonder Productions

WOW Report Archives Productions About WOW Air Dates Search

Try Harder, Honey

August 10, 2012 at 3:30 pm

tags airport style, dirty words, LAX, Marilyn Manson, snap!

James St. James

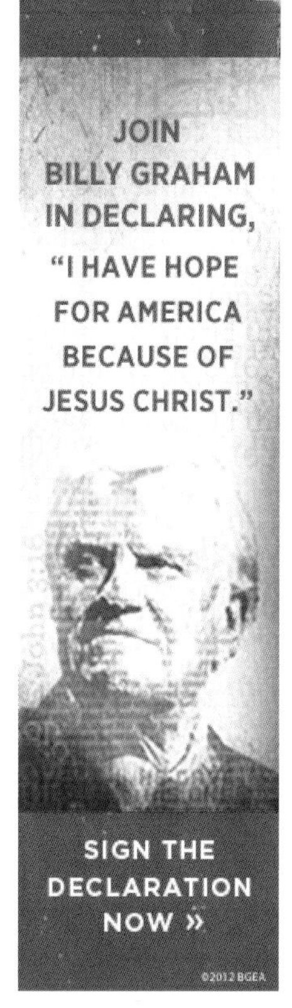

Marilyn Manson quickly scrawls "FUCK YOU" on his face for the photographers waiting for him at LAX, apparently under the impression that they won't be able to sell profanity-laden pics. HA! Little does he realize that we LOVE Marilyn and we LOVE potty mouths and we LIVE for this type of childish behavior here at the WOW Report. (Photo bought from Pacific Coast News)

twitter

the BOYS are back in town
– THE FABULOUS –
BEEKMAN BOYS

THURS sept 20 10pm ON COOKING CHANNEL

Related Posts

See WOW Elsewhere

Manifesto

We believe the Sixteenth minute can be better than the

J S J: And the owls. When we were told we were doing owls, we were like, What? That ended up being absolutely fabulous. We had giant trees in the gallery.

S S: What was the country-and-western one?

J S J: "Dollypop!" We did Dolly Parton.

S S: With the big bale of hay.

J S J: And live chickens at the opening!

T S: Remember, that space was available and Randy and Fenton just said figure it out.

J S J: That's actually how *Daily Freak Show* started. It was just a big empty space and I had my book *Freak Show* coming out, so I said, "Why don't we just film me for 24 hours taking phone calls." It was a live feed. We had bands come in and perform. We had strippers and everything. And I got drunk about 10 o'clock in the morning.

S S: Actually, one of my favorite things we ever did was *Ring My Bell.* I loved that so much. And it was in that little room in the lobby, that cute little room with the clock on the wall, and people would call in live.

J S J: And sometimes they would not call and you had to vamp, and you had to stretch it out for an entire hour.

S S: And it was always some really low-budget celebrity we had in there.

J S J: We had Prince Poppycock.

T S: Arianna Huffington did it.

J S J: Did she?

S S: She did?

J S J: Who else?

T S: Ummm. Alec Mapa.

J S J: Ross the Intern. Selene Luna.

S S: But, see, these are not like Cher.

J S J: *Ring My Bell* was based on a show they did in England that Laurie Pike was the host of and actually had Boy George. Who were some of the other celebrities?

T S: The Queen of England.

J S J: The Queen of England did not do it!

T S: A look-alike drag queen.

J S J: (*Laughs*) Wait a minute! You are wearing my Jem and the Holograms T-shirt! Where did you get that?

T S: I wondered where this came from. I just found it in my cubicle. Anyway, we are off the topic.

J S J: Snuggies! What do you have to say about Snuggies?

S S: I think that WOW has a very strong streak of irony, shall we say, and I like to think the whole Snuggie obsession was ironic.

J S J: And yet it fed into the mania surrounding it at the time and stopped being ironic and started being real.

S S: It didn't stop being ironic for me.

J S J: Well that's because you don't wear yours. I wear mine all the time.

THIS PAGE: Laurie Pike with Gabriel Rotello; James St James with Michael Pressman; Steve Moore, Douglas Rushkoff, and Jake Fogelnest at the Edinburgh Television Festival, August 23, 1997

OPPOSITE PAGE: Joelle Pezely, RuPaul's longtime business manager, and Mathu Andersen; Rebel Steiner with RuPaul; Ed Magaña at his desk in the Crossroads of the World offices, Hollywood

S S: Actually, I never got one. I have a regular robe at home.

J S J: Excuse meeeee!

T S: That's another thing you didn't want to be photographed for.

S S: Nobody asked me.

T S: Yes!

S S: For the box? No.

T S: Yeah.

S S: No.

T S: Yeah.

S S: No.

T S: Yeah.

S S: No.

J S J: Oh my God! So this is a whole page of like no, no, no, nos?

S S: I wasn't asked.

T S: You said no.

S S: I did not say no! We can edit this out. This is not precious!

T S: I'm not gonna be in it anyway. This is just between you two.

J S J: I have a feeling you are gonna be in this because you won't shut up is what it is! So you are in this. What I was about to say is World of Wonder is entering into sort of a mainstream period now where they are not doing as many underground things. We have *The Fabulous Beekman Boys.*

T S: Gay *Green Acres.*

J S J: For somebody who doesn't want to be in this.... I tell you what. *Million Dollar Listing* – how much do we love each and every one of those boys? I want to put that little Chad Michael in my pocket right now.

T S: His name is Chad Rogers.

J S J: I want to put that little Chad Rogers in my pocket and just take him home with me.

S S: Is he the haircut?

J S J: Yes.

S S: He has left the show.

J S J: They replaced Chad Rogers? Fine. I want to talk about Carnie Wilson.

S S: It's one of the shows that didn't make it. Is that what you were gonna say?

J S J: I was talking about wonderful women!

S S: Aww.

J S J: The wonderful women of World of Wonder! Carnie Wilson! Whadda ya got?

S S: Nothing.

J S J: OK, then we're moving on! All the people at World of Wonder! It takes a village! You know it's funny, 'cause over the years there have been so many

Ve became infatuated with the Snuggie and decided o produce our own custom version to celebrate the olidays in 2009. Steven Corfe slaved over faithfully ecreating the box down to the last detail

The Blanket That Has Sleeves!™

Snuggie™

Keeps You Warm And Your Hands Free!

The Blanket That Has Sleeves!™

Snuggie™

AS SEEN ON TV

- Better Than TiVo
- Perfect For Re-Gifting
- As Seen In The Pacific Trash Gyre

Reduces Office Heating Bills

Improves Staff Morale

The Blanket That Has Sleeves!™

Snuggie™

AS SEEN ON TV

- Keeps You Warm and Your Hands Free
- Perfect For Punching Executives
- Madonna Has Two

Special Bonus!

Limited Edition Box!

The Blanket That Has Sleeves!™

Snuggie™

- Completely Handmade By Machines
- 100% Pointless
- Ruins Your Sex Life

The Blanket That Has Sleeves!™

This is a limited edition Snuggie imbued with special powers to transform your life.

- Million Dollar Snuggie
- Tori & Dean: Snug Sweet Hollywood
- RuPaul's Snug Race
- Fan-snug-tasia For Real
- Man Wraps Globe
- Carnie Wilson: Unsnuggled
- 25iest Snuggies
- Fabulous Beeksnug Boys
- Design Snug School
- Snuggies of Malice
- The Snug Beekeeper
- Ghetto Snug Ballet
- Snuggi-Loggers
- Deeper Snuggie Throat

WARNING!
Use only as directed. Potentially fatal if ingested. May cause loss of dignity, projectile vomiting, existential angst, loss of purpose and/or will to live. Has been shown to cause sudden gay urges.

After the Snuggie, we became obsessed with real-wax remote-control battery-operated flameless candles and the concept of the Glow Job Kit was born. Featured on the box (left to right, top to bottom) are Amber Prochaska, Rudy Garcia, Rushie Perera, Chris McKim, Chris Wereski, Mary Ann Heagerty, Blake Jacobs, and Keely McCullough

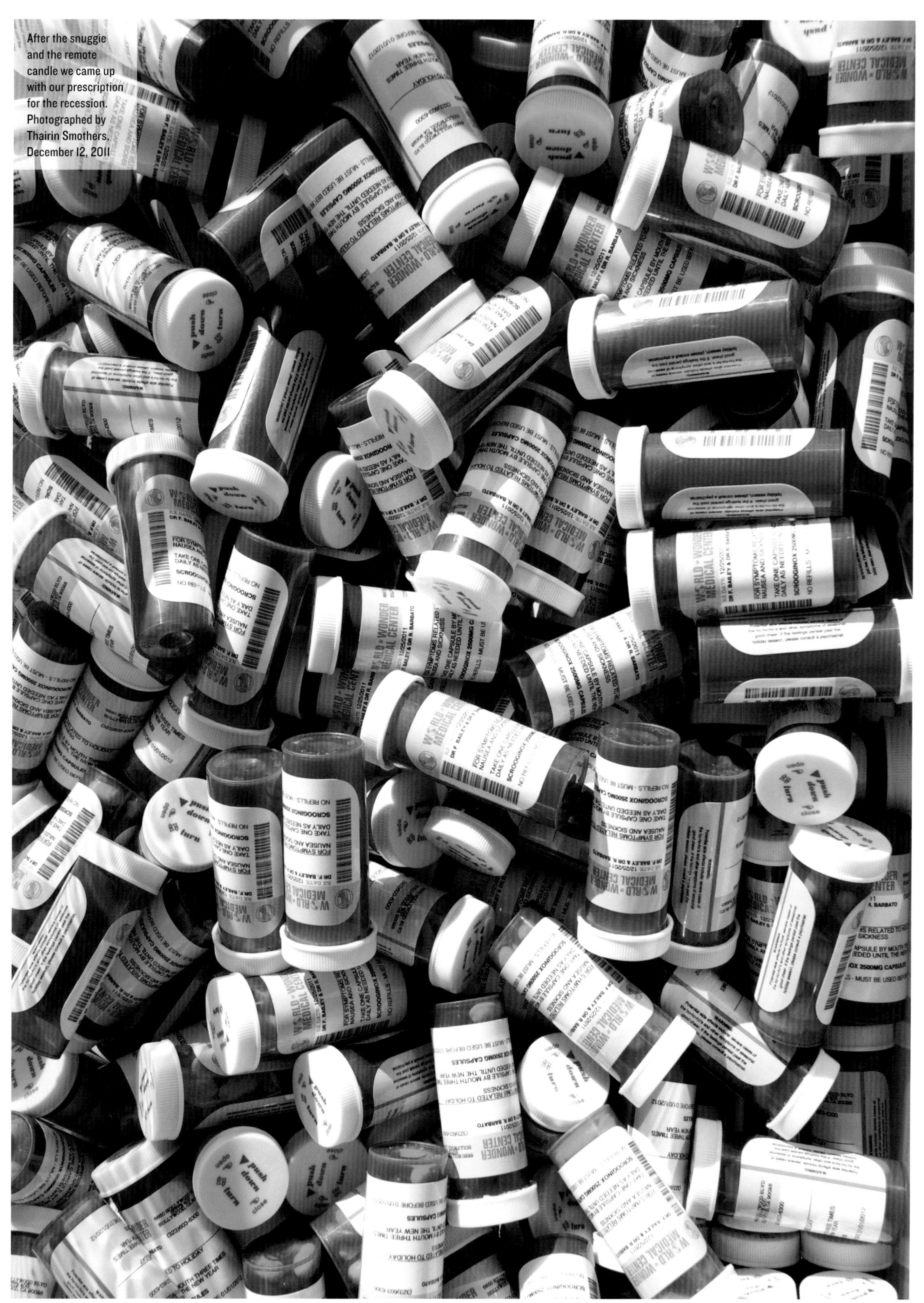

After the snuggie and the remote candle we came up with our prescription for the recession. Photographed by Thairin Smothers, December 12, 2011

If you are a disenchanted or dienfranchised outsider, come to World of Wonder and you will be embraced

people, like Jim Galasso, Moye, Lydia....

S S: I know. Classics!

J S J: Classics! The people we love! Nicole Flowers! Nicole and Liz! God, we love them! I love David Keeps! David Schiff! I love me some David Schiff! The thing is, we get really attached to certain people here and then they're gone.

S S: They move up. All the receptionists become producers.

J S J: It's true. Mary Ann, if you remember, came in to do reception and a month later she was running the joint!

S S: Transsexual receptionist.

J S J: Kiana Moore.

S S: Delightful, right?

J S J: Jeffrey Onassis. He looked fucking fabulous! Am I right? Every day!

T S: The phone would be ringing and she would be staring at her mirror.

S S: And Ed!

J S J: Ed! Oh my God! Ed Magaña! I can't believe we have waited this long to mention Ed!

T S: Ed is the oldest employee.

S S: Well, Ed has *been here* the longest.

J S J: Ricardo! He's the second longest.

T S: He's celebrating his tenth year. Ed is the first. I am the second, and Ricardo is the third!

J S J: Tiffany Flynn? God bless Tiffany Flynn? Tiffany was so much fun! Courtney Love before there was Courtney Love!

S S: What did she do?

T S: She went from running the front desk to becoming a producer.

S S: What happened to her?

T S: She started her own company.

J S J: And I think it got bought out by a Japanese consortium, or something like that.

S S: So now she's a millionaire?

T S: And retired in New York City.

J S J: If you are a disenchanted disenfranchised outsider, or a quirky individual, come to World of Wonder and you will be embraced.

S S: If you have been bullied your whole life. Come here and we will hire you!

J S J: Exactly!

T S: I didn't start out as a receptionist. I had sent video footage of Angel that I had –

J S J: OK, let's turn this into the Thairin Smothers hour.

T S: Well, I just want to say that I was a researcher first, then I got a full-time job as the receptionist.

J S J: And Thairin gets the last word! Goodbye!

END TAPE

THIS PAGE: The fabulous Beekman boys in their Snuggies, Christmas Day, 2009; Tori and Dean's baby, Stella, luxuriates in her Snuggie; Thairin Smothers cuts through the red (er, purple) tape in the World of Wonder Storefront Gallery

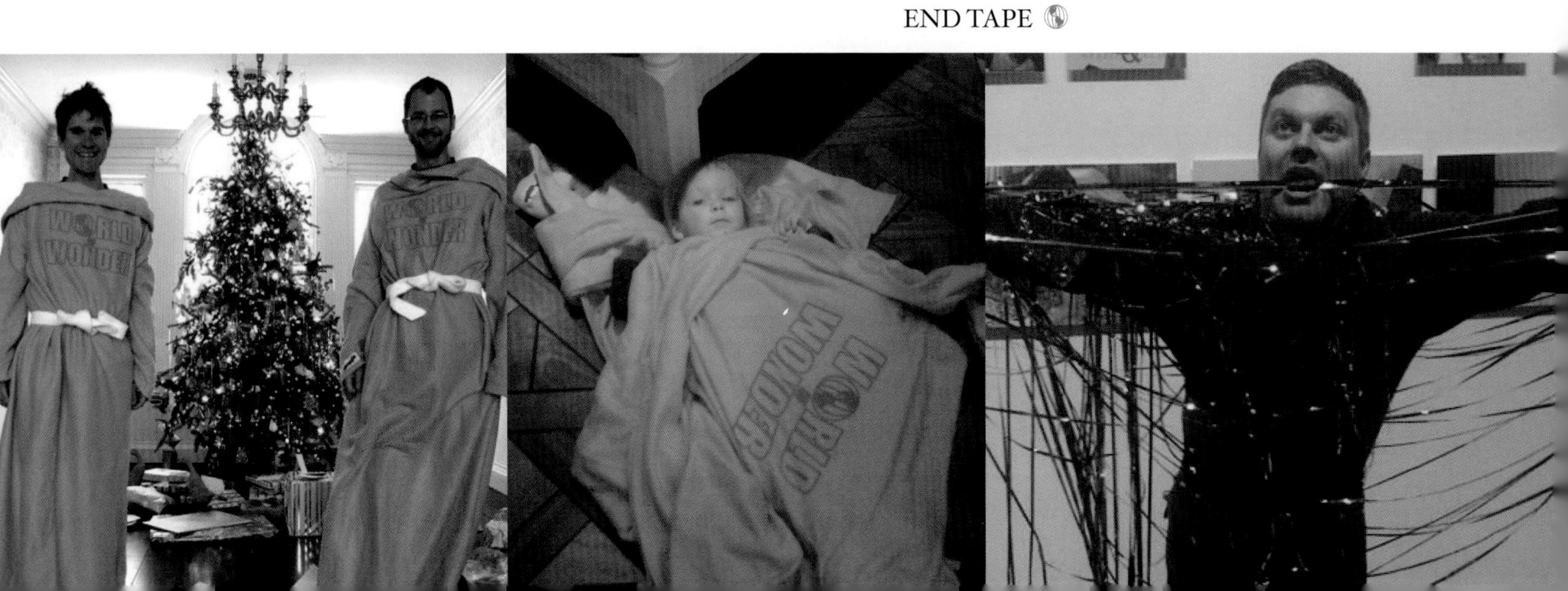

Idris + Tony

PHOTOGRAPHERS

Idris Rheubottom and Tony Craig worked for years taking photographs of all the wow-lebrities. And all along we kept reminding them about their picture, until it got to the point that we didn't think they were ever going to take it. This self-portrait, a brilliant composite of their two faces is the last picture they took for the book, and it was worth the wait!

PHOTOGRAPHED BY IDRIS + TONY
THEIR STUDIO, BROOKLYN, NEW YORK,
APRIL 22, 2012

WOW Staff

On these and the following pages are a selection of current and former World of Wonder staffers: Rushie Perera, Stephen Nugent, Michelle Palmer, Amber Prochaska, Andrew Berg, Keely McCullough, Sara Kordy, Ted Roze, Chris Diaz, Alfonso Espinosa, Kevin Andreu, Ricardo Gonzalez, Chris Skura, Theresa Slowskei, Alex Garcia, Chris Wereski, Mary Ann Heagerty, Michael Roha, Trevor Bailey, Steve Sims, Rudy Garcia, Michael Pressman, John Blair, Jennifer Burke, Jason Rasmussen, Scott Edelman

PHOTOGRAPHED BY IDRIS + TONY
WORLD OF WONDER PRODUCTIONS,
HOLLYWOOD, CALIFORNIA, JANUARY 26, 2010

Sally Miles
TV DISTRIBUTOR

Since launching her company Passion in 2008, Sally has built a formidable outfit that distributes all of World of Wonder's shows. Every year she does a Christmas card updating everyone on the status of her puddings and she is one of our closest friends

PHOTOGRAPHED BY ALEX GRACE
AT HOME, PARSONS GREEN, LONDON,
MARCH 4, 2010

Blake Jacobs
WORLD OF WONDER RUNNER

Lindsey Hager
FORMER WORLD OF WONDER RECEPTIONIST

"Good morning! World of Wonder!" The disembodied voices made flesh

PHOTOGRAPHED BY IDRIS + TONY
WORLD OF WONDER PRODUCTIONS,
HOLLYWOOD, CALIFORNIA, JULY 15, 2009

Michael Lucid aka Damiana Garcia

PRODUCER OF THE *DAILY FREAK SHOW*, TV PRESENTER

Michael shoots and edits *The Daily Freak Show* and also presents his own digital series *The Damiana Files*, hosted by his alter ego Damiana Garcia

PHOTOGRAPHED BY IDRIS + TONY
WORLD OF WONDER PRODUCTIONS,
HOLLYWOOD, CALIFORNIA, NOVEMBER 17, 2009

Marjorie Conrad
RECEPTIONIST

When asked how she felt about being kicked off *America's Next Top Model....*

PHOTOGRAPHED BY IDRIS + TONY BOARDNERS, HOLLYWOOD, CALIFORNIA, APRIL 19, 2012

Heidi Ewing

DIRECTOR

Heidi got her start in the business at World of Wonder and has gone on with her own production company, Loki Films, to become a successful award-winning documentary filmmaker

PHOTOGRAPHED BY IDRIS + TONY
SILVER LAKE, CALIFORNIA, JULY 15, 2010

Cooper Green

FORMER MANAGER OF DEVELOPMENT, WORLD OF WONDER

Cooper had a golden touch when it came to charm and politeness. He also looks better than most of us would covered in gold paint

PHOTOGRAPHED BY IDRIS + TONY
WORLD OF WONDER PRODUCTIONS, HOLLYWOOD, CALIFORNIA, JULY 16, 2010

A J Bernard

INTERIOR DESIGNER

When we moved our offices to Hollywood Boulevard, Bernard, the former New York nightlife legend, designed the raw space

PHOTOGRAPHED BY IDRIS + TONY
WORLD OF WONDER PRODUCTIONS,
HOLLYWOOD, CALIFORNIA,
JANUARY 21, 2010

Mark Itkin

AGENT

Mark represented us at William Morris Enterprises for 10 years and still believes that *Ring My Bell* could be a hit show

PHOTOGRAPHED BY IDRIS + TONY
HOLLYWOOD, CALIFORNIA,
AUGUST 4, 2009

Bobcat Goldthwait
COMEDIAN

Tasha Goldthwait
ACTRESS

Bobcat's daughter Tasha interned at World of Wonder and seems to have suffered no lasting ill effects

PHOTOGRAPHED BY IDRIS + TONY
FAKE GALLERY IN SILVER LAKE, CALIFORNIA, JANUARY 23, 2010

David Steinberg
COMPOSER

Mona Card
PRODUCER

David has created beautiful scores for many of our documentaries, many of which were produced by Mona

PHOTOGRAPHED BY IDRIS + TONY
AT HOME, HOLLYWOOD, CALIFORNIA,
JANUARY 24, 2010

Top left clockwise:

Scott Shatsky

PRODUCER

Scott was the showrunner on several of our series: *Carnie Wilson: Unstapled, Dresscue Me @ Shareen Vintage,* and *The Arrangement.* But then he decided to relocate to New York. Sad trombone

PHOTOGRAPHED BY IDRIS + TONY
SILVER LAKE, CALIFORNIA,
JULY 15, 2010

Dan Gold

TATTOO ARTIST

Dan starred in several seasons of *London Ink,* our UK-based tattoo show. Dan bristled under the disciplinarian eye of bossman Louis

PHOTOGRAPHED BY JOHNNI JAVIER
LONDON,
JANUARY 26, 2010

Rob Bonfigilio

MUSICIAN

Rob is Carnie's TDF husband and a musician in his own right

PHOTOGRAPHED BY IDRIS + TONY
WOODLAND HILLS, CALIFORNIA,
NOVEMBER 16, 2009

Top left clockwise:

Peter Asher

MANAGER

Peter came into our lives in his capacity as Pamela Anderson's manager. As charming a Brit as you will ever hope to meet, he has a storied past as one half of Peter and Gordon, who are best known for the hit "World Without Love." He also introduced John Lennon to Yoko Ono, which some argue led to the break-up of The Beatles.

PHOTOGRAPHED BY IDRIS + TONY
MALIBU, CALIFORNIA,
NOVEMBER 18, 2009

Daniel Combs & Brian Dahl

SALON OWNERS

Daniel and Brian are a couple and run The

Syndicate, which, sinister as it sounds, is a fabulous hair salon in Calabasas. Everyone needs a BFF in the form of a gay hairdresser, and Carnie Wilson who frequents the place like it's a second home, has two

PHOTOGRAPHED BY IDRIS + TONY
LOS ANGELES, CALIFORNIA
NOVEMBER 16, 2009

Mickey Shapiro

MANAGER

Mickey is Carnie Wilson's manager. Hey Mickey, you're so fine you blow my mind, hey Mickey!

PHOTOGRAPHED BY IDRIS + TONY
LOS ANGELES, CALIFORNIA,
NOVEMBER 18, 2009

Jason Mecier

ARTIST

His fabulous objet trouve work was often featured in our gallery shows. Your junk, his art. Priceless. Here he works on his partner Adam J Ansell

PHOTOGRAPHED BY IDRIS + TONY
AT HOME, SAN FRANCISCO, CALIFORNIA,
JULY 6, 2010

Sham of Hollywood

ARTIST

When Sham came to us and asked if he could use the vacant storefront in our building for a one-man show, an idea was born – the World of Wonder Storefront Gallery

PHOTOGRAPHED BY IDRIS + TONY AT HOME, HOLLYWOOD, CALIFORNIA, NOVEMBER 11, 2009

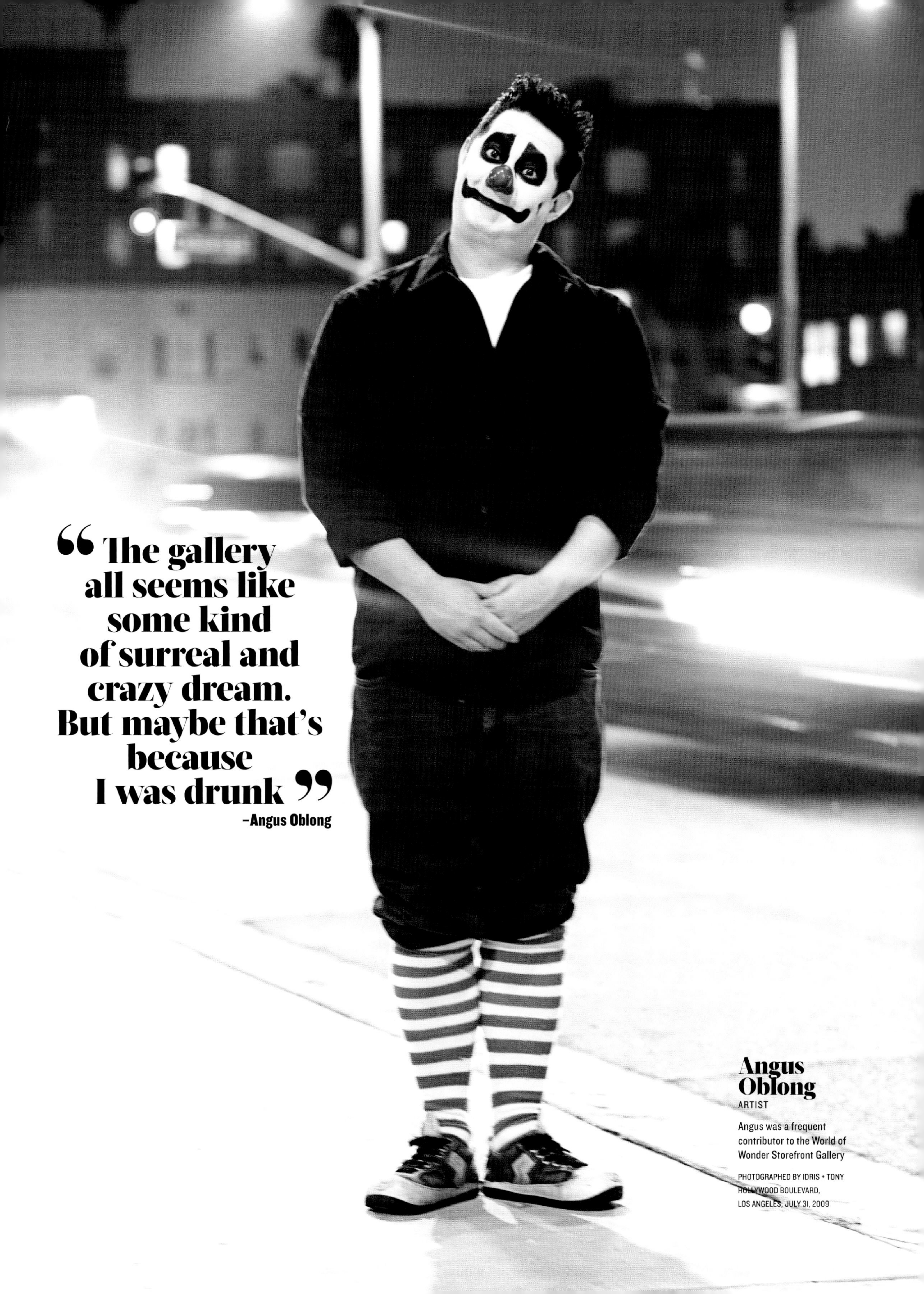

“The gallery all seems like some kind of surreal and crazy dream. But maybe that’s because I was drunk”

–Angus Oblong

Angus Oblong

ARTIST

Angus was a frequent contributor to the World of Wonder Storefront Gallery

PHOTOGRAPHED BY IDRIS + TONY
HOLLYWOOD BOULEVARD,
LOS ANGELES, JULY 31, 2009

Norman Korpi
ARTIST

Besides being an artist who appeared in several group shows at the World of Wonder Storefront Gallery, Norm was also a cast member in the first-ever season of MTV's *The Real World*, making him something of an institution in reality television

PHOTOGRAPHED BY IDRIS + TONY
AT HOME, LOS ANGELES, CALIFORNIA,
JANUARY 21, 2010

Greg Gorman

PHOTOGRAPHER

Fab photographer Greg was featured in our film *The Eyes of Tammy Faye* and – from one extreme to another – in our Heidi Fleiss documentary

PHOTOGRAPHED BY IDRIS + TONY
AT HOME, HOLLYWOOD HILLS,
CALIFORNIA, JANUARY 22 2010

Lenora Claire

GALLERY CURATOR

Lenora curated the "Golden Gals Gone Wild," "Merry Titmass," and "Bettie Page: Heaven Bound" shows at the World Of Wonder Storefront Gallery

PHOTOGRAPHED BY IDRIS + TONY
CALIFORNIA INSTITUTE OF ABNORMAL ARTS, BURBANK, CALIFORNIA, APRIL 13, 2009

Selene Luna
COMEDIAN AND ACTRESS

Selene is rightly infamous for her pitch perfect parodies of Madonna's daughter Lourdes. Her work was also featured at the World of Wonder Storefront Gallery

PHOTOGRAPHED BY IDRIS + TONY
AT HOME, HOLLYWOOD, CALIFORNIA,
APRIL 21, 2011

Pierre Brogan, Jonathan Swaden, Lee Horvitz

AGENTS

Our three main agents at CAA. They are our Three Muskateers, and are on the phone making us money right now

PHOTOGRAPHED BY IDRIS + TONY
HOLLYWOOD DELL, CALIFORNIA,
JULY 14, 2009

Rebel Steiner

LAWYER

Our attorney at Loeb and Loeb. He not only negotiates great deals he also mixes a killer cocktail

PHOTOGRAPHED BY IDRIS + TONY
CENTURY CITY, CALIFORNIA,
AUGUST 4, 2010

James McGowan

PRODUCTION DESIGNER

Steven Corfe

PRODUCER

James is set designer for many of our shows, and Steven is the showrunner of *Drag U* and *Untucked*. They met in 2003 and got married in 2012

PHOTOGRAPHED BY IDRIS + TONY WITH THEIR PUGS, STELLA AND CRACKERS, AT HOME. SILVER LAKE, CALIFORNIA, NOVEMBER 20, 2009

Erik Rudy

STYLIST

Erik was on our UK series *Rock Around the Block* and has been an indispensable and fun fashionista on many of our shows

PHOTOGRAPHED BY IDRIS + TONY
HOLLYWOOD AND HIGHLAND CENTER,
LOS ANGELES, CALIFORNIA,
JULY 12, 2010

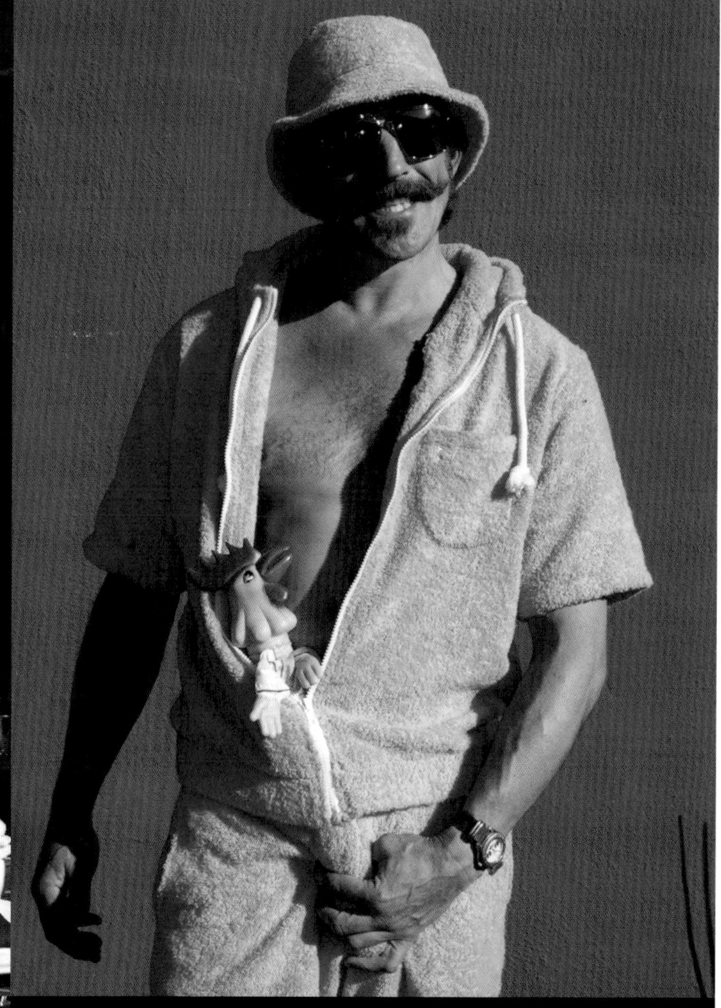

Top left clockwise:

Ami Copeland & Gemma Cairney

PERFORMERS

Ami and Gemma were two of the fearless fun and feisty hosts of our digital show *Bite*

PHOTOGRAPHED BY ALEX GRACE
LONDON, MAY 13, 2009

Brian Friend

PERFORMER

When David joined up with Simon Morley he became the second penis puppeteer

PHOTOGRAPHED BY THAIRIN SMOTHERS
LOS ANGELES, CALIFORNIA
MAY 29, 2010

Marco Marco

DESIGNER

Designer extraordinaire, Marco Marco has been a costume designer for *Drag Race* and *Drag U*. His studio is just around the corner from WOW HQ

PHOTOGRAPHED BY IDRIS + TONY
HOLLYWOOD, CALIFORNIA,
JANUARY 21, 2010

Top left clockwise:

Kitten Natividad

ACTRESS

Legendary vixen, actress, and patron of the World of Wonder Storefront Gallery

PHOTOGRAPHED BY IDRIS + TONY
LOS ANGELES, CALIFORNIA,
JANUARY 25, 2010

Louis Malloy

TATTOIST

Louis was the bossman on *London Ink*. He was tough-talking but had a big soft heart. I hope he doesn't read this caption because he'll probably berate us for saying such a thing

PHOTOGRAPHED BY ALEX GRACE
MIDDLETON, UK
MARCH 22, 2010

Kim & Jordan Mosley

CATERER, ACTRESS

Beloved mother and daughter, stars of our Bravo series *Showbiz Moms & Dads*. No table-flipping from these two!

PHOTOGRAPHED BY IDRIS + TONY
INGLEWOOD, CALIFORNIA,
JANUARY 23, 2010

Elise Duran

TV PRODUCER, DIRECTOR

Elise showran *Girls Who Like Boys Who Like Boys* and *Finding Sarah*. She is someone who claims to love dogs more than people and we would have no reason not to believe her if she wasn't such a big softie

PHOTOGRAPHED BY IDRIS + TONY
AT HOME, HOLLYWOOD HILLS,
CALIFORNIA, APRIL 24, 2011

Donal Coonan

PERFORMER

Donal invented and presented our digital series *This Is a Knife*. While taking a break, he went off and trained as a professional clown. He can also play the ukelele

PHOTOGRAPHED BY ALEX GRACE
WATERLOO, LONDON,
FEBRUARY 24, 2010

Ed Magaña

MANAGER OF POST PRODUCTION AT WORLD OF WONDER

Alicia Magaña

TV PRODUCER

Ed and Alicia met and fell in love at WOW. Their wedding in 2007 was a magical affair

PHOTOGRAPHED BY IDRIS + TONY
WORLD OF WONDER PRODUCTIONS,
HOLLYWOOD, CALIFORNIA, JULY 16, 2009

“We are WONDER! I wonder who made up that word?”

–Alicia Magaña

Tom Wolf

CHIEF ADMINISTRATIVE OFFICER AT WORLD OF WONDER PRODUCTIONS

Tom prefers not to fly, so he took the train from Chicago for his job interview and could only afford a one-way ticket. Luckily he got the job!

PHOTOGRAPHED BY IDRIS + TONY
WORLD OF WONDER PRODUCTIONS,
HOLLYWOOD, CALIFORNIA,
JULY 9, 2009

Top left clockwise:

Phillip Bloch

STYLIST

Odd, you might think, for a stylist as renowned as Phillip to appear all but naked, unless of course he has some fabulously lucrative deal with Chanel. But as Coco herself said, "It is always better to be slightly underdressed"

PHOTOGRAPHED BY IDRIS + TONY
BROOKLYN, NEW YORK,
MAY 13, 2009

Brian Heinberg

PAINTER, BLOGGER

Brian is our pup culture expert contributing insightful pieces on indie music, design, and doggies to the WOW Report

PHOTOGRAPHED BY IDRIS + TONY
RUNYON CANYON, LOS ANGELES, CALIFORNIA
NOVEMBER 19, 2009

Marc Malkin

REPORTER

The E! online blogger curated the "Dolly Pop" art show at the World of Wonder Storefront Galley

PHOTOGRAPHED BY IDRIS + TONY
SPOTLIGHT BAR, HOLLYWOOD, CALIFORNIA,
NOVEMBER 17, 2009

Stephen Saban

CO-EDITOR OF THE WOW REPORT

Last century, when Stephen was the nightlife editor at the original *Details* magazine and we were the Pop Tarts, we would send him press releases and materials in the hopes that he would write about us. But he never did. Well, maybe he did once. The solution was to lure him to Hollywood to write for and edit The WOW Report

PHOTOGRAPHED BY IDRIS + TONY
WORLD OF WONDER PRODUCTIONS,
HOLLYWOOD, CALIFORNIA,
APRIL 13, 2009

Angelyne

HOLLYWOOD ICON

Angelyne appeared in our two-hour special *History of the Cleavage* (A&E). She was a pioneer of self-promotion and branding in the days before reality TV and the internet. Hollywood would be a little less pink without her

PHOTOGRAPHED BY IDRIS + TONY
WORLD OF WONDER PRODUCTIONS,
HOLLYWOOD, CALIFORNIA,
JULY 11, 2010

Maria Conchita Alonso

ACTRESS

Maria starred in our Latin house reality competition elimination show, more sexily known as *¡Viva Hollywood!*

PHOTOGRAPHED BY IDRIS + TONY
MALIBU, CALIFORNIA,
NOVEMBER 19, 2009

Victor Gutierrez

REPORTER, AUTHOR

In 1994, long before Michael Jackson was charged with anything, Victor wrote and self-published the book *Michael Jackson Was My Lover* that told the story of Jackson's relationship with Jordie Chandler. We thought the book was so incredible we bought the rights and wrote a script. So far we have not been able to finance the movie. But we will

PHOTOGRAPHED BY MATHU ANDERSEN
WORLD OF WONDER PRODUCTIONS,
HOLLYWOOD, CALIFORNIA, APRIL 22, 2010

Clancy Cavnar
COUNSELOR, ARTIST

Regular contributor to the WOW Storefront Gallery. One of our favorite shows was "Owls" that featured over 100 of her owl paintings

PHOTOGRAPHED BY IDRIS + TONY AT HOME, SAN FRANCISCO, CALIFORNIA, JULY 6, 2010.

Dawn Airey
TV EXECUTIVE

Jacquie Lawrence
FORMER HEAD OF DEVELOPMENT AT WORLD OF WONDER PRODUCTIONS UK

When Jacquie was at WOW she met and fell in love with Dawn. Jacquie, then a cosmopolitan girl who wouldn't be seen dead on a farm let alone nurse a baby, did an abrupt 180 and ended up becoming not just a mom but the best one anyone could wish for. Their daughter Dulcie is on the left

PHOTOGRAPHED BY ALEX GRACE
OXFORDSHIRE, ENGLAND,
FEBRUARY 27, 2010

WOW! It's a Wrap

OVER THE YEARS WE'VE BEEN ASKED TO NAME our favorite show. That is so Sophie's Choice. They have all been made with love. Yet from the 1,580 episodes and 216 original series made for 41 different networks, we actually do have favorites. The ones we've never made. Yet. They take on a ghostly presence in our lives. Hovering on the margins, a gleam in our eye.

Like *Past Life Makeovers*. How do you know where you are going if you don't know where you've been? In each episode someone facing a problem does regression therapy to find out who they were in their past life. Then we whisk them off for an immersive experience in all the details of that life – what they would have worn, eaten, where they would have slept. Finally they return to their everyday life. What have they learned? Do they now feel able to face the problem daunting them?

Or there is *Michael Jackson Was My Lover*, a jaw-dropping account of a young teenager's relationship with Michael Jackson. The startling thing about this book (written and self-published by journalist Victor Gutierrez in 1994), is that it came out long before the now-famous trial that was the final nail in Michael Jackson's reputation. We thought the book was so incredible we bought the rights and wrote a script. Who wouldn't want to watch that movie, right?

OPPOSITE PAGE: Randy (giving the finger) and Fenton wear Matt Scott's fantastic Golden Girls heads in a photo shoot for *Paper* magazine. Swaravski walker by Zackary Drucker. Photographed by Luke Gilford, World of Wonder Gallery, August 5, 2007

HOLLYWOOD
VIA RODEO
N. RODEO DR
UNIVERSAL
Universal Studios Hollywood

Fenton Bailey

WOW CO-FOUNDER

Fenton is the proud owner of a plushie version of the Facehugger from Alien

PHOTOGRAPHED BY IDRIS + TONY
WORLD OF WONDER PRODUCTIONS,
HOLLYWOOD, CALIFORNIA,
APRIL 19, 2011

Randy Barbato
WOW CO-FOUNDER

In space noone can hear you blow bubbles

PHOTOGRAPHED BY IDRIS + TONY, WORLD OF WONDER PRODUCTIONS, HOLLYWOOD, CALIFORNIA, APRIL 19, 2010

Classic
RC

If this montage of pictures of Randy giving the finger needs a caption, you aren't getting the message.

And how about *Cannibal Chef*? That '70s movie *Soylent Green* always had a profound effect on us, especially the last line (spoiler alert) "Soylent Green is people." Well, what other delicious dishes can be made out of people? Each episode a world class chef works with one ingredient – the human body – to prepare and produce a cannibal feast for viewers in the audience.

It's OK that none of these have been made yet. It is an immutable law of the medium that television is on a mission to render everything visible. And don't forget, No is always the beginning of Yes.

And the point of all this – since this really is the last word – is that it's all about unfinishedness. The world of wonder we all live in is, by definition, infinite and incomplete.

We asked everyone in the book what the idea of a world of wonder means to them, and here are some of their answers...

Michael Musto: After all these years, I can still feel wonder whenever I see a powerful play or film and think, 'This thing drips with inspiration. It was clearly made by angels!' Or go to a club filled with my kindred freaks and fabulosities and feel, 'I am truly home! I belong here!' Or get emailed an adorable shot of a kitten with antlers...and promptly delete it! THAT'S wonder."

Kim Roth: "I can't *imagine* a world without wonder."

Allan Brocka: "People are obsessed with all kinds of peculiar, fucked-up, or mundane things. I, for example, am obsessed with other people's obsessions. So as long as there are people and shit that fascinates them, this will be a world of wonder for me."

Lenora Claire: "Whoever declared there are seven wonders of the world was way off. There are almost seven billion people on the earth, each one weirder than the next. I want to hear all of their stories."

And finally, when it came to our own idea of what World of Wonder means to us, Simon Doonan put it so much better than we ever could:

"World of Wonder is a rank, twisted Bauhaus of perverse creativity, dedicated to celebrating everything which is squalid and marginal. In doing so, WOW has become the ultimate antidote to the smarmy, prosaic naff-ness of red-carpet Hollywood. I salute my brothers and sisters at WOW and wish them continued success in their quest to spotlight the beauty which resides in the gutter."

Thank you Simon, and thank you everyone for making this a world of wonder.

The Wowie

At one point we thought Hollywood needed one more award show. Then we came to our senses. But we would like to give YOU this award for getting to the end of this book

PHOTOGRAPHED BY IDRIS + TONY
WORLD OF WONDER PRODUCTIONS
JULY 9, 2009

from the eye of the storm

1991

MAR 3, Rodney King is beaten by the LAPD. A bystander captures the incident on video.
MAY 1, Manhattan Cable, 9x45' - C 4 (UK)
MAY 24, Truth or Dare is released.
Fall, Wigstock (The Late Show), 1x15' - BBC2 (UK)
OCT 26, Ring My Bell, 7x45' - C 4 (UK)
DEC 26, Manhattan Cable's Christmas Extravaganza, 1x50' - C4 (UK)

1992

FEB 12, Milken and the Media (Edge), 1x15' - PBS
MAR 30, The Silence of the Lambs sweeps the Academy Awards.
APR 24, Made in the USA, 7x45' - C 4 (UK)
MAY 21, MTV premieres the first season of The Real World.
NOV 12, Absolutely Fabulous premieres in the UK.
NOV 17, RuPaul - Supermodel (Music Video)

1993

APR 25, LA Stories: From the Eye of the Storm, 1x135' - BBC2 (UK)
MAY 18, RuPaul - Back to My Roots (Music Video)
JUN 4, McDonald's introduces "Dino-Size" fries and drinks as a tie-in with Jurassic Park. Afterwards, it is renamed "Supersize."
SEP 7, RuPaul - A Shade Shady (Music Video)
SEP 27, Mosaic, the first graphical web browser, is released to public beta.
DEC 14, Shock Video 1: Videos, Vigilantes and Voyeurism, 1x60' - HBO
DEC 21, RuPaul's Christmas Ball, 1x60' - C 4 (UK)

DAILY PLAÑET

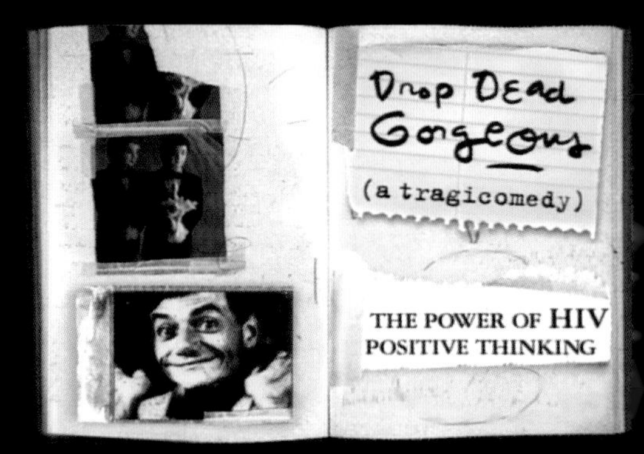

THE DIVINE DAVID PRESENTS...

1996

MAR 24, Showgirls wins seven Razzies.
APR 13, RuPaul's Party Machine, 1x240' - VH1
JUN 23, Super Mario 64 is released in Japan.
JUL 12, Takeover TV (Season 2), 8x30' - C 4 (UK)
AUG 7, Wrinklyvision, 1x45' - BBC2 (UK)
AUG 19, TV Latino, 1x35' - C 4 (UK)
SEP 17, RuPaul - Snapshot (Music Video)
OCT 12, The RuPaul Show, 12x30' - VH1
DEC 6, The Adam & Joe Show, 4x30' - C 4 (UK)
DEC 7, Shock Video 4: Turn On TV '96, 1x60' - HBO
DEC 24, God in the House, 7x30' - C 4 (UK)

1997

JAN 12, TV Pizza, 4x45' - C 4 (UK)
FEB 18, For the Love of..., 6x60' - C 4 (UK)
FEB 25, RuPaul - A Little Bit of Love (Music Video)
MAR 31, Ultra Naté - Free (Music Video)
APR 30, Ellen DeGeneres comes out on her primetime series Ellen.
MAY 24, Tickled Pink, 1x60' - C 4 (UK)
JUN 15, Drop Dead Gorgeous: The Power of HIV Positive Thinking, 1x60' - HBO
JUN 19, The RuPaul Show (Season 2), 59x30', 1x60 - VH1
JUN 23, Hot Property, 28x30' - C 5 (UK)
JUN 30, Harry Potter and the Philospher's Stone by J.K Rowling is published in London
AUG 15, For the Love of... (Season 2), 5x60' - C 4 (UK)
AUG 31, Diana, Princess of Wales, is killed in Paris during a car chase with paparazzi.
SEP 13, Survivor premieres in Sweden, under its original title Expedition Robinson.
NOV 22, The Adam & Joe Show (Season 2), 6x30' - C 4 (UK)
DEC 12, Shock Video 5: Turn On TV '97, 1x60' - HBO
DEC 31, Adam & Joe's Fourmative Years, 1x60' - C 4 (UK)

THE EYES OF
Tammy
Faye

THE
SECRET RULERS
OF
THE WORLD

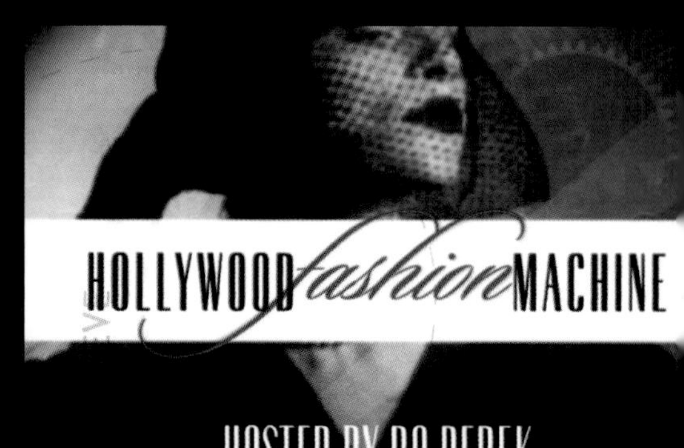

1994

FEB 12, United States of TV, 6x45' - C 4 (UK)
FEB 14, Elton John & RuPaul - Don't Go Breaking My Heart (Music Video)
MAR 1, Justin Drew Bieber is born.
APR 5, Kurt Cobain commits suicide.
JUN 17, OJ Simpson leads police on a freeway chase in his white Ford Bronco.
JUL 15, Shock Video 2: The Show Business of Crime and Punishment, 1x60' - HBO
JUL 31, Nelson Sullivan's World of Wonder, 1x60' - C 4 (UK)
AUG 26, Natural Born Killers is released.
SEP 12, OJ Mania: The Media Trial of OJ Simpson (The Late Show), 1x45' - BBC2 (UK)

1995

OCT 12, Shock Video 3: Turn On TV, 1x60' - HBO
MAR 19, Daily Planet, 1x90' - C 4 (UK)
MAY 6, Takeover TV, 8x30' - C 4 (UK)
JUN 9-18, Shantay, 1x15' - 19th SF Int'l Lesbian and Gay Film Festival
JUL, Amazon.com sells its first book.
JUL 16, TV Afrika, 1x50' - BBC2 (UK)
AUG 24, Takeover TV: The Sci-Fi Experience, 1x60' - C 4 (UK)

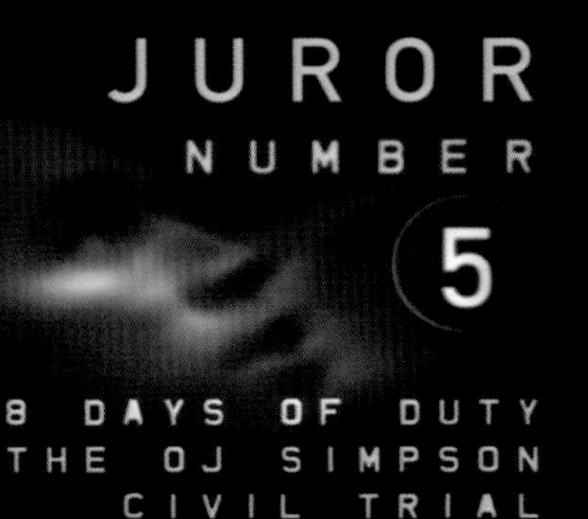

1998

JAN 19, Housebusters, 13x30' - C 5 (UK)
FEB, Potato chips with Olestra are introduced with the warning: "Olestra MAY cause abdominal cramping and loose stools."
FEB 23, For the Love of... (Season 3), 7x60' - C 4 (UK)
MAR 21, The RuPaul Show (Season 3), 27x30' - VH1
MAR 27, Viagra is approved for use in treating erectile dysfunction.
APR 25, The Real Ellen Story, 1x60' - C 4 (UK) / Bravo
MAY 4, Hot Property (Season 2), 16x30' - C 5 (UK)
AUG 25, Vinyl Justice, 8x30' - VH1
SEP 4, Google, Inc is formally incorporated.
SEP 13, Party Monster: The Shockumentary, 1x60' - C 4 (UK)
SEP 21, Will & Grace premieres.
OCT 23, For the Love of... (Season 4), 9x60' - C 4 (UK)
DEC 5, The Divine David Presents..., 6x30' - C 4 (UK)
DEC 5, Shock Video 6: Turn On TV '98, 1x60' - HBO

1999

MAR 25, Viva Espana, 8x30' - C 5 (UK)
APR 16, The Adam & Joe Show (Season 3), 6x30' - C 4 (UK)
APR 26, The Hollywood Fashion Machine, 10x30' - AMC
MAY 1, Juror #5: 58 Days of Duty in the OJ Civil Trial, 1x60' - HBO
JUL 30, The Blair Witch Project is released.
AUG 2, The New Klan, 1x60' - C 4 (UK)
SEP 16, Big Brother premieres in the Netherlands.
OCT 14, Pornography: The Secret History of Civilisation, 6x60' - C 4 (UK)
NOV 12, Mission Divine, 6x60' - C 4 (UK)

FROM THE WAIST DOWN
MEN, WOMEN & MUSIC

Lesbians go mad in LESBOS

HACKERS IN WONDERLAND

DEC 11, Video Killed the Radio Star: The History of the Music Video, 1x120' - C 4 (UK) / 5x60' - VH1
DEC 18, Shock Video 2000, 1x60' - HBO
Winter, Film Preservation Classics with Jodie Foster, 1x60' - AMC
DEC 31, Y2K.

2000

JAN 6, The Adam & Joe Toy Movie Special, 1x45' - C 4 (UK)
JAN 24, The Hollywood Fashion Machine (Season 2), 6x30' - AMC
MAR 4, Naked Players Meet the People, 1x30' - HBO / C 4 (UK)
MAR 9, Ferris wheel The London Eye opens.
MAR 21, The Hollywood Fashion Machine: Costume Preservation, 1x60' - AMC
JUN 21, Who Would Want to Marry a Millionaire, 1x60' - C 4 (UK)
AUG 12, Backstory: Bonnie & Clyde, 1x30' - AMC
AUG 21, 20 to 1, 12x60' - VH1
AUG 28, 101 Rent Boys, 1x80' - Cinemax / C 4 (UK)
SEP 16, Inside Big Brother, 1x60' - C 4 (UK)
OCT 9, 100 Greatest Dance Songs of Rock & Roll, 5x60' - VH1
NOV 28, The Eyes of Tammy Faye, 1x80' - Cinemax / C 4 (UK)
DEC 16, Shock Video 2001: A Sex Odyssey, 1x60' - HBO

backstory
BONNIE AND CLYDE

J K ROWLING AND THE HARRY POTTER EXPRESS

THE AWARD SHOW Awards SHOW
NARRATED BY TATUM O'NEAL

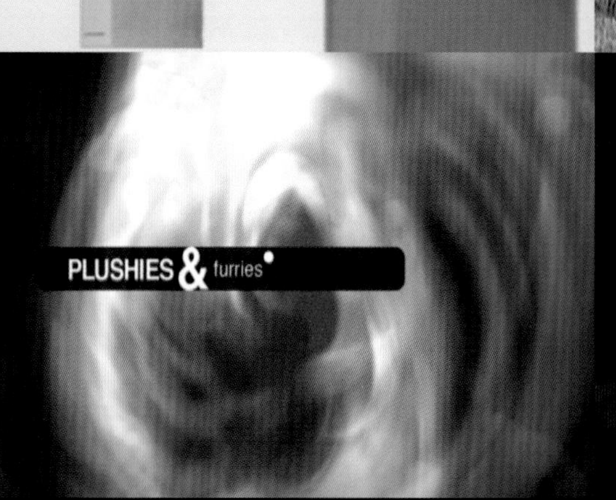

X-Rated Ambition: The Traci Lords Story

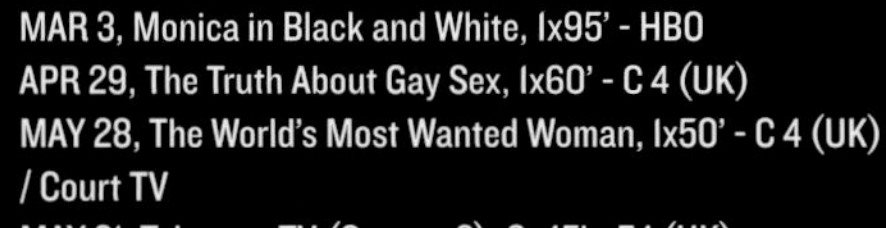

MAR 3, Monica in Black and White, 1x95' - HBO
APR 29, The Truth About Gay Sex, 1x60' - C 4 (UK)
MAY 28, The World's Most Wanted Woman, 1x50' - C 4 (UK) / Court TV
MAY 31, Takeover TV (Season 3), 8x45' - E4 (UK)
JUN 11, Fox premieres American Idol.
JUN 12, TV's Most Censored Moments, 1x90' - Trio!
JUN 20, Hot Property (Season 4), 13x30' - C 5 (UK)
JUL 4, Lesbians Olé, 1x60' - C 5 (UK)
JUL 29, Bollywood for Beginners, 1x30' - C 4 (UK)
AUG 4, The Anna Nicole Show debuts on E!
OCT, SCI FI Field Guide to UFOs, 1x60' - SciFi
OCT 21, Uncut: The True Story of Hair, 1x120' - A&E
NOV 9, Shock Video Refried: The Best of the Worst: America Undercover, 1x60' - HBO
NOV 18, The History of Masturbation, 1x60' - C 5 (UK)
DEC 8, Brilliant But Cancelled: The Perfect Pitch, 1x30' - Trio!
DEC 10, Cleavage, 1x120' - A&E / 1x60' C 5 (UK)

2003

JAN 25, Kidneys For Jesus, 1x50' - C 4 (UK)
FEB, Heroes of Bad Taste, 1x60' - VH1
FEB 17, Aircrash, 3x60' - C 4 (UK) / 1x90' - A&E
MAR 18, The Da Vinci Code is published.
MAR 9, The Real Cliff Richard, 1x60' - C 4 (UK)
MAR 16, The Blockbuster Imperative, 1x80' - Trio!
APR 11, Hot Property (Season 5), 13x30' - C 5 (UK)
APR 17, School's Out: The Life of a Gay High School in Texas (True Life), 1x60' - MTV
MAY 5, Dark Roots: The Unauthorized Anna Nicole, 1x90' - Showtime / C 4 (UK)

Brilliant but
CANCELLED
Narrated By Andy Richter

OUT OF THE CLOSET
OFF THE SCREEN
the life of william haines

2001

JAN 11, Lesbians Go Mad on Lesbos, 1x60' - C 5 (UK)
JAN 24, The Adam & Joe Show (Season 4), 6x30' - C 4 (UK)
FEB 24, Hackers in Wonderland, 1x60' - C 4 (UK)
MAR 10, Shock Video with Adam & Joe, 8x30' - E4 (UK)
MAR 18, Lesbians Behaving Badly, 1x60' - Sky One (UK)
MAR 21, Britain's Bitchiest Babes, 1x60' - C 5 (UK)
APR 29, The Secret Rulers of the World, 5x60' - C 4 (UK)
JUN 5, Divorce: Hollywood Style, 1x60' - C 4 (UK)
JUN 28, Downloaded, 4x30' - C 5 (UK)
AUG 5, History of Surveillance, 4x60' - C 4 (UK)
AUG 6, From the Waist Down: Men, Women & Music, 5x60' - VH1
AUG 26, JK Rowling and the Harry Potter Express, 1x60' - C 5 (UK)
OCT 23, Apple launches the iPod.
NOV 5, Hot Property (Season 3), 6x30' - C 5 (UK)
NOV 14, Punishment: Cruel and Unusual, 1x60' - Court TV / 3x60' - C 5 (UK)
DEC 22, Shock Video 2002: America Undercover, 1x60' - HBO

2002

JAN 2, I Am a Talkshow Survivor, 1x60' - C 5 (UK)
JAN 3, Plushies & Furries, 1x30' - MTV
JAN 27, Andy Warhol: The Complete Picture, 1x90', 2x60' - C 4 (UK) / 1x120' - Bravo
FEB, Penis Puppeteers (Real Sex 29), 1x10' - HBO
FEB, Shock Video with Adam & Joe (Season 2), 8x30' -E4 (UK)
FEB 5, Out of the Closet, Off the Screen: The Life of William Haines, 1x60' - AMC
FEB 11, The Double Life of Jonathan King, 1x75' - C 4 (UK)
FEB 26, Masters of Darkness: The Marquis de Sade, 1x70' - C 4 (UK)

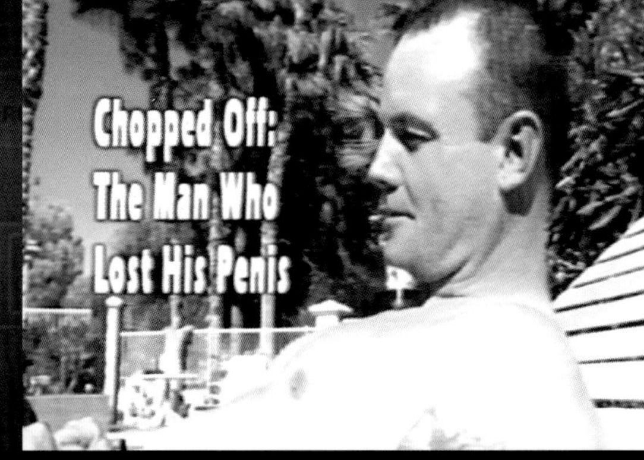

MAY 7, Wired For Sex, 13x30' - TechTV
MAY 12, Women on Top: Hollywood & Power, 1x60' - AMC
MAY 22, X-Rated Ambition: The Traci Lords Story, 1x60' - C 5 (UK)
JUL 20, Good Clean Porn, 3x30' - Trio!
AUG 11, Gay Hollywood, 1x90' - AMC
AUG 18, Totally Gay!, 1x60' - VH1
SEP 3, Brilliant But Cancelled: Pilot Season, 1x80' - Trio!
SEP 5, Party Monster, 1x98' - Strand Releasing
SEP 8, The Reality of Reality, 4x60' - Bravo
NOV 17, Arnold Schwarzenegger is sworn in as California's "Governator."
NOV 23, Matt's Old Masters, 4x60' - C 4 (UK)
NOV 26, Epic TV: The Top Ten Miniseries of All Time, 1x60' - Trio!
DEC 6, Shock Video 2004: Too Hot for the Box, 1x60' – HBO
DEC 7, The Award Show Awards Show, 1x90' - Trio!

2004

JAN 11, Vivid Valley, 13x30' - C 4 (UK) / PlayboyTV
FEB 4, Facebook launches.
FEB 14, Super Secret Movie Rules, 7x30' - VH1
MAR 10, Totally Gayer, 1x60' - VH1
APR 3, The Art Show, 7x30', 1x60' - C 4 (UK)
APR 13, Showbiz Moms & Dads, 7x60' - Bravo
APR 20, Hidden Fuhrer: Debating the Enigma of Hitler's Sexuality, 1x90' - Cinemax / C 5 (UK)
APR 30, House of Clues, 6x30' - Court TV
MAY 31, Hardcore: The Larry Flynt Story, 1x60' - C 5 (UK)
JUN 5, Former President Ronald Reagan dies.

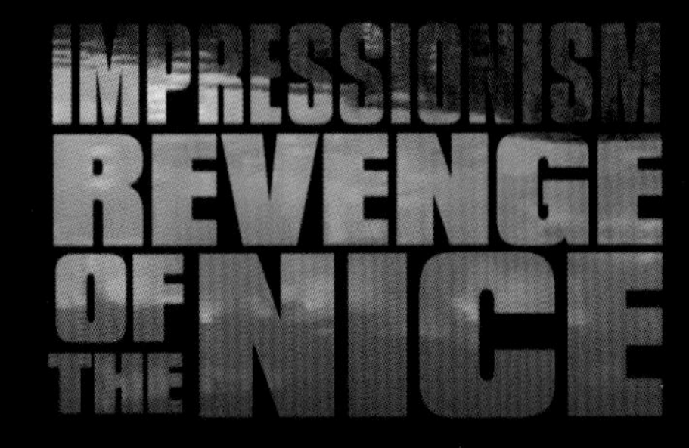

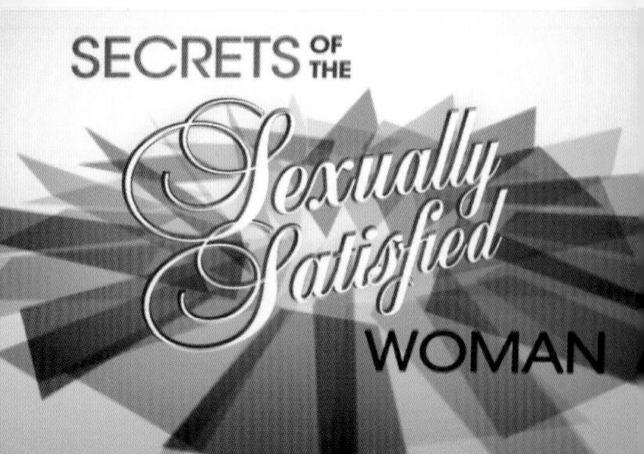

JUN 6, Flops 101: Lessons from the Biz, 1x60' - Trio!
JUN 15, Paris Hilton's sex tape, 1 Night in Paris, is released.
NOV 7, The Crazy Rulers of the World, 3x60' - C 4 (UK)
NOV 7, House of Clues (Season 2), 6x30' - Court TV
NOV 16, Made in Britain: Babel, 1x30' - C 4 (UK)
NOV 19, What Leonard Cohen Did For Me, 1x30' - BBC4 (UK)
NOV 19, Housebusters (Season 2), 7x30' - C 5 (UK)
NOV 20, Gay Republicans, 1x60' - Trio!
DEC, Shock Video 2005: Naughty by Nation, 1x60' - HBO
DEC 14, The Christmas Special Christmas Special, 1x60' - Trio!

2005

JAN 21, Inside Deep Throat, 1x90' - Universal
JAN 31, Sex in the 70's: Oo-Er-Missus, 1x60' - C 4 (UK)
FEB 14, YouTube is launched.
MAR 4, Martha Stewart is released from prison.
MAR 15, HG Wells and Me, 1x30' - BBC4 (UK)
MAR 22, Joseph Beuys and Me, 1x30' - BBC4 (UK)
MAR 30, Showdog Moms & Dads, 8x60' - Bravo
APR 9, Impressionism: Revenge of the Nice, 1x120' - C 4 (UK)
APR 11, Secrets of the Sexually Satisfied Woman, 1x60' - Lifetime
MAY 29, Power Lesbians, 1x60' - Sky One (UK)

FRANK LLOYD
WRIGHT
MURDER, MYTH
& MODERNISM

WHAT PEREZ SEZ

JUN 7, Pop Sex: Sex in the 80's, 1x60' - C 4 (UK)
JUL 27, Getting on the Property Ladder, 5x60' - C 5 (UK)
AUG 7, My Kid's Psychic, 1x60' - C 4 (UK)
AUG 16, Ted Bundy: Natural Porn Killer, 1x60' - C 4 (UK)
AUG 17, Dart Tarts, 1x60' - BBC3 (UK)
AUG 27, TransGeneration Reunion, 1x30' - Sundance Ch.
AUG 29, Million Dollar Listing, 6x60' - Bravo
SEP 26, Generation Boom, 4x30' - TVLand
OCT 12, Terror From Tokyo (IFC News), 1x30' - IFC
NOV 30, Pete Burns: Unspun, 1x60' - Living TV (UK)
DEC 13, One Punk Under God, 6x30' - Sundance Ch.
DEC 30, My Husband's Secret, 1x50' - A&E

2007

JAN 10, From Ranch to Raunch, 1x60' - BBC4 (UK)
FEB 8, Anna Nicole Smith is found dead at the Hard Rock Hotel in Hollywood, Florida.
FEB 16, Britney Spears shaves her head.
FEB 18, The Last 48 Hours of Kurt Cobain, 1x60' - BBC2 (UK)
FEB 21, Vivid releases Kim Kardashian's sex tape.
MAR 9, Debbie Does Dallas... Again, 7x30' - Showtime
MAR 20, Tori & Dean: Inn Love, 8x30' - Oxygen
APR 20, Wife, Mom, Bounty Hunter, 11x30' - WE TV
MAY 10, Hitler: The Comedy Years, 1x60' - C 4 (UK)
MAY 23, Sex Change Hospital, 6x60' - More4 (UK) / WE TV

My Kid's Psychic

JUN 1, Sports Kids Moms & Dads, 8x60' - Bravo
JUN 3, Housebusters (Season 3), 7x30' - C 5 (UK)
JUN 5, The Comeback, starring Lisa Kudrow, premieres.
JUN 5, I Do Diaries: Royal Weddings, 1x60' - Lifetime
JUN 6, Camp Michael Jackson, 1x45' - Sky One (UK)
JUL 16, Rock Around the Block, 6x60' - ITV1 (UK)
JUL 25, Tammy Faye: Death Defying, 1x90' - WE TV
SEP 9, Movies That Shook the World, 12x30' - AMC
SEP 10, Self Portraits: The Me Generation, 3x60' - C 4 (UK)
SEP 10, Most Irresistible Women, 1x60' - Spike TV
SEP 20, TransGeneration, 8x30' - Sundance Ch.

OCT 5, Twilight is published.
NOV, The I Do Diaries: Beg, Borrow & Steal, 1x60' - Lifetime
DEC 1, This is a Knife (Web Series), Motorola / C4.com
DEC 6, Party / Party, 8x60' - Bravo
DEC 11, Angelina: Saint or Sinner, 1x60' - Sky One (UK)

2006

JAN 4, The Smoking Gun exposes the lies in James Frey's memoir, A Million Little Pieces.
JAN 30, The Perfect Penis, 1x60' - C 4 (UK)
JAN 31, Chopped Off: The Man Who Lost His Penis, 1x90' - C 4 (UK)
FEB 1, The World's Biggest Penis, 1x60' - C 4 (UK)
MAR 5, Brokeback Mountain fails to win the Academy Award for Best Picture.
MAY 11, Frank Lloyd Wright: Murder, Myth & Modernism, 1x60' - BBC4 (UK)
JUN 2, History of Prostitution, 3x60' - Sky One (UK)

JUN 3, Paris Hilton goes to jail.
JUN 29, Apple launches the iPhone.
AUG 5, The Minor Accomplishments of Jackie Woodman (Season 2), 8x30' - IFC
AUG 14, Tori & Dean: Inn Love (Season 2), 10x30' - Oxygen
SEP 5, Children of God: Lost and Found, 1x75' - Cinemax
SEP 11, What Perez Sez, 4x60' - VH1
SEP 23, London Ink, 6x60' - Discovery Real Time (UK)
OCT 7, Art and the City, 6x30' - Ovation
OCT 8, Pete's PA, 10x60' - Living TV (UK)
NOV 13, Miss Navajo (Independent Lens), 1x60' - PBS

NOV 21, I, Videogame, 5x60' - Discovery
DEC, Dictators By Design, 1x60' - Discovery Times
DEC 28, Wired for Sex (Season 2), 3x30' - G4

2008

FEB 11, Transamerican Love Story, 8x60' - Logo
FEB 20, Bite (Web Series), Ford / C4.com
MAR 18, James St. James' Daily Freak Show (Web Series), WorldOfWonder.net
MAR 29, David Ogilvy: Original Mad Man, 1x60' - BBC4 (UK)
APR 13, ¡Viva Hollywood!, 8x60' - VH1
MAY 8, Relative Madness, 6x60' - SoapNet
MAY 19, Reverend Death, 1x75' - C 4 (UK)
JUN 10, 25iest: Power Couples, 1x60' - Oxygen
JUN 16, Same-sex marriage becomes legal in California.
JUN 17, Tori & Dean: Home Sweet Hollywood S3, 10x60' - Oxygen

DAVID OGILVY
Original Mad Man

JUN 25, When I Knew, 1x40' - HBO
JUL 15, Stanley Kubrick's Boxes, 1x50' - More4 (UK) / Sundance Ch.
JUL 21, Heidi Fleiss: The Would-Be Madam of Crystal, 1x69' - HBO
AUG 3, Pam: Girl on the Loose, 8x60' - E!
AUG 5, Million Dollar Listing (Season 2), 6x60' - Bravo
SEP 12, Get Your Island On (Web Series), Malibu/Yahoo! UK
SEP 13, Tina Fey returns to Saturday Night Live to debut her impersonation of Sarah Palin.
SEP 14, The Hunger Games is published.
SEP 23, Machines of Malice, 3x60' - Discovery
OCT 14, Beyoncé releases her video for "Single Ladies."
OCT 15, Charo - España Cañí (Music Video),
OCT 19, London Ink (Season 2), 6x60' - Discovery Real Time (UK)
OCT 28, Victoria Silvstedt: My Perfect Life, 8x60' - E! (Int'l)
NOV 5, Same-sex marriage becomes illegal in Califonia.
DEC 6, Dancing with Dogs, 1x120' - Animal Planet
DEC 9, 25iest: Bad Girls Gone Wild, 1x60' - Oxygen

2009

FEB 2, RuPaul's Drag Race, 8x60' - Logo
FEB 5, Heli-Loggers, 10x60' - TLC
FEB 14, Deeper Throat, 6x30' - Showtime
MAR 25, Grindr launches.
MAY 11, RuPaul - Jealous of My Boogie featuring Chi Chi La Rue (Music Video)
MAY 19, Tori & Dean: Home Sweet Hollywood (Season 4), 12x60' - Oxygen
JUN 11, Chastity Bono comes out as transgendered.
JUN 25, Michael Jackson dies.
JUL 14, 25iest: Celeb-U-Tots, 1x60' - Oxygen

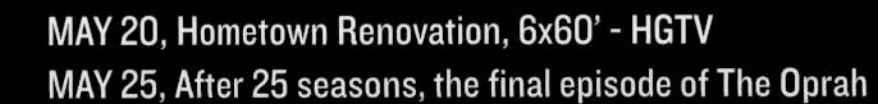

2011

JAN 22, Grab, 1x60' - Sundance Film Festival
JAN 24, RuPaul's Drag Race (Season 3), 1x90, 15x60' - Logo
JAN 24, RuPaul's Drag Race: Untucked (Season 2), 13x30' - Logo
FEB 3, Million Dollar Listing (Season 4), 9x60' - Bravo
MAR 22, The Fabulous Beekman Boys (Season 2), 10x30' - Planet Green
APR 6, Tori & Dean: sTORIbook Weddings, 9x60' - Oxygen
APR 19, Dresscue Me @ Shareen Vintage, 8x30' - Planet Green
MAY 10, Becoming Chaz, 1x90' - OWN
MAY 20, Hometown Renovation, 6x60' - HGTV
MAY 25, After 25 seasons, the final episode of The Oprah Winfrey Show is broadcast.
JUN 12, Finding Sarah, 6x60' - OWN
JUN 20, RuPaul's Drag U (Season 2), 10x60' - Logo
AUG 25, Standard & Poor's downgrades the United States credit rating for the first time in the history of ratings.
SEP 20, The Strange History of Don't Ask, Don't Tell, 1x80' - HBO
NOV 18, Girls Who Like Boys Who Like Boys: Nashville (Season 2), 12x30' - Sundance Ch.
NOV 27, Being Chaz, 1x90' - OWN
NOV 29, Tori & Dean: Home Sweet Hollywood (Season 6), 9x60' - Oxygen

girls WHO LIKE boys WHO LIKE boys

2010

SEP 12, The Last Beekeeper, 1x66' - Planet Green
SEP 14, Machines of Malice (Season 2), 3x60' - Discovery
OCT 7, Man Shops Globe, 8x60' - Sundance Ch.
OCT 12, Million Dollar Listing (Season 3), 9x60' - Bravo
NOV 10, Lady Gaga's video for "Bad Romance" premieres.
DEC 9, RuPaul - Devil Made Me Do It (Music Video)
DEC 18, 25iest: Hollywood's Most Outrageous Holiday Gifts, 1x60' - Oxygen
DEC 22, RuPaul - Tranny Chaser (Music Video)
DEC 30, Ghetto Ballet, 1x35' - HBO

JAN 11, Fantasia For Real, 9x30' - VH1
JAN 14, Carnie Wilson: Unstapled, 9x30' - GSN
FEB 1, RuPaul's Drag Race (Season 2), 12x60' - Logo
FEB 1, RuPaul's Drag Race: Untucked, 10x30' - Logo
FEB 11, Alexander McQueen commits suicide.
APR 5, Tori & Dean: Home Sweet Hollywood (Season 5), 10x60' - Oxygen
MAY 23, The final episode of Lost airs.
JUN 1, Design School, 10x60' - HGTV Canada / HGTV
JUN 3, Rue McClanahan passes away, leaving Betty White as the sole surviving Golden Girl.

JUN 16, The Fabulous Beekman Boys, 10x30' - Planet Green
JUN 30, Man Shops Globe (Season 2), 8x60' - Sundance Ch.
JUL 19, RuPaul's Drag U, 8x60' - Logo
JUL 20, 25iest: Jersey Celebs, 1x60' - Oxygen
SEP 19, Fantasia For Real (Season 2), 11x30' - VH1
OCT 4, The Arrangement, 8x60' - Logo
DEC 7, Girls Who Like Boys Who Like Boys, 8x60' - Sundance Ch.
DEC 8, The Fabulous Beekman Boys Holiday Special, 1x60' - Planet Green
DEC 12, Wishful Drinking, 1x90' - HBO

SEX CHANGE HOSPITAL

2012

JAN 30, RuPaul's Drag Race (Season 4), 1x90', 13x60' – Logo
JAN 30, RuPaul's Drag Race: Untucked (Season 3), 12x30' – Logo
FEB 5, Madonna is the Halftime show for the 2012 Superbowl.
MAR 7, Million Dollar Listing: New York, 9x60' - Bravo
MAY 6, Tattoo School, 8x30' - TLC
JUNE 6, Million Dollar Listing: Los Angeles, 10x60' - Bravo
JUNE 18, RuPaul's Drag U S3, 8x60' - Logo

JULY 31, All the Right Moves, 8x60' - Oxygen
AUG 18, 10 Kids 2 Dads, 2x60' - OWN
OCT 22, RuPaul's All Stars Drag Race, 6x60' - Logo
OCT 22, All Stars:Untucked, 6x60' - Logo
DEC 6, Vogue, 1x60' - HBO
DEC 8, Mario & Courtney's Wedding Fiesta - 1x120' - TLC

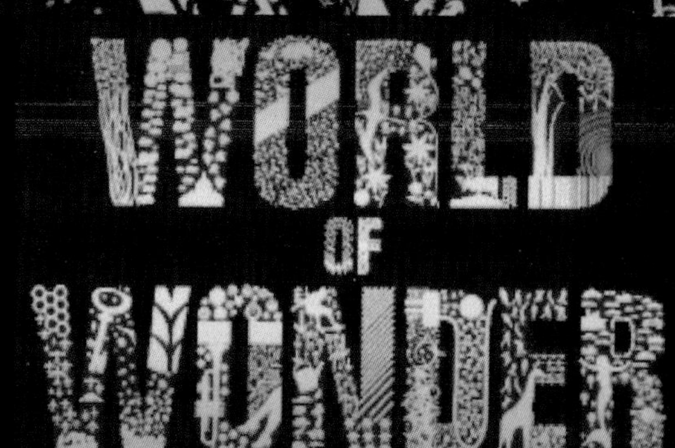

WORLD OF WONDERS

FIRST EDITION

ISBN #978-0-9855834-0-8
PRINTED IN THE USA

TEXT - Fenton Bailey & Randy Barbato
PHOTOGRAPHY - Idris Rheubottom & Tony Craig
ADDITIONAL PHOTOGRAPHY - Mathu Andersen, Alex Grace
ART DIRECTION - Trey Speegle
DESIGNER - Emiliano Neri
COPY EDITOR - Stephen Saban
PRINTER - Almaden Press
PRODUCTION COORDINATORS - Thairin Smothers, Chris Wereski, Tom Wolf